OUT OF HIS Abundance

366 DEVOTIONALS FOR WOMEN

REBECCA MARTIN

OUT OF HIS ABUNDANCE

Christian Light Publications

Harrisonburg, Virginia 22802

©2022 Christian Light Publications, Inc.

Printed in the United States of America

ISBN: 978-0-87813-361-1

Cover & Inside Design: Lanette Steiner

Cover & Interior Graphics: 123RF

SPIRITUAL NEW YEAR

DAILY BIBLE READING: EXODUS 12:1-7

"It shall be the first month of the year to you" (Exodus 12:2).

Did you know that the Israelites celebrated two new years? Before the Exodus, their year began in the autumn. New Year's Day, for them, was in the month we now call September. But in Exodus 12, God now told Moses that the spiritual New Year was to begin in the spring, in the month we call April.

Why? Was it because spring is when the earth quickens and becomes renewed? Certainly, even nature agrees that spring is a good time to begin anew.

But God had a far deeper reason for instituting this New Year's Day. It signified the beginning of Israel's life as a redeemed people. This is a glorious truth, just as powerful for us today as for the Israelite multitude redeemed from Egypt.

How was Israel redeemed? By the sacrifice of a spotless lamb. Sinful ones redeemed by sinless ones. Oh, Israel, did you truly realize what a wonderful new year you were beginning as you sacrificed those innocent lambs?

That is exactly how our own spiritual New Year—or new life—begins. When we place our trust wholly in the sinless Lamb who gave His life for us, we, too, begin our lives as redeemed ones.

Peter reminds us in 1 Peter 3:18 that Jesus, the just, suffered for the unjust (which means us). He died for us, and by faith we take part in His death. This death, for us, is not a once-and-for-all thing, but something we experience daily. Continually, daily, our flesh is being put to death; continually, daily, our spirit is being quickened—made alive—by the Holy Spirit.

That is the life of the redeemed—life in the spiritual New Year.

"For Christ also hath once suffered for sins, the just for the unjust, that he might bring us to God, being put to death in the flesh, but quickened by the Spirit" (1 Peter 3:18).

WHAT REALLY DREW HER?

DAILY BIBLE READING: RUTH 1:14-18

"But Ruth clave unto her" (Ruth 1:14).

Can we grasp how much Ruth gave up when she made this decision to cleave to her mother-in-law? She was giving up her homeland of Moab. She was giving up her family—parents, brothers, sisters. Very likely she would never again see any of them.

What's more, Ruth was giving up any hope of security. In those days the plight of a widow was desperate. Unless a widow remarried, she was doomed to poverty. That is why Naomi urged her two daughters-in-law to return to Moab; there they would have hopes of remarrying.

Basically, then, we could say that Ruth was giving up everything. What inspired her to do this? What was it about Naomi that made Ruth love her so much?

In Naomi, Ruth saw a woman who held to her faith in spite of severe hardships. Naomi's husband and sons had died and she was left desolate, but she clung to God. From Naomi's careworn features shone with the radiance that can only adorn the face that is uplifted to God.

So we arrive at this conclusion: Ruth was actually drawn to the Lord. She recognized in Naomi's faith the true God, and she realized He had far more to offer than the gods of Moab.

The question for you and me is this: do our lives shine forth the light of faith? Are others attracted to Jesus because of something they see in us? Let's pray like Moses did in Psalm 90:17, "Let the beauty of the LORD our God be upon us." And the only way to absorb the Lord's beauty is to dwell constantly in His presence.

"That I may dwell in the house of the LORD all the days of my life, to behold the beauty of the LORD" (Psalm 27:4).

ALL THINGS WORK TOGETHER

DAILY READING GUIDE: RUTH 1:19-22

"Call me not Naomi, call me Mara" (Ruth 1:20).

The people of Bethlehem were excited to hear about Naomi's return. Perhaps they had memories of a happy, laughing woman. (The name *Naomi* means "pleasant.")

But now Naomi is back; and when Bethlehem's citizens hurry out to greet her, they see terrible anguish of soul in this woman they once knew. "Don't call me pleasant—call me bitter!" she exclaims.

Indeed, Naomi had seen harsh circumstances. She had dwelt for years among strange people who worshipped strange gods. There she had lost her husband and both sons. Three graves she had left behind when she turned her face once more toward Bethlehem.

Those experiences were hard, but the saddest part is that Naomi felt forsaken by God. She felt His hand was against her. "The Lord hath testified against me, and the Almighty hath afflicted me." Naomi had apparently fallen to the depths of desolation—and there, bitterness overtook her.

We may never encounter circumstances as dire as Naomi's. Yet we, too, are sometimes tempted to despair, tempted even to feel forsaken of God. "Why did this have to happen to me?" we wail.

But we are so shortsighted. Think again of Naomi. Even while she wallowed in bitterness, God's hand was at work, setting in motion a chain of events that would bring blessings beyond Naomi's wildest dreams. She and Ruth arrived in Bethlehem at the beginning of the barley harvest—and that was the start. In those barley fields, God would work out a marvelous salvation for these two destitute widows!

"And we know that all things work together for good to them that love God, to them who are the called according to his purpose" (Romans 8:28).

NO TASK TOO HUMBLE

DAILY BIBLE READING: RUTH 2:1-7

"And she went, and came, and gleaned in the field after the reapers" (Ruth 2:3).

Do you sometimes have to perform tasks that you don't like? Jobs that are very tiring or very boring or very dirty? Let's look at the work Ruth did to support her mother-in-law. We may find that our own work is easy by comparison.

To begin with, gleaning must have been humiliating. Only poor people went gleaning. Deuteronomy 24:19 gave God's instructions to farmers about leaving some grain in the fields or fruit on the trees: "It shall be for the stranger, for the fatherless, and for the widow." Ruth willingly did this humblest of tasks so she could bring food home to Naomi.

Gleaning was certainly wearisome! Imagine walking, stooping over a stubble field in search of any stray grains. Ruth did it from dawn to dusk. Boaz's servants told him, "She came, and hath continued even from the morning until now" (verse 7).

Ruth had to be brave, to go into this stranger's field and start gleaning. What if the harvesters mocked her or treated her roughly? What if the field's owner resented her presence? But Ruth trod underfoot all her "what ifs" and went forth to glean.

In performing this difficult, demeaning, and humble task, Ruth shows us the kind of qualities any woman should wish for. Ruth was faithful: she persisted all day. She was hardworking. In her care for Naomi she was loving and kind. And Ruth was brave.

Does it seem that God asks you to do tasks that are beneath your abilities or almost too humble? Perform them faithfully. God wants to develop in you the same qualities He fostered in Ruth.

"And now, my daughter, fear not . . . for all the city of my people doth know that thou art a virtuous woman" (Ruth 3:11).

 *Day* 5

OUT OF HIS ABUNDANCE

DAILY BIBLE READING: RUTH 2:10-16

"Let her glean even among the sheaves, and reproach her not" (Ruth 2:15).

The story of Ruth gives us a vivid picture of how it is when we come to Jesus. When Ruth realized what Boaz intended to do for her, she was overwhelmed. Falling on her face, she exclaimed, "I'm only a stranger. Why have I found grace in your sight?"

Boaz's reply? She had found grace because she willingly forsook all for the Lord, "under whose wings thou art come to trust."

Thereupon follows a beautiful scene. Picture Ruth, invited to sit with the reapers at mealtime. Picture Boaz, giving her special attention and passing her a bowl of parched corn. Imagine the wonder and gratitude in this once-destitute widow's heart as she partook of her kinsman's kindness!

The abundance of Boaz knew no bounds. He even told the harvesters to drop some extra grain. "Let her glean," he said, "even among the sheaves"—a rare favor, since usually the gleaners had to wait until the field was bare.

Once we recognize our sinfulness and unworthiness, do not we also fall in humility and gratitude at the feet of our Saviour? Are we not also willing to forsake all and follow Him?

Wonder of wonders, Jesus issues His invitation to come and dine. And as we daily come to the pages of His Word, we hear in our hearts the echo of that command: "Let her glean." Out of Christ's abundance, our puny efforts will be rewarded far beyond anything we deserve.

"Now unto him that is able to do exceeding abundantly above all that we ask or think . . . unto him be glory" (Ephesians 3:20, 21).

JUST A SMALL KIND DEED

DAILY BIBLE READING: RUTH 2:19-23

"Blessed be he of the L<small>ORD</small>*, who hath not left off his kindness to the living and to the dead" (Ruth 2:20).*

Remember the Naomi we met in Chapter 1? She was so embittered by adversity that she told people to call her Mara. She felt God had "testified against her" and "afflicted" her. In fact, she felt forsaken and forgotten.

Now look at Naomi on the day Ruth comes home with a whole basket of grain. In wonder she listens as Ruth tells of Boaz's kindness. A sparkle enters Naomi's eyes at this evidence of human love; it rekindles her faith in God's love and God's purpose. "Blessed be he of the L<small>ORD</small>," she exclaims, "who hath not left off his kindness" (verse 20). Despite her bitterness, Naomi had not stopped believing in God. She had only lost sight of His love. Now that vision of His love had been restored to her.

And how? All it took was one small act of kindness on the part of Boaz. Oh, if there is any kindness we can show to people around us, let us do it with an eager heart! We never know when a thoughtful gesture will be the means of restoring a flame of faith to some heart's candle that has flickered low.

How brightly Naomi's faith burned now! For she knew this man Boaz; he was a kinsman. Naomi could see that Ruth's happening upon this man's field was no mere accident, but the providence of a faithful God.

"He restoreth my soul . . . Thou preparest a table before me" (Psalm 23:3, 5).

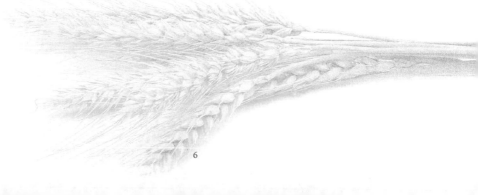

Day 7

HE COULD NOT REST

DAILY BIBLE READING: RUTH 4:9-12

"The man will not be in rest, until he have finished the thing this day" (Ruth 3:18).

If you want a picture of Christ as Redeemer, consider Boaz. Redeeming Ruth—claiming her for his wife—was no easy matter. Start reading at Ruth 3:12, and you will discover that there was also another man who could have claimed Ruth. So Boaz set himself the task of straightening things out. And, as Naomi predicted, he wasn't going to rest until the thing was done!

First, Boaz sought out that other relative and held a discussion with him. "If you want to redeem Naomi's land, you also have to marry Ruth." That made the other relative back down. He had no love for Ruth. There at the city gate, Boaz called the elders to witness the transaction. The thing was done, and it was done well.

What Boaz did to redeem Ruth pales when compared with what Christ did to redeem us from sin. Let's consider the steps He took. He left His home in Heaven, where at the Father's right hand He was King of the universe. He came to earth a helpless baby and grew up in a home that was far from wealthy. For three years He wore out His sandals traveling around Palestine on preaching tours and errands of mercy. During those three years He often encountered hatred and scorn from His enemies.

But His work was not finished. Jesus knew He could not claim His bride, the church, until the devil's claims had been cut off. Only the cross could do that. So Jesus did not rest, but forged ahead with the Father's plan. He allowed cruel hands to nail Him to the cross. He hung there in horrible pain, forsaken even by His disciples and mocked by His enemies. And then—just before His spirit returned to the Father—Christ cried out: "It is finished" (John 19:30). The thing was done, and it was done well.

"I have finished the work which thou gavest me to do" (John 17:4).

ONE WITH HIM

"And he shall be unto thee a restorer of thy life" (Ruth 4:15).

Don't we all like stories with happy endings? The scene here at the end of the Book of Ruth certainly is a happy one. Two women who once had trodden together the valley of the shadow of death now are dwelling in the light of the mountaintop. Picture Naomi, adorned with a beautiful grandmotherly smile as she cuddles her new grandson. Picture Ruth, glowing in the love and kindness of her husband Boaz.

Gone are the days when Ruth must go out and work the fields for food. Gone are the days of anguish and uncertainty. Ruth has been redeemed—she is one with her redeemer! Now all his fields are hers. All his riches are at her disposal.

What a picture of new life in Christ! No longer do we have to work for redemption. Jesus has done that; He has redeemed us, and through faith we are one with Him.

We who believe can now say of Jesus our kinsman, "We have redemption through his blood, the forgiveness of sins, according to the riches of his grace" (Ephesians 1:7). His riches are ours. Our life is bathed with the sunlight of His love.

What then? What is the outcome of so great a redemption, so great a love? Paul gives the answer in Romans 7:4: "That ye should be married . . . to him who is raised from the dead, that we should bring forth fruit unto God." Just as it was Ruth's destiny to bear a son whose lineage would bless mankind, so, when we are one with Christ, it is our destiny to bring forth the fruit of a godly life.

"But the fruit of the Spirit is love, joy, peace, longsuffering, gentleness, goodness, faith, meekness, temperance" (Galatians 5:22, 23).

ETERNAL PERSPECTIVE

DAILY BIBLE READING: RUTH 1:1-6

"They took them wives of the women of Moab" (Ruth 1:4).

Why have we returned to the bleak landscape of the story's opening? Why think again of those dark days when Naomi lost her husband and sons?

Because it is often good to view the beginning from the end. Once we know the end of a story, we can look back over the chapters and trace the author's design, woven into every happening. We can say, "Ah, yes, that's what he was getting to."

Think of it. Ruth was from Moab, a land despised by Israel, yet God made her one of the ancestors of Jesus Christ. She became part of a grand design to enrich the whole world. What an honor for a desolate widow from a foreign land!

But Ruth had to endure much before she was ready for that high honor. She lost her husband. She experienced her mother-in-law's anguish. She went away to a foreign land, leaving behind all that was dear to her. Perhaps she endured loneliness and homesickness.

Treading through those dark valleys, could Ruth realize what God had in store for her? Did she guess at God's purpose? Did she dream that through her God was making preparations to send the Messiah? Hardly.

When we pass through valleys of trial and temptation, we will not fathom God's purpose either. Only from the perspective of eternity, at the end of our earthly life's story, will we clearly see God's grand design.

"In whom also we have obtained an inheritance, being predestinated according to the purpose of him who worketh all things after the counsel of his own will" (Ephesians 1:11).

Day 10

ROOTED IN HIM

DAILY BIBLE READING: COLOSSIANS 2:6, 7

"Walk ye in him: rooted and built up in him" (Colossians 2:6, 7).

Do you sometimes feel discouraged about your spiritual life? Does it seem that your progress is slow or even nonexistent?

Let me tell you about the little pine tree that grows on the rocky bluff behind our house. It has not seemed to grow higher at all in the months since we moved here. Did you notice what I said though? That little tree is literally growing on a rock. There must be a crack, and there must be some soil, or else no tree could grow. Even though all I can see is rock, the tree must be drawing sustenance from somewhere. I picture its roots reaching downward and outward, slowly but surely, ever deeper into the cleft of the rock.

If you cling to Jesus, your roots will grow. Let them grow ever deeper into Christ, the sure foundation. Believe that you are being built up in Him.

The more you are rooted and built up in Him, the more "stablished" you will be. Your faith will grow strong in the truths you have been taught. While your roots are growing secretly, your outward walk and behavior will grow too, even if it is only the slow growth of a little pine tree.

Never forget how greatly you need Jesus. That is what the first words of today's reading mean: "As ye have therefore received Christ . . . so walk ye in him." We receive Him because we need Him, and we keep on walking in Him because we need Him every hour.

"That Rock was Christ" (1 Corinthians 10:4).

THE SECRET OF THE LORD

DAILY BIBLE READING: PSALM 25:8-14

"The secret of the LORD is with them that fear him" (Psalm 25:14).

It should come as no surprise that God has secrets. His ways and His thoughts are so much higher than our ways. Of course He knows many, many things that we cannot fathom.

The surprising part—the wonderful part—is that God wants to tell us His secrets. Just as you and I long to confide in a friend, so God wants to show us the mysteries of His love and mercy. Could any privilege compare with the privilege of having the Creator of heaven and earth as our Friend and Confidant?

There are conditions we must meet if we want to know God's mysteries. "The meek will he guide in judgment" (verse 9). "Such as keep his covenant and his testimonies" are shown God's path (verse 10). "He that feareth the LORD" shall be taught in God's ways (verse 12).

If we are meek, if we keep His testimonies, and if we fear the Lord, we can be friends with God, just as Abraham was. Of him God said, "Shall I hide from Abraham that thing which I do? . . . For I know him" (Genesis 18:17, 19).

Paul acknowledged that God has secrets. "But we speak the wisdom of God in a mystery, even the hidden wisdom . . . Eye hath not seen, nor ear heard, neither have entered into the heart of man, the things which God hath prepared for them that love him" (1 Corinthians 2:7, 9).

Then Paul went on with this glorious truth: "But God hath revealed them unto us by his Spirit" (1 Corinthians 2:10). God, through the work of Jesus and the Holy Spirit, has revealed "the secret of the LORD" as never before.

"The secret things belong unto the LORD our God: but those things which are revealed belong unto us and to our children for ever" (Deuteronomy 29:29).

UPHELD BY HIS HAND

DAILY BIBLE READING: PSALM 37:23, 24

"The Lord upholdeth him with his hand" (Psalm 37:24).

When I read these two verses, I picture a father striding along with big steps. At his side is his little daughter. Her short legs must trot very fast to keep up with Daddy. Suddenly she stumbles, but she does not fall flat on her face. Why not? Because her hand is held fast in her father's.

That's how God is toward us. We may stumble. We may fail Him. But He keeps hold of us. Why? Because He delights in our ways, as the psalmist says in verse 23. Imagine that! God takes delight in every detail of our lives. He has a plan for us. He orders our steps.

The Bible has other similar promises. When Hannah sang her song of praise to God, she said: "He will keep the feet of his saints" (1 Samuel 2:9). That reminds us of the words in 1 Peter 1:5: we are "kept by the power of God." Perhaps you feel like protesting, "But this promise is only for a good man. See? The psalmist says that the steps of a good man are ordered by the Lord. And I am not very good at all."

It's true that we are all sinners. But this is what God wants of us: that we see our need, seek after Him, and follow Him as best we can. Do you think the daddy in our story upheld his little girl because she was perfect? Hardly. He cared for her because she needed him, and he knew it.

"He will not suffer thy foot to be moved" (Psalm 121:3).

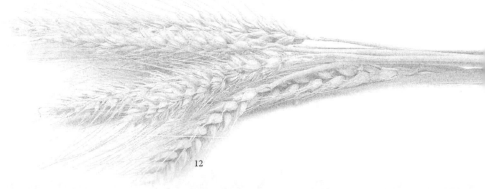

DEALING WITH STRESS AND TEMPTATION

DAILY BIBLE READING: MARK 14:36, 37

"Watch ye and pray, lest ye enter into temptation" (Mark 14:38).

Jesus faced tremendous stress there in the Garden of Gethsemane. As God's Son and yet a man, He experienced enormous pressure and temptation. You and I will never experience anything like it.

But we do face stress, and we do face temptation. We are willing—oh, yes, we are willing—to do the right. So was Peter; but we know what happened to him. Then how shall *we* cope? We are no better than Peter.

Jesus gave us a magnificent example. Let's notice four things He did or recommended as a means of dealing with stress and temptation.

First, He *prayed*. Oh, how we need to bring everything to God in prayer. Jesus told His Father exactly how He felt about His looming trial.

Jesus also *asked for support* from His loved ones. True, they didn't do a very good job of supporting Him, but that's beside the point. We all need each other. Let's not forget to ask our friends for help.

Then too, Jesus *focused on God's will.* Yes, He also thought about the terrible things He faced; but through it all He maintained His focus on the purpose of God.

Finally, *watch.* Jesus did it. We, too, must be vigilant and aware if we do not want to be overtaken by temptation.

Pray. Ask loved ones for support. Focus on God's will. And *watch!* That is the Bible way of dealing with stress and temptation.

"The spirit truly is ready [willing], but the flesh is weak" (Mark 14:38).

Day 14

OUT OF WEAKNESS

"Out of weakness were made strong" (Hebrews 11:34).

We tend to feel small when we read the "heroes of faith" chapter. What great things those patriarchs wrought for the Lord! Noah, Abraham, Isaac, Jacob, Moses, David—compared to us they seem like giants. Verses 33 and 34 list some things they accomplished through their faith. Most of those things may appear unattainable to you and me, but there is one phrase we can cling to: "out of weakness were made strong."

Many of these "heroes" were actually weak in themselves. Moses, for instance. When God called him to lead Israel, he protested, "Who am I . . . that I should bring forth the children of Israel out of Egypt?" (Exodus 3:11). Or consider Gideon. He was aghast at God's announcement that he would save Israel. "I am the least in my father's house" (Judges 6:15).

David certainly had his weaknesses. Just think how deeply into sin he fell. Solomon was no better. As for Rahab, it's amazing that a woman like her should be listed among the heroes of faith.

Weakness. We all have it in one form or another. God, however, is a master hand at turning weaknesses into strengths. If we bring our weakness to Him, He can transform it by His strength.

But that can never happen as long as we don't admit our weakness. We must recognize and confess our weakness and bring it all to God in faith. That's the only way to be made strong.

"My strength is made perfect in weakness" (2 Corinthians 12:9).

Day 15

THERE CAME A CLOUD

DAILY BIBLE READING: LUKE 9:34-36

"There came a cloud . . . and they feared as they entered into the cloud" (Luke 9:34).

We certainly can't blame the disciples for being frightened. This experience was so new, so strange. Up on a mountain with Jesus, barely awake from their sleep, bedazzled with a strange vision of Moses and Elijah . . . then "there came a cloud."

Maybe the disciples didn't realize that this was the Shekinah cloud, the very cloud used by God for centuries to show His presence. God was in that cloud!

Sometimes a cloud overshadows your life or mine: a trial, a time of testing, something new and unknown that inspires fear in our hearts. Oh, we of little faith. Why can we not sense the presence of God in these clouds? Why do we fear to enter it when Jesus is by our side?

As the cloud passes by, we will find that it has wrought in us a new awareness. God has spoken to our hearts from that dreaded cloud. He has pointed us anew to Jesus. He has spoken to us the very words He spoke to Peter, James, and John on the Mount of Transfiguration: "This is my beloved Son: hear him."

Every cloud will be worth it, if it draws us more fully to the beloved Son, if it inspires us to hear Him and Him alone. Moses and Elijah are in the past. Today, Jesus is here. Let us hear Him.

"The LORD is on my side: I will not fear" (Psalm 118:6).

A REAL MAN

DAILY BIBLE READING: HEBREWS 2:14-17

"Forasmuch then as the children are partakers of flesh and blood, he also himself likewise took part of the same" (Hebrews 2:14).

The Bible never uses the word *incarnation,* yet there is hardly another single word that so fully expresses the main message of the Bible. *Incarnate* means "made manifest in the flesh." Was there a more important event in all history than the coming of God's Son into the world as a man?

He stayed God's Son. He kept His divinity. Yet He became a human like you and me. The Bible gives us many indications that Jesus was subject to the same limitations we are. As God, He had the power to be everywhere at once. But as man, He accepted the limitations of time and place: when He was in Galilee, He could not be in Jerusalem, and so on.

Jesus even limited His knowledge when He became a man. As God, He was all-knowing. But as a man, He accepted, followed, and submitted to God's will as a human. Isn't that amazing?

Jesus experienced sorrow, just as we do. In Matthew 26:37 we find him "sorrowful and very heavy."

Jesus knew what it was like to be hungry. After forty days without food, He "hungered" (Luke 4:2).

Christ's human body must have needed sleep as much as ours do. Why else would He have fallen asleep in a boat on a stormy sea (Luke 8:23)?

The Creator of the universe even endured poverty for our sakes: He had no home of His own (Luke 9:58).

But God Incarnate never had sin. In that respect Jesus was not like the rest of humanity. And that's why He could be the supreme sacrifice to take away our sin.

"And the Word was made flesh, and dwelt among us, (and we beheld his glory, the glory as of the only begotten of the Father,) full of grace and truth" (John 1:14).

LAID UP IN OUR HEARTS

DAILY BIBLE READING: DEUTERONOMY 11:18-21

"Therefore shall ye lay up these words in your heart" (Deuteronomy 11:18).

What a powerful weapon is the Word of God in our battles with the enemy! That is why we want to acquaint ourselves with the Scriptures, reading them daily in order to "lay them up" in our hearts.

But it is not enough merely to memorize Scripture. Even the devil knows God's Word. Satan quoted verse after verse when he tempted Jesus in the wilderness. Yes indeed, the devil knows God's Word—but he doesn't obey it. He twists and warps it to suit his own evil purposes.

"Thy word have I hid in mine heart" says the psalmist in 119:11. Jesus is our great example for having the Word hidden in the heart. Under attack from the devil's cunning abuse of Scripture, Jesus was able to withstand each volley. He drew on the fountain of God's Word that welled up from deep within Him. Jesus not only knew God's Word, but He obeyed it.

Reverently, even fearfully, let us hide in our hearts the precious ammunition of God's Word. Let us obey it. Let us receive it as life and health and power. Above all, let us believe what God says in His Word; because it is only as we believe that the power of the Word is released for obedience.

"Ye shall diligently keep all these commandments which I command you, to do them, to love the LORD your God, to walk in all his ways, and to cleave unto him" (Deuteronomy 11:22).

Day 18

A HEALING TONGUE

"A wholesome tongue is a tree of life" (Proverbs 15:4).

We could use the word *healing* in place of *wholesome* in this verse. How can you have a "healing" tongue rather than one that wounds?

Verse 1 gives us a good answer to that question. A healing tongue will not argue. We all know what it feels like to be stirred to anger by an unfair accusation or an unexpected challenge. Inwardly, we feel angry; will we allow that anger to escape, to lash out? Then we are creating an argument. Harsh words stir up mutual anger that slaps back and forth. Quite the opposite of a healing tongue!

"Don't raise your voice!" my grandmother used to warn when we children began exchanging heated words. It's a warning that can check many an argument. Have you ever tried arguing in whispers? If you have, I'm guessing the argument didn't last long. Either it died away for lack of momentum or it escalated into something louder than whispers. So don't raise your voice. Give a soft, healing reply. Then you, too, can have the "tongue of the wise," a healing tongue rather than a mouth that "poureth out foolishness." After all, God sees and hears everything. We wouldn't argue in His presence, would we?

"A wrathful man stirreth up strife: but he that is slow to anger appeaseth strife" (Proverbs 15:18).

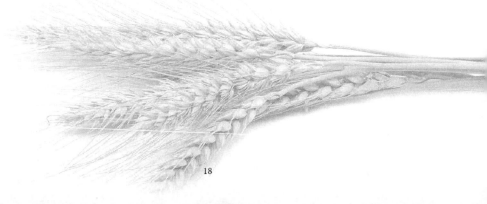

Day 19

BETWEEN THE VERSES

DAILY BIBLE READING: LUKE 1:26-28

"The angel came in unto her, and said, Hail, thou that art highly favoured, the Lord is with thee: blessed art thou among women" (Luke 1:28).

Like Mary, you and I are also greatly blessed and highly favored. If we have repented, confessed our sins, and been received into the church of the redeemed, we have inherited blessings beyond anything we could earn. Before us lies the shining vista of blessings that will last throughout eternity.

But does this high favor mean we will never suffer pain? Do God's blessings guarantee us a life free of suffering?

It was certainly not so for Mary. Read verse 31 again: that tells of Christ's birth. Then read verses 32 and 33, where we see Jesus clad in His resurrection glory, reigning over the whole earth. Then think of all that took place between those verses—between Christ's birth and His resurrection. Think of all the human, earthly pain that came to Mary! She probably lost many of her friends. No doubt she endured mocking and contempt. Later she suffered the pain of seeing her Son rejected by His own people. And can we even begin to fathom the sword that twisted her heart when her Son was crucified?

Yet none of this pain changed the fact that Mary was blessed and highly favored. The same is true for you and me. Pain does not detract from blessing.

"Wherein ye greatly rejoice, though now for a season, if need be, ye are in heaviness through manifold temptations" (1 Peter 1:6).

EXPECT THE UNEXPECTED

DAILY BIBLE READING: LUKE 1:29-38

"She was troubled at his saying, and cast in her mind what manner of salutation this should be" (Luke 1:29).

How did Mary feel when confronted by the angel Gabriel? Obviously she was startled. We can also gather that she was confused, perhaps even disturbed. One thing is certain—the angel's visit was quite unexpected. Mary was just an ordinary girl, going about her everyday life. Suddenly an angel came to announce that she would be the mother of God's Son!

On the one hand, the angel's visit was unexpected. On the other hand, I believe there was deep within Mary an expectation that every Jewish woman shared. God had promised that one day the Messiah would be born. Holy expectation dwelt in Mary's heart, ready to be awakened by just such an unexpected visit as this.

We can draw a parallel in our own lives. We meet plenty of unexpected happenings. How do we react? Do we fret and complain? Or do we respond as Mary did, saying humbly, "Behold the handmaid of the Lord; be it unto me according to thy word"?

Deep inside our hearts we, too, harbor a holy expectation. We long to become more like Jesus. We want His life to be formed in ours. Humbly submitting to unexpected frustrations is one way to realize our expectation of holiness. In obedience and submission our character can become more godly. Trials and temptations are meant for our betterment. So let's expect the unexpected; God has great things in store for us!

"My little children, of whom I travail in birth again until Christ be formed in you" (Galatians 4:19).

SEVEN REASONS WHY WE ARE ONE

DAILY BIBLE READING: EPHESIANS 4:4-6

"One body, and one Spirit" (Ephesians 4:4).

These have been called the "oneness verses." Seven times in these three verses we find the word *one* used to point out seven things as the reality of the believers' oneness.

First, we are *one body.* That's because we all, as many members, have the same Head—Jesus Christ. The body is the church.

Second, we are one because the *same Spirit* activates us. The Holy Spirit gives life to all.

Third, we are *one in hope.* For all of us, our hope is in Christ alone. He alone gives salvation. He alone, through the calling of the Spirit, gives us hope for eternal life.

Fourth, we are one because we are all *subject to one Lord*—Jesus Christ. Obedience to Him binds us as one.

Fifth, we have *one faith.* We all believe that we are saved by grace. We all cling to the same Gospel. We are all committed to Jesus Christ.

Sixth, we are *one in baptism.* This sacrament is what brings us into the oneness of the body of Christ. Baptized in the name of the Father, the Son, and the Holy Spirit, our oneness is complete.

It's significant that the seventh bond of oneness is the greatest. Seven is the number of completeness, of perfection. *God* is the crowning unity! He is our Father. Not only is He *above* us all, but He pervades everything by being *in* and *through* us all.

Bound together in such a oneness, we need not let petty differences and disagreements disturb and destroy us.

"That ye stand fast in one spirit, with one mind, striving together for the faith of the gospel" (Philippians 1:27).

PERSIST

DAILY BIBLE READING: MATTHEW 9:27-30

"Believe ye that I am able to do this?" (Matthew 9:28).

When I read this story, I get the picture that Jesus paid no attention to the two blind men when they first called out. Even though He heard their shouts, He just kept walking until He reached the house where He was staying. Jesus forced those men to persist. And persist they did. They followed and apparently burst unceremoniously into the house after Him.

Jesus had already tested their faith by not responding immediately; now He tested it further by asking a question: "Do you believe I'm able?"

Why did Jesus test these men so? We don't know all His reasons. But one reason may simply have been that He knew they did have faith. By further testing that faith, He was strengthening it!

Jesus still tests our faith today. He still challenges us to persist, even when the gates of Heaven seem to clang shut in our faces. To say that He pays no attention when we pray is false; God always pays attention when His children cry out to Him. But at times it may seem like He's not listening. Our suffering just goes on—our load is not lightened—deliverance is delayed.

Take heart! Jesus is testing you. "Do you believe that I can bless you and heal you?"

Even though our fragile faith trembles, let us answer yes! In His own good time, God will send deliverance. Only persist.

"Men ought always to pray, and not to faint" (Luke 18:1).

THE EYES OF THE HEART

DAILY BIBLE READING: MATTHEW 20:29-34

"Have mercy on us, O Lord, thou Son of David" (Matthew 20:30).

Today we also have two blind men calling out for healing, this time just outside of Jericho. Both pairs of blind men were persistent. In today's account, although the multitude tried to hush the men, they would not be silenced.

But I want you to notice the most significant similarity of all: in both stories, the blind men addressed Jesus as "Son of David."

Why is this significant? It shows what good spiritual vision these blind men had. Though physically blind, the eyes of their hearts were open much wider than those of many seeing people who thronged after Jesus.

Why does using "Son of David" prove their spiritual eyesight? It shows that they recognized Jesus as the Saviour. They knew that the Messiah would be born in the lineage of King David; that's why they called Him "Son of David." They also knew what the prophets had said of the Messiah: "Behold, your God will come . . . he will come and save you. Then the eyes of the blind shall be opened" (Isaiah 35:4, 5).

How many years had these blind men sat by Jericho's gate, treasuring with their spiritual eyesight the promise that the Messiah would come and restore their vision? We do not know, but we marvel that those who were blind to the earth had excellent vision in the eyes of their hearts.

Pray that God would make you blind to the earth so that the eyes of your heart can be enlightened.

"That the God of our Lord Jesus Christ, the Father of glory, may give unto you the spirit of wisdom and revelation in the knowledge of him: the eyes of your understanding being enlightened" (Ephesians 1:17, 18).

THE TREES OR THE FOREST?

DAILY BIBLE READING: ISAIAH 51:12-14

"Who art thou, that thou shouldest be afraid of a man that shall die?" (Isaiah 51:12).

In this chapter we find the Lord speaking to His people when they were captives in Babylon. After two generations in captivity, it seems Israel had become a fearful people. In these verses God rebukes them severely for their misplaced fear of man.

Those rebukes point just as sharply at us today. We are also prone to fear our fellow men. But why should we fear mortal man, who like grass blooms today and withers tomorrow? Such fear is absurd.

Worse still, such fear keeps us in bondage, if we fear "continually every day." There may be times in life when we have reason to momentarily fear wicked men. But there is no need to live in constant terror. That only makes us like those of whom Paul speaks in Hebrews 2:15, "who through fear of death were all their lifetime subject to bondage."

Worst of all, fear of man makes us forget God. A misplaced fear, indeed. It's like the saying "He can't see the forest for the trees." If our eyes are constantly on petty fears around us, we become blind to the great power of our Creator God, who "stretched forth the heavens, and laid the foundations of the earth" (verse 13). What a loss, to allow earthly fears to keep us captive when our great God is offering freedom!

So let's stop glancing fearfully at all the little "trees." Let's see the "forest" instead—the greatness and goodness of God.

"But I am the LORD thy God, that divided the sea, whose waves roared: The LORD of hosts is his name" (Isaiah 51:15).

WHY STAND YE GAZING?

DAILY BIBLE READING: ACTS 1:9-11; LUKE 19:11-27

"They looked stedfastly toward heaven as he went up" (Acts 1:10).

We can't blame the disciples for gazing into Heaven; you and I would also have gazed longingly after our dear Master if we had been there. Still, the angel's words carry a mild rebuke. "Why are you just standing around?" he seems to ask. "Jesus will come again, and in the meantime, you have work to do!"

That holds true for us as well. And what is it that we ought to be doing until our Saviour returns?

For answer we turn to Christ's parable of the ten talents in Luke 19. "Occupy till I come," the nobleman told his people. When he returned, he harshly scolded the man who didn't bother to use his talent. Why?

The one-talent man displayed a lack of trust. He also failed to actively further his master's kingdom while he was gone. And he was very self-centered.

Rather than standing around doing nothing, we should stay acutely aware that Christ may return at any time. Our whole focus should be to help His kingdom grow. Our trust in Him should be total and unflinching. And while we occupy till He comes, we should always be more concerned about others than ourselves.

"For I say unto you, That unto every one which hath shall be given: and from him that hath not, even that he hath shall be taken away from him" (Luke 19:26).

WHAT HAPPENED TO MARK?

DAILY BIBLE READING: ACTS 13:13-16

"And John departing from them returned to Jerusalem" (Acts 13:13).

Most of the time, the writer of Acts gives a thorough account of life in the early church. But occasionally we read a verse that leaves us full of curious questions.

Acts 13:13 is one such verse. Why did John part ways with Paul and Barnabas? John, also known as John Mark, had been chosen to assist Paul and Barnabas when they set out on their first missionary trip. John Mark must have felt honored. Then why did he return to Jerusalem when their planned journey had just begun?

Maybe John Mark had some of the same weaknesses you and I struggle with. Maybe he got homesick. Maybe he found the rigors of missionary travel a bit too much. Maybe he was just plain discouraged.

Whatever the reason for John Mark's desertion, Paul didn't like it one bit. Later on, when Barnabas again suggested taking John Mark as an assistant on a journey, Paul objected. "But Paul thought not good to take him with them, who departed from them from Pamphyllia, and went not with them to the work" (Acts 15:38).

This gives us reason to think that John Mark's desertion had been a grave mistake. We all know what it's like to make mistakes and wrong decisions.

Still, the story of John Mark can encourage us because he moved beyond his mistakes. He may have fallen, but he didn't stay down.

How do we know? John Mark was the man who wrote the Gospel of Mark. Also, we know that Paul later expressed great appreciation for this young man who had once sorely disappointed him:

"Take Mark, and bring him with thee: for he is profitable to me for the ministry" *(2 Timothy 4:11).*

GOD IS HERE

DAILY BIBLE READING: EXODUS 13:20-22

"In the edge of the wilderness ... the LORD went before them" (Exodus 13:20, 21).

Sometimes I get a wistful feeling as I read about this wonderful pillar of cloud that lighted the night and shadowed the day. What a comfort it must have been! Every minute of the day and night, the cloud reminded Israel, *God is here.* I think it would be nice to have such a sublime daily proof of God's presence on my own pathway.

But why be wistful? We, too, have assurances of God's presence.

One is the Holy Spirit, of whom Jesus said, "The Comforter, which is the Holy Ghost, whom the Father will send in my name, he shall teach you all things, and bring all things to your remembrance" (John 14:26).

Another reassurance God has given us is His holy Word, the Bible. Day or night, we can look to God's Word to light our path, just as the fiery cloud did for Israel. And just as the cloud stood between Israel and her enemies, so God's Word protects us from evil if we obey it.

What's more, the guidance of God's Word is as sure as the guidance of the cloud. As for inspiration, can we get any less inspiration from God's Word than Israel did from the cloud? Surely not.

God is here. That is the message of the Bible as surely as it was the message of the fiery pillar.

"Who went in the way before you ... in fire by night, to shew you by what way ye should go, and in a cloud by day" (Deuteronomy 1:33).

I'M LISTENING, LORD

DAILY BIBLE READING: 1 SAMUEL 3:1-10

"So Samuel went and lay down in his place" (1 Samuel 3:9).

When he first heard the voice, Samuel didn't realize what was happening. In his startled, perturbed state, he did what came naturally. He ran to Eli and asked, "Did you call me?"

Picture the old man rising bleary-eyed on one elbow. Was his voice a wee bit impatient? "No, I didn't call you. Go back to sleep."

In a way, this is the story of every person awakening to the drawing of God upon the heart. At first we are not sure what's going on. We barely understand our inner tumult. Our hearts are full of questions.

Like Samuel, we make mistakes. We don't recognize that these testings, these turbulences, are the voice of a loving God seeking our soul's salvation.

You are wise if you confide your questions and struggles to an elder. And the elder (perhaps your mother) is wise if she advises you to relax. Don't run hither and thither in agitation. Lie down again; wait upon God. He will keep on calling. So be sure to reply, "I'm listening, Lord!"

You may feel that you are young and ignorant and blind. But if you are willing to truly listen to God, He will do as He promised Paul in Acts 26:18.

"To open their eyes, and to turn them from darkness to light, and from the power of Satan unto God, that they may receive forgiveness of sins, and inheritance among them which are sanctified by faith that is in me" (Acts 26:18).

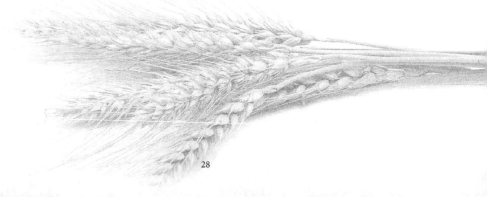

NO FUEL NEEDED

DAILY BIBLE READING: EXODUS 3:1-3

"The bush burned with fire, and the bush was not consumed" (Exodus 3:2).

This burning bush is one of the Bible's great mysteries. I don't pretend to understand all its symbolism, but one way we can think of the burning bush is as a picture of God's love. God's love needs no fuel!

To help us understand this idea, let's think about our own human love. In order to survive, our love mostly needs some type of fuel. We love others—if they love us. We love our children—because they are part of us. We love our parents, brothers, and sisters—because they're our family. We love our church brethren—because of the oneness we feel.

In each of those instances, we could say that our love is fueled by something, whether ties of family or ties of faith. There's something for our love to feed upon.

But God's love is its own fuel! It burned brightly toward the Israelites with a plan to deliver them. It burns brightly toward us. Through Jesus He offers deliverance from sin—all because of His unquenchable love that is its own fuel.

We, too, need a love that can burn without fuel. Jesus said, "But I say unto you, Love your enemies, bless them that curse you, do good to them that hate you. For if ye love them which love you, what reward have ye?" (Matthew 5:44, 46).

Obviously, it takes more than human love to love like God. It takes His love in our hearts, burning brightly even when there is no fuel.

"That ye may be the children of your Father which is in heaven: for he maketh his sun to rise on the evil and on the good, and sendeth rain on the just and on the unjust" (Matthew 5:45).

THEY STILL HAD MUCH TO LEARN

DAILY BIBLE READING: JOHN 1:41-51

"Rabbi, thou art the Son of God; thou art the King of Israel" (John 1:49).

Notice what the disciples call Jesus in these verses. It's amazing that in the first three days of knowing Jesus, they already recognized Him as Lamb of God, Messiah, Rabbi, King of Israel—and Son of God. We could think their faith was already fully developed in those early days.

But was it really? Even though they used these exalted names for Him, the disciples still had a lot to learn about Jesus and His purpose. Throughout the Gospels we read of times when the disciples doubted Him or clumsily thwarted His purpose through their ignorance. The three years the disciples spent with Jesus on earth included plenty of fumbles and blunders.

Jesus knew it would be so. That's part of what He meant in verse 51: "Hereafter ye shall see heaven open, and the angels of God ascending and descending upon the Son of man." In other words, "through your experiences as you walk with Me, you will learn a great deal about Me. As your spiritual insight grows, you will recognize Me as the One who connects man to God, like the ladder of Jacob's day."

We are like those disciples. Early on, we profess our faith in Jesus the Saviour, but it is through experience that we truly learn to know Him as Lord.

"God hath made that same Jesus . . . both Lord and Christ" (Acts 2:36).

TAKING HIS PROMISES IN VAIN

DAILY BIBLE READING: EXODUS 16:6-8

"He heareth your murmurings against the LORD" (Exodus 16:7).

That word *murmuring* is used quite a few times in the first half of Exodus 16. What does murmuring mean? My Bible gives a very plain—and sobering—definition in the margin, a word we're all familiar with: grumbling. Who has never grumbled about something?

Just because it's so common and universal doesn't mean that grumbling is excusable. It is never okay to grumble about our lot! This saying has jolted me into recognizing how serious grumbling is: "To swear is wicked because it is taking God's name in vain. To murmur is likewise wicked, for it takes God's promises in vain."

Oh no, we would never take God's name in vain. That would mean we are abusing His name, calling it futile, empty, even false. How terrible!

Yet when Israel grumbled, they were taking God's promises in vain. God had promised to bring them out of Egypt to "the land which the LORD will give you, according as he hath promised" (Exodus 12:25). By their murmurings, the children of Israel said they didn't believe God's promises.

Has not God given us wonderful promises in Jesus Christ? Read the first few verses of Ephesians 1. Through faith in Jesus we are promised adoption as children, acceptance in the beloved, redemption through His blood . . . The list goes on. Shall we faithlessly murmur, thus saying that God's promises are in vain?

"Neither murmur ye, as some of them also murmured, and were destroyed of the destroyer" (1 Corinthians 10:10).

THE THIRTEEN COMMANDMENTS

DAILY BIBLE READING: HEBREWS 13:1-6

"Let brotherly love continue" (Hebrews 13:1).

Hebrews 13 is such an imperative chapter. Remember? *Imperative* is another word for "command." Anyone who thinks the Christian faith is a "free" religion that makes no demands upon us ought to read Hebrews 13. God makes superhuman demands upon the Christian! And rightly so. If we are in Christ and He in us, what else should we do but live the Christ-life? (Which is but another way of saying that we must live a superhuman life.)

Let's go over the chapter, repeating in our own words the thirteen commandments given here. Some are worded more gently than others—but each one carries a charge.

1. Keep on loving each other as brethren (verse l). (This is the prime command that takes in all the others.)
2. Follow the example of faithful leaders (verse 1)
3. Be hospitable (verse 2).
4. Do what you can for those in prison (verse 3).
5. Don't be covetous (verse 5).
6. Be content with what you have (verse 5).
7. Don't get carried away by erroneous teachings (verse 9).
8. Be willing to follow Jesus even if it means persecution (verse 13).
9. Praise God continually (verse 15).
10. Give willingly to the needy (verse 16).
11. Obey those who have the rule over you (verse 17).
12. Pray for all (verse 18).
13. Willingly receive exhortation (verse 22).

What a list of commandments! Because we know our human weakness, it's enough to make us quail. But the same chapter gives us beautiful encouragement:

"Now the God of peace . . . make you perfect in every good work to do his will, working in you that which is wellpleasing in his sight, through Jesus Christ" (Hebrews 13:20, 21).

WAITING AND LOOKING

DAILY BIBLE READING: TITUS 2:12-15

"Looking for that blessed hope, and the glorious appearing of the great God and our Saviour Jesus Christ" (Titus 2:13).

A small boy once ran inside to his big sister, exclaiming, "Come quick! I want to show you something!"

So she hurried with him to the door. "There!" cried the child, pointing to the sky. "See that bright light? It can't be a star, because it's daytime. Could it be—" and he stopped to catch his breath. "Could it be that Jesus is coming back?"

Big sister squinted at the distant, gleaming object. Then she chuckled. "David, that's just an airplane. The reason it shines so is because the sun reflects from its wings."

"Oh," said David, crestfallen. His shoulders drooped as he walked away.

Returning to her work, his sister felt remorseful. Why had she laughed? "I should be more like him," she told herself. "He's eager to see Jesus coming back. I tend to forget about Christ's Second Coming. Maybe I'm too preoccupied with earthly things."

That goes for us all, doesn't it? But really, our life should be full of expectation. Let's eagerly look and wait for Christ's return! We, too, can long to see Him, yearning to be freed once and for all from our sinful nature.

Verse 12 tells us how to live so as to sustain a vibrant expectation of Christ's return: denying ungodliness and worldly lusts, we should live soberly, righteously, and godly in this present world.

"So that ye come behind in no gift; waiting for the coming of our Lord Jesus Christ" (1 Corinthians. 1:7).

Day 34

OPPORTUNITIES FOR JOY

DAILY BIBLE READING: JAMES 1:1-4

"My brethren, count it all joy" (James 1:2).

As Christians, we are so blessed. We have far more opportunities for joy than unbelievers do. Do you know why? Because even our troubles are opportunities for joy. And life seems to contain a lot of troubles, in all shapes and sizes and varieties. What a privilege, then, to count each trial a joy! Don't forget—James says, "Count it *all* joy."

This can be hard to understand: in our human nature, we think troubles do not bring joy at all. Is it true that every frustration, every temptation, every battle with sin and self, can be counted as an opportunity for joy?

Yes, it really is true. Verse 3 explains why. Trials test our faith. The testing of our faith gives our patience, or endurance, a chance to grow.

How do we react to trials and pressures? Our reactions are the best indicator of our endurance level. Sure, we can be kind when people are nice to us—but what happens when they're not? Our true character will show in the difficult situations.

The best part is that God won't leave us to battle alone. We can ask Him for strength to endure. So James is right. Troubles are opportunities for joy—they give our endurance a chance to grow. The more our endurance grows, the more we can be ready for anything, and the more joy we can have.

"But rejoice, inasmuch as ye are partakers of Christ's sufferings; that, when his glory shall be revealed, ye may be glad also with exceeding joy" (1 Peter 4:13).

CONSTRUCTIVE ANGER

DAILY BIBLE READING: EPHESIANS 4:26, 27

"Be ye angry, and sin not" (Ephesians 4:26).

In the King James Version, these are puzzling words. They become clearer when translated thus: "In your anger do not sin" (NIV).

Anger in itself is not necessarily sin. But uncontrolled anger can do so much damage. By nursing angry grudges, we allow the devil to come between friends. If we angrily "let off steam," we hurt others. Anger can destroy relationships. And if we bottle up our anger, it can destroy us from within.

Really, the only time anger is good is when it's directed at sin or mistreatment. Consider these two examples of righteous anger. Unless the anger you experience is similar to these, then it's an anger you need to get rid of.

First, an incident from the early days of King Saul's reign. The Ammonites threatened to disgrace Israel by making them slaves and gouging out their right eyes. When this news reached Saul, he was out in the field plowing. Immediately Saul realized that radical action was needed. He butchered his oxen and sent the pieces throughout the land along with the message: "This is what will happen to the oxen of anyone who refuses to follow Saul and Samuel into battle!" The army that answered his summons soundly defeated the Ammonites.

For a gentler example of righteous anger, we go to Mark 3. Here we find Jesus in a synagogue, noticing a man with a deformed hand. What made Jesus angry? The hypocritical Pharisees were more concerned about Sabbath-keeping than the healing of a fellow man. Christ's anger kindled His healing love, and the man was made whole.

"He . . . looked round about on them with anger, being grieved for the hardness of their hearts" (Mark 3:5).

GOOD LOOKS WILL SAVE YOU

DAILY BIBLE READING: ISAIAH 45:22-25

"Look unto me, and be ye saved" (Isaiah 45:22).

Are you surprised by today's title? What? Surely we can't be saved because we're good-looking!"

No, we must understand the words differently. If we turn our eyes and look the right way, we will be saved. That is a "good look." Remember the brass serpent God told Moses to lift up when many Israelites lay dying from poisonous snakebites? One look—one pleading, faith-filled look—could bring healing to a dying man.

"Look unto me, and be ye saved." Those are the words of the Lord here in Isaiah 45. The original Hebrew word translated *look* actually had a meaning closer to "turn." Turn unto me—turn away from self and sin and idols—turn to Jesus who died on the cross to save.

Three "good looks" are necessary for salvation. The first one is looking unto Jesus on the cross for redemption. The second is found in Hebrews 12:2: "Looking unto Jesus the author and finisher of our faith; who . . . is set down at the right hand . . . of God." This is a lifelong look. Constantly, daily, hourly, we must look to Jesus for grace and victory in the battle of life.

Our third "good look" is found in Titus 2:13: "Looking for that blessed hope, and the glorious appearing of the great God and our Saviour Jesus Christ." This, too, is a constant looking, a constant watching and waiting for our Saviour to come again.

The poet John Parker wrote, "There is life in a look." In ourselves we are without spiritual life and strength. Let us look to the Lord and receive all we need!

"They looked unto him, and were lightened: and their faces were not ashamed" (Psalm 34:5).

THEY DIDN'T TAKE LUNCH

DAILY BIBLE READING: MARK 6:32-36

"They have nothing to eat" (Mark 6:36).

Reading these verses, I'm struck with how eager people were to follow Jesus. Imagine yourself in a similar situation. Suppose you heard of a certain speaker who would speak at a town some miles away. Because the journey there and back will take awhile, you'll be gone all day. Would you be so eager to hear this speaker that you would drop whatever were doing and walk (or run) to hear him? Would you leave so quickly that you'd forget to take a lunch?

I have a hard time picturing myself going off with nothing to eat. But that's what these Galileans did. When they saw Jesus and His disciples entering a boat on the lake and realized He was leaving, they dropped their work and hastened on foot along the lakeshore to meet Him where He landed.

They were well-rewarded for their efforts. Though Jesus could have been offended at their intrusion into His privacy, He welcomed them instead. He saw them for what they were: sheep without a shepherd and in need of food. Spiritual food first of all, but once their lunchless state became apparent, Jesus provided physical food as well.

Let's follow our Lord with such abandonment! Let's not worry overmuch about earthly provisions. Let's focus on Him and His great love. Let's believe it: lunch will be provided.

"I am the bread of life: he that cometh to me shall never hunger" (John 6:35).

GIVE ME DISCERNMENT

"If thou criest after knowledge . . . then shalt thou understand" (Proverbs 2:3, 5).

Suppose you went to the doctor because you were experiencing stomach pain. Suppose he gave you a prescription, and you went home with a bottle of pills. Would you set that bottle on a shelf and never open it? Would you hope that just having those pills in the house would cure your pain?

The Bible is God's prescription for us, a medication for all our ills. But will God's Word do any good if we just leave it lying on a shelf?

"Oh, I don't do that," you may protest. "I read the Bible every day."

Fact is, we can read God's Word daily and still not gain much value from it. What does it take for God's medicine to really work on our spiritual ills? We need to apply the Word to our everyday situations. We need to practice and obey His loving commands in the nitty-gritty of life.

That's not easy. It takes spiritual understanding to know how God's medicine should be applied. We need to cry after understanding, diligently seeking it. "Give me discernment," pleads the psalmist in Psalm 119:125 (NIV).

So let this be our daily prayer: that along with His prescription, the Great Physician will dispense discernment and understanding so we can apply what He prescribes.

"Making mention of you in my prayers; that the God of our Lord Jesus Christ . . . may give unto you the spirit of wisdom . . . the eyes of your understanding being enlightened" (Ephesians 1:16-18).

 Day 39

HANDS AND FEET FOR FAITH

DAILY BIBLE READING: JAMES 2:14-20

"I will shew thee my faith by my works" (James 2:18).

Believe—trust—have faith. Those three terms are more or less interchangeable. In today's reading we find James using *faith* and *believe* alternately. To *believe* in Jesus is to rely on Him, adhere to Him, and hope only in Him. *Faith* means conviction and commitment. *Trust* refers to an unshakable hope for Heaven.

But all these definitions are abstract. They exist inside our heads. Faith, trust, and belief are real, yes—but what proves they are real? How are they shown to be actual and true?

That's the question James is answering in these verses. Unless faith is expressed in daily living, it isn't real. Our belief and trust need to be implemented and operating. Our faith needs hands and feet!

A faith—a trust—a belief that is real and righteous before God is a busy thing. It cannot merely talk of good things that need to be done. It must work, doing all it can for one's fellow man. True faith does more than transform our thoughts. True faith changes us, transforming our conduct from selfishness to selfless serving.

"Your work of faith, and labour of love, and patience of hope in our Lord Jesus Christ" *(1 Thessalonians 1:3).*

Day 40

SPIRIT AND LIFE

DAILY BIBLE READING: JOHN 6:53-66

"The words that I speak unto you, they are spirit, and they are life" (John 6:63).

The Jews were constantly challenging Jesus. Here in John 6 they reminded Him of the manna God sent to Israel and challenged Him to provide a similar miraculous sign. Jesus replied, "I am the bread of life. You can't even have life unless you eat my flesh and drink my blood." For these literal-minded Jews, it was a shocking message. Was Jesus promoting cannibalism? If only they could have understood that Jesus was speaking of spiritual realities!

What about us? Do we recognize the full spiritual meaning of "drinking Christ's blood and eating His flesh"?

Eating this living bread from Heaven means becoming united with Christ, receiving Him into our lives. His life becomes ours. How do we become united with Christ? First, believe in His death and resurrection for salvation from sin; second, live our daily lives as He requires.

But none of this is possible without the Holy Spirit. That's why Jesus said in verse 65, "No man can come unto me, except it were given unto him of my Father." God alone gives spiritual life. He reveals truth to us, dwells in us, and enables us to live according to the truth.

"Even the Spirit of truth; whom the world cannot receive, because it seeth him not, neither knoweth him: but ye know him; for he dwelleth with you, and shall be in you" (John 14:17).

Day 41

THE WORD AT WORK

DAILY BIBLE READING: 1 THESSALONIANS 2:13

"The word of God, which effectually worketh also in you" (1 Thessalonians 2:13).

God has a tool for working in us: the Word of God, which Paul describes in another place as "quick, and powerful" (Hebrews 4:12). But He can't operate this tool in our lives unless we receive it.

Twice in this verse, Paul uses the word *receive*. In the Greek, those are two different words. The first means to receive formally, outwardly. In other words, using our ears to listen or our eyes to read the Word of God.

But true receiving goes deeper than that. The second *receive* means to welcome, to take willingly into our hearts. That is when the Word can start working!

However, like an electric tool that must be plugged in before it operates, so must we be connected to the source of power before God's Word can be effective. God, of course, is the source of power. And our faith is the cord, the plug that connects us. As Paul says, the Word works effectively "in you that believe."

Once we have willingly received it and are connected to the power source, the Word "pierces even to the dividing asunder of soul and spirit...and is a discerner of the thoughts and intents of the heart" (Hebrews 4:12). The Word of God penetrates. It reveals evil. It transforms our lives at the deepest part of our being.

What a privilege to be in the hands of such a Surgeon who wields such a dynamic tool.

"Being born again ... by the word of God, which liveth and abideth for ever" (1 Peter 1:23).

PERFECT—FOR THIS STAGE

DAILY BIBLE READING: MATTHEW 5:43-48

"Be ye therefore perfect" (Matthew 5:48).

"Perfect?" you gasp. "How can I be perfect? I still have so much to learn."

If you go to the orchard in June, you won't find an apple that's fully mature. In fact, it might still be quite small and green. But that doesn't mean it isn't perfect. Though immature, the apple is perfect for the stage it's expected to be in June.

Yes, it's true that you and I still have much to learn. We still struggle with a tendency to sin. But must that tendency prevent us from striving to be like Christ? Must it keep us from the spiritual exercise of disciplining ourselves? Because if we seek excellence in spiritual things, discipline is definitely what we need.

No, we can't become Christlike overnight—no more than an apple can be ripe in June. But God does expect us to strive for perfection at the stage we're in right now.

What a beautiful incentive God gives! He promises that if we strive for perfection, we shall one day truly be perfect, even as Christ is perfect. "Beloved," wrote John the apostle, "now are we the sons of God, and it doth not yet appear what we shall be"—the apple is still green—"but we know that, when he shall appear, we shall be like him" (1 John 3:2).

"And every man that hath this hope in him purifieth himself, even as he is pure" (1 John 3:3).

CONTAINERS

DAILY BIBLE READING: JEREMIAH 18:1-6

"So he made it again another vessel, as seemed good to the potter to make it" (Jeremiah 18:4).

What does a potter make? Pots, of course. Or, to use Bible language, *vessels.* Today we might say *containers.*

God is the potter. Mankind is the clay. And God's purpose in creating mankind has never been anything but container-ship.

In our vanity, we want self-importance. We think we can accomplish many things. We are deluded with the thought that we are something, in and of ourselves. That's the mistake Adam and Eve made, and humans have been making it ever since.

What folly! We are meant for container-ship. We are intended as vessels to contain the life of God. Unless we become emptied of ourselves, we are not accomplishing anything. Even Jesus emptied Himself of human ambition: "made himself of no reputation" (Philippians 2:7).

Think about the different aspects of container-ship mentioned in the Scriptures. We are temples for the Spirit of God (1 Corinthians 3:16). We are earthen vessels to contain the light of the knowledge of the glory of God (2 Corinthians 4:7). We are branches for containing the "sap" of God's power and love flowing from the Vine Himself (John 15).

Back in Eden, when man fell, our container-ship was shattered. But Jesus came to restore our relationship with God. And now, through faith, we can know the reality of Colossians 1:27:

"Christ in you, the hope of glory" (Colossians 1:27).

LIVING SACRIFICE

DAILY BIBLE READING: ROMANS 12:1, 2

"Present your bodies a living sacrifice" (Romans 12:1).

Those two words, *living sacrifice,* express the paradox of the Christian life. A paradox is a statement that seems to say two opposite things. Certainly the Jews would have said that the words *living* and *sacrifice* contradicted each other. How can you sacrifice something to God without killing it? The Jewish altars held dead bodies, ran red with the blood of endless sacrifices.

But God wants no more dead sacrifices. He himself provided the supreme sacrifice—the life of His own Son. This Lamb of God has swept away all those slain sacrifices demanded by the Law; and in their place is a compelling love that draws us to sacrifice our lives—a living sacrifice!

However, as D.L. Moody whimsically put it, the trouble with a living sacrifice is that it's still able to crawl off the altar. Our earthly self is still alive, still ready to rebel against the promptings of the Holy Spirit.

That's why being a living sacrifice is something we have to constantly work at. It's why Paul said, "I die daily" (1 Corinthians 15:31). It's also why he said in Romans 6:11, "Reckon ye also yourselves to be dead indeed unto sin, but alive unto God through Jesus Christ our Lord."

So how can we be a living sacrifice? The living part refers to the life of Christ in our spirits. And the sacrifice part refers to Paul's words in Romans 6:13: "Yield yourselves unto God, as those who are alive from the dead, and your members as instruments of righteousness unto God."

"But to do good and to communicate forget not: for with such sacrifices God is well pleased" (Hebrews 13:16).

Day 45

GUARDING YOUR HEART

DAILY BIBLE READING: PROVERBS 4:23-27

"Keep thy heart with all diligence" (Proverbs 4:23).

The original Hebrew could also be translated, "Keep thy heart above all keeping." This is a very earnest charge. Above all, keep your heart! Guard it with every means available.

But what does Solomon mean by the word *heart?* He doesn't mean our blood-pumping organ. He isn't urging us to have regular checkups with a heart specialist or to get bypass surgery done if there are blockages. The word *heart* is used over nine hundred times in Scripture, but it almost never refers to man's literal heart.

Heart as used in the Bible can have different meanings. It can refer to our minds, our emotions, our wills, our feelings, or our affections. Perhaps it would be safe to say that when the Biblical writers use *heart*, they are referring to the inner man.

Now we can see why guarding the heart is so important. What we think, feel, and desire will determine how we live. Jesus said, "Where your treasure is, there will your heart be also" (Matthew 6:21). So let us keep our hearts from being defiled by sin or disturbed by trouble. Let us refrain from hurting the hearts of others, while protecting our own hearts from the damage Satan would inflict upon it.

But Jeremiah says something about the heart that can bring us almost to despair: "The heart is deceitful above all things, and desperately wicked: who can know it?" (Jeremiah 17:9). How can we guard such a heart from harm? There is only one answer, and that is God's promise in Ezekiel 36:26: "A new heart also will I give you"—and this He does through Jesus Christ.

"And the peace of God . . . shall keep your hearts and minds through Christ Jesus" (Philippians 4:7).

THE GREATEST RIVER

DAILY BIBLE READING: REVELATION 22:1-6

"He shewed me a pure river of water of life, clear as crystal, proceeding out of the throne of God" (Revelation 22:1).

If I asked you to name the world's largest river, you might mention the Nile or the Amazon. But have you heard of the Gulf Stream? It has been called a "river in the ocean" because it is a distinct current that follows a distinct route. The Gulf Stream originates in the Caribbean Sea and follows the coastline of North America before crossing the Atlantic toward northern Europe. It carries fifty times as much water as all the world's rivers combined!

We may be puzzled by the thought of a river flowing through the ocean. Can it actually be distinguished from the surrounding water? Yes, indeed. A satellite photo will show the Gulf Stream as a much deeper blue than the rest of the ocean. You see, the water of the Gulf Stream is exceptionally clear and, because of its southern origin, up to eighteen degrees warmer than surrounding waters. Certain European countries have a warmer climate than others in the same latitude because of the warming influence of the Gulf Stream.

The Gulf Stream is beneficial in other ways: its strong current carries many nutrients for fish, and it has a cleansing effect, sweeping away pollutants.

Isn't all this a lovely illustration of God's river of water of life? That river flowing from the throne of God is certainly greater by far than any of the world's rivers. It is completely pure and crystal clear. It brings the warmth of God's love and the cleansing of His grace. Praise God for the river of His Holy Spirit!

"There is a river, the streams whereof shall make glad the city of God" (Psalm 46:4).

ACCORDING TO THY MERCY

DAILY BIBLE READING: PSALM 25:6-11

"According to thy mercy remember thou me" (Psalm 25:7).

What is the single most important realization a person must have before she can truly be a Christian? It is this: to realize how great is our sin. First and foremost, we must be conscious of sin! We must see that sin has made us rotten to the core.

David knew this. "O LORD, pardon mine iniquity; for it is great," he says in verse 11. In Psalm 51:3 he writes, "I acknowledge my transgressions: and my sin is ever before me."

Why is it so important to be conscious of sin? Because without that consciousness, we cannot see the Lord for who He really is: a loving, merciful God. It is the darkness of sin that brings out the pure light of God's love and mercy.

As long as we do not properly recognize our sin, our religion will be shallow. We will go about with a vague idea that we can be our own redeemer by doing good works; we do not understand how greatly we need the Saviour.

But once we do recognize our need and our sin—what a blessed state we achieve! Now we can cry with David, "According to thy mercy remember thou me." Not according to anything we deserve; not according to any obligation God has toward us. No, no—it is only by His mercy that we can find grace in His sight.

And then the promise is ours: "The meek will he teach his way" (Psalm 25:9). Made meek by the realization of our sin and God's mercy, we are ready for Him to teach us the ways of righteousness.

"According unto the multitude of thy tender mercies blot out my transgressions" (Psalm 51:1).

HE BELIEVED

DAILY BIBLE READING: GENESIS 15:1-6

"And he believed in the LORD; and he counted it to him for righteousness" (Genesis 15:6).

Did you know that here in Genesis 15 is the very first time the word *believed* is used in the Bible? What a powerful word it is! For Abraham, believing made the difference between despair and joy.

Abraham must have been close to despair. We can detect that in verses 2 and 3, where he explained to the Lord that his servant would probably inherit all his possessions.

Then came God's astounding promise: "You will have descendants as innumerable as the stars of the sky!" What would you and I have done in the face of such an incomprehensible promise? Would we, like Abraham, have believed?

Because of Abraham's faith, God's promises were as good as done. Blessings as unimaginable as the sand on the seashore and the stars in the sky were his.

And best of all, as the Apostle Paul reminds us in Romans 4, Abraham's faith was counted to him as righteousness. Abraham had probably performed many good deeds in his life, but that isn't what made him right with God. His faith did that—faith in the righteousness of God.

You and I have a promise just as stupendous as the one God gave to Abraham: the promise of redemption through the blood of Christ! We can't comprehend that promise, but will we believe? If we do, our faith will be counted to us for righteousness.

"Faith was reckoned to Abraham for righteousness" (Romans 4:9).

THE FIRST RECORDED PRAYER

DAILY BIBLE READING: GENESIS 18:23-26

"Shall not the Judge of all the earth do right?" (Genesis 18:25).

In this chapter we find recorded the first lengthy, solemn prayer of the Bible. What a beautiful picture of prayer it is, with Abraham drawing near to commune with God! We can learn many things from this prayer, but today, let's focus on just one point.

Notice how Abraham gave a reason for his request. He pleaded, "God, You are the Judge of all the earth, and You are righteous; how then could You slay the righteous with the wicked?" That was the foundation for Abraham's supplication.

You and I must often come before God to plead for His mercy toward our failings. Like Abraham, we need a foundation for our requests.

But what reason can we bring to God that will ensure His mercy? Can we tell Him He is obligated to forgive us? Can we speak of our own righteousness as a reason for Him to be merciful toward us?

No, no. There is only one reason we can offer to God when we approach His throne of grace. And that reason is Jesus Christ. His great sacrifice is the infinite reason why every penitent sinner can expect to find mercy. Armed with this precious "reason," we can "come boldly to the throne of grace."

"The prayer of the upright is his delight" (Proverbs 15:8).

Day 50

DUST AND ASHES

DAILY BIBLE READING: GENESIS 18:27-33

"Behold now, I have taken upon me to speak unto the Lord, which am but dust and ashes" (Genesis 18:27).

We marvel at the humility of Abraham. He could have been puffed up with pride: God had come in person to visit him! But no, Abraham considered himself of the lowest, nothing but dust and ashes.

It is true of all of us. In the Garden of Eden, God said to our first parents, "Dust thou art, and unto dust shalt thou return" (Genesis 3:19). We are as nothing before such a righteous, exalted God. Job felt the same. "I . . . repent in dust and ashes" (Job 42:6). And King David said in 2 Samuel 7:18, "Who am I, O Lord God . . . that thou hast brought me hitherto?"

However, that is only one side of the story. God does want us to recognize our lowliness. But at the same time, He wants us to "come boldly unto the throne of grace" (Hebrews 4:16) to make our requests known. That is what Abraham did here in Genesis 18. Though estimating himself as lowly as the dust, he nevertheless interceded for the doomed city and for the few righteous that still lived there.

Today it is Jesus who makes it possible for us to "draw near . . . in full assurance of faith" (Hebrews 10:22). Praise God, we who are but "dust and ashes" can have "boldness to enter into the holiest by the blood of Jesus" (Hebrews 10:19).

"Unto me, who am less than the least of all saints, is this grace given" (Ephesians 3:8).

ESCAPE FOR YOUR LIFE

DAILY BIBLE READING: GENESIS 19:17-21

"Look not behind thee, neither stay thou in all the plain; escape to the mountain" *(Genesis 19:17).*

Two things stand out in this story of Lot's deliverance from Sodom: the urgency of the angels and the weakness of the man they were helping. Listen to the emphatic, urgent words used by the angels: Escape for your life! Don't look behind you. Don't linger in the plains. Escape to the mountains, or you will die.

Yet how weak Lot was. He hesitated and lingered. The angels literally took his hand to pull him out. And he protested the command to flee to the mountains, "Please don't make me go that far! Disaster might catch up with me! Let me stop at a little village instead."

Aren't we all like Lot when it comes to the saving of our souls? We hesitate and linger, but God takes hold and saves us through His mercy and grace.

His commands to us are urgent too. Don't look back to sin and Satan! Don't "stay in the plain" by depending on self and the world. Reach up to Christ Himself, the mountain of refuge.

Shall we be like Lot and insist on our own ideas rather than fully obeying the urgings of the Holy Spirit? Let us not give in to such folly. Let us rather "press toward the mark for the prize of the high calling of God in Christ Jesus" (Philippians 3:14).

"But we are not of them who draw back unto perdition [destruction]; but of them that believe to the saving of the soul" (Hebrews 10:39).

PATIENCE AND ANGER

"Brimstone and fire from the LORD out of heaven" (Genesis 19:24).

In this sobering story of Sodom's destruction, we notice two things about God: His patience and His anger.

Imagine the patience God had—agreeing to spare a whole city if only ten righteous people could be found in it! We cannot comprehend how patient God is. But if it were not for His patience, there would be no hope for us. In Romans 15:5 Paul calls our heavenly Father "the God of patience." How thankful we should be for divine patience.

But there is another side to God; and we can be thankful for this side too. This is the side of God's anger toward sin. One glance at the fire and brimstone raining from Heaven shows us the magnitude of God's anger. Sin is an abomination to Him.

The Old Testament refers many times to God's anger. For example, "I shall execute judgments in thee in anger and in fury and in furious rebukes. I the LORD have spoken it" (Ezekiel 5:15).

Once—only once—is the word *anger* used in the New Testament in connection with Jesus. We read about it in Mark 3. Jesus was angry at the synagogue attendants because of the hardness of their hearts; in other words, because of their sin. Praise God for His anger against sin, because His power can give us victory over it!

"The LORD is slow to anger, and great in power, and will not at all acquit the wicked" (Nahum 1:3).

THE PRAYER OF A RIGHTEOUS MAN

DAILY BIBLE READING: GENESIS 19:27-29

"God remembered Abraham, and sent Lot out" (Genesis 19:29).

Had Abraham slept that night? The Bible doesn't tell us, but it does say that he got up early the next morning. Breathless with urgency, Abraham climbed to the heights of Hebron, the very spot where he had spoken with the Lord the day before. One question must have consumed his mind: were his prayers answered? Did God find ten righteous men and spare those cities?

But no. From the plain rose awful billows of smoke. What a fearsome sight that must have been! Not only the wicked cities, but all the country round about, was being consumed by that fire from Heaven.

Time and again the Scriptures allude to this terrible morning when Sodom and Gomorrah were destroyed. Isaiah speaks of it, and so does Jude. Jesus Himself reminded us of Lot's wife. In Revelation we read of Babylon's destruction, and it makes us think of Sodom: "When they shall see the smoke of her burning, standing afar off for the fear of her torment, saying, Alas, alas, that great city Babylon, that mighty city! for in one hour is thy judgment come" (18:9, 10).

Did Abraham know when he saw the smoke that Lot had been saved? Was he aware that God had answered his prayer by rescuing Lot from the burning?

Truly, the "effectual fervent prayer of a righteous man availeth much" (James 5:16). May we all do like Abraham and pray mightily that souls can be saved from the bottomless pit of eternal fire.

"Sodom and Gomorrah, and the cities about them in like manner . . . are set forth for an example, suffering the vengeance of eternal fire" (Jude 7).

SEALED

DAILY BIBLE READING: REVELATION 7:1-3

"Hurt not the earth...till we have sealed the servants of our God in their foreheads"
(Revelation 7:3).

Here is a wonderful picture of how God takes care of His own. Can we imagine those four angels, standing on the four corners of the earth and holding the power of the four winds in their hands? Once the angels unleashed that power, great havoc would be wrought.

But wait! The four angels were arrested by the voice of still another angel. "Don't harm anything until we've sealed God's children!" the fifth angel cried.

Sealed. It is such a comforting word. We read about being sealed in 2 Corinthians 1:22: God, "who hath also sealed us, and given the earnest of the Spirit in our hearts." Long ago, officials used to seal letters by putting their stamp on them. By giving us His Spirit, God puts the stamp of His divine likeness on us.

The seal of the Holy Spirit is God's guarantee for His promises. That's why Paul says in that same chapter of 2 Corinthians 1, "All the promises of God in him are yea, and in him Amen" (verse 20). The Holy Spirit is our hope of salvation, our foretaste of Heaven, and our premise for help in life's struggles.

Because the struggles will come; we are all familiar with the storms of life. But praise God! He has sealed us into His tender care.

"In whom also after that ye believed, ye were sealed with that holy Spirit of promise"
(Ephesians 1:13).

HOW TO VIEW YOUR CIRCUMSTANCES

DAILY BIBLE READING: PSALM 31:22-24

"The LORD preserveth the faithful" (Psalm 31:23).

Do your circumstances today look gloomy to you? They can hardly be worse than the circumstances David describes in Psalm 31. If you read the whole psalm, you'll hear him speak of trouble, grief, sighing, slander, and fear. He says he feels forgotten, broken, weak, consumed.

What a dark cloud these circumstances could have cast over David's day! But David didn't let those circumstances get between him and God. He didn't look at God through his circumstances; he looked at his circumstances through God.

How do we know that? Because, in spite of his complaints, David's main theme in this psalm is the presence of the Lord. Like a shining golden haze, that presence hovers over everything. God's presence sheds healing rays over the darkest circumstances!

Viewing his circumstances through God didn't come naturally for David. In verse 22 we see him reacting just like we do when something unpleasant happens: in sudden fear we feel God has forsaken us. "For I said in my haste, I am cut off from before thine eyes."

But let's emulate David's courageous *nevertheless*. "Nevertheless thou heardest the voice of my supplications when I cried unto thee." Let's keep calling upon God. The light of His mercy can conquer our gloom.

"LORD, lift thou up the light of thy countenance upon us" (Psalm 4:6).

NOT WHO, BUT WHY

DAILY BIBLE READING: JOHN 1:19-24

"I am the voice of one crying in the wilderness, Make straight the way of the Lord"
(John 1:23).

Who are you?

That's a question we face every now and then. Perhaps seeing us for the first time, people ask, "Are you Amish? Mennonite?" They're like the Pharisees who sent messengers to inquire about the identity of the stranger who was baptizing on the banks of the Jordan. "Are you Elijah? Are you a prophet? Are you the Christ?"

But the Pharisees missed the point. They wanted to know who *John* was, but John wanted them to know who *Jesus* was!

So John didn't directly answer the Pharisees' question. He didn't tell them who he was. He simply told them *why* he had come. He told them he was merely a "voice," preparing the way for one far greater than he—and thus he pointed them to Christ.

When curious people inquire about our identity, we do well to remember John's example. Exactly who we are or what label we carry is not that important. Forget about the who; think about the why! The purpose of our life is to show forth at least a little bit of Christ in the wilderness of this world.

"He was a burning and a shining light" (John 5:35).

LESS THAN A SLAVE

DAILY BIBLE READING: JOHN 1:25-28

"Whose shoe's latchet I am not worthy to unloose" (John 1:27).

We would all agree that John the Baptist was a great man, an important messenger of God. Jesus even said of John that the earth had seen no greater prophet (Luke 7:28).

But did John consider himself important? Did he go about putting on airs? Was he eager and proud to administer baptism to Jesus?

No indeed. Comparing himself with Jesus, John said, "I'm not worthy to stoop and help Jesus remove His shoes." In other words, John was saying he wasn't even worthy to be Christ's slave. Helping his master unbind his sandals was a slave's job. John felt unworthy for even such a menial task.

How much more should you and I lay aside our pride to serve Christ! The truth is, once we really understand who Jesus is and what He did for us, our pride and self-importance melt away. John knew. He was so dazzled by Christ's greatness that his own importance dwindled to nothing. You and I should be the same.

"He must increase, but I must decrease" (John 3:30).

TWO-SIDED REALITY

DAILY BIBLE READING: ROMANS 5:1-5

"Rejoice in hope of the glory of God. And not only so, but we glory in tribulations also" *(Romans 5:2, 3).*

By taking the last part of verse 2 and the first part of verse 3 together, we can see it clearly: there are two sides to the Christian life. On the one hand, we are justified: we have faith, we have peace, we have access, we stand in grace, we rejoice in hope—all because of Jesus. What a glorious reality! We are complete in Christ, accepted by God. We stand in a highly privileged place. Instead of being God's enemies because of sin, we have become His friends; yes, even His dearly beloved children.

Yet on the other hand, we're still human. We still need to grow. Problems and tribulations accost us daily. Such a two-sided reality! At the same time, we have the status of kings and the duties of slaves. We enjoy the presence of Christ, even while fully aware of the pressure of sin.

Can we reconcile these two sides? Indeed, Paul tells us we can rejoice and glory. The tribulations help us grow. God uses the problems to develop our perseverance. This in turn strengthens our character and deepens our trust in God. Every day we can learn more about the power of Christ, who dwells in us through His Spirit. Let's never forget—we are complete in Him, yet we still need to grow.

"Knowing this, that the trying of your faith worketh patience" (James 1:3).

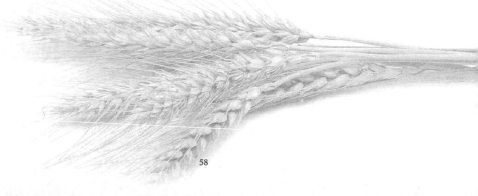

CHRIST THE WARRIOR

DAILY BIBLE READING: PSALM 45:2-5

"Gird thy sword upon thy thigh, O most mighty, with thy glory and thy majesty"
(Psalm 45:3).

What royal language this psalm uses to describe the glory of Jesus Christ! In this picture of Jesus the warrior, we are reminded of Revelation 19:13-15: "And he was clothed with a vesture dipped in blood: and his name is called The Word of God. And the armies which were in heaven followed him upon white horses, clothed in fine linen, white and clean. And out of his mouth goeth a sharp sword."

Glory and majesty and prosperity—all are promised to the warrior. But this is not the earthly kind of warrior. Christ's glory is in His cross. He shed His own blood to save His army. Christ's majesty is in His meekness, and His prosperity stands upon the truth. No wonder that His right hand will teach us wondrous things.

"Thine arrows are sharp . . . whereby the people fall under thee" (verse 5). How can we reconcile this warlike statement with our lowly, merciful Saviour? His arrows are tipped with love. It is love that pierces our hearts and makes us ready to die to self that we might live to Him.

How joyfully we hearken to the grace that pours from our Captain's lips, as Luke says, "And all . . . wondered at the gracious words which proceeded out of his mouth" (4:22).

"And take the helmet of salvation, and the sword of the Spirit, which is the word of God"
(Ephesians 6:17).

CHRIST THE KING

DAILY BIBLE READING: PSALM 45:6, 7

"Thy throne, O God, is for ever and ever" (Psalm 45:6).

Next the writer of Psalm 45 portrays Christ as King. "Thy throne, O God, is for ever and ever." How do we know that these words point to Jesus? Hebrews quotes these words, saying that God spoke them to His Son. "But unto the Son he saith, Thy throne, O God, is for ever and ever" (1:8). In Psalm 93:2 the psalmist said it this way: "Thy throne is established of old: thou art from everlasting."

As for that great scepter of righteousness in the hand of the King, Balaam had prophesied, "There shall come a Star out of Jacob, and a Sceptre shall rise out of Israel" (Numbers 24:17). Earlier still, we have the prophesy of the patriarch Jacob: "The sceptre shall not depart from Judah . . . until Shiloh come; and unto him shall the gathering of the people be" (Genesis 49:10).

Verse 7 pictures Christ anointed as King. We read in the Gospel of John that the Holy Spirit came to rest upon Jesus like a dove; was not that His divine anointing? Yes, it was as the psalmist says, "the oil of gladness above thy fellows"—yet we as followers of the King may share in His anointing. The oil of the Holy Spirit drips down over His kingly robes and reaches even to us. "The anointing which ye have received of him abideth in you" (1 John 2:27).

"The king shall joy in thy strength, O LORD; and in thy salvation how greatly shall he rejoice! Honour and majesty hast thou laid upon him" (Psalm 21:1, 5).

CHRIST THE BRIDEGROOM

DAILY BIBLE READING: PSALM 45:8-15

"She shall be brought unto the king in raiment of needlework . . . with gladness and rejoicing shall they be brought" (Psalm 45:14, 15).

Finally, the psalmist describes Christ as Bridegroom. If the pictures of Warrior and King seemed vivid, this picture of the Bridegroom is the most vivid of all!

In ancient Eastern weddings, the groom was more important than the bride. He led the procession, while the bride stayed secluded in her chamber. The guests followed in the procession, craning their necks to see the marvelous garments of the groom. That's why the psalmist spoke of the garments that smelled of spices. Indeed, our heavenly Bridegroom comes with the sweet savor of salvation from the ivory palaces of Heaven!

At last the groom and the bride stand side by side. "Upon thy right hand did stand the queen in gold of Ophir" (Psalm 45:9). The bride's raiment glistens with gold; yet by nature she had neither beauty nor gold—it is all the gift of her kingly groom, making her "all glorious within."

Is that not the picture given us by Paul in Ephesians 5? Did not Christ give His life for the church, that He might present her to Himself as a glorious bride? May we all be present for this great wedding feast of Christ the Bridegroom and the church as bride!

"The king hath brought me into his chambers: we will be glad and rejoice in thee" (Song of Solomon 1:4).

Day 62

TWO DIFFERENT STOCKPILES

DAILY BIBLE READING: ROMANS 2:5-10

"Treasurest up unto thyself wrath against the day of . . . judgment" (Romans 2:5).

Have you noticed that whenever the New Testament speaks of judgment, works are almost always mentioned too? Judgment and works go hand in hand. When it comes to the day of judgment, it's by our works that we will be judged. Here in Romans 2 we get the picture of two very different stockpiles. What is a stockpile? It's a store, a treasury, an accumulation of something we will refer to in the future.

In the sight of God, our works build the stockpile that will determine our eternal destiny. Do we want to stockpile glory, honor, and peace, as in Romans 2:10? Or do we want to stockpile indignation, wrath, tribulation, and anguish?

"Patient continuance in well-doing"—that contributes to the first stockpile. Disobedience to the truth, contentiousness, evil—all those contribute to the second stockpile.

"But aren't we saved by grace?" we might ask. Oh, yes, Jesus alone redeems—but it is our works that show whether or not we are trusting in that redemption.

"Lay up for yourselves treasures in heaven" (Matthew 6:20).

A GOD WHO LEADS AND DRAWS

DAILY BIBLE READING: EXODUS 34:5, 6; ROMANS 2:4

*"And the L*ORD *passed by before him, and proclaimed, The L*ORD*, The L*ORD *God, merciful and gracious, longsuffering, and abundant in goodness and truth" (Exodus 34:6).*

Two men tried to move a flock of sheep from one field to another. One man got behind the sheep and began shouting at them, hoping to drive them by sheer force through the gate. The sheep scattered in confusion.

The other man took up a position at the front of the flock. With gentle, coaxing words he called them while he walked ahead to lead. The sheep came willingly after him to their new pasture.

You and I need to "change pastures." We need to leave the old life of serving self; we need to move on to the pastures of repentance and amendment through the grace of God. God is our Shepherd. Which of the two men better shows God's ways as He guides us unto Himself?

In Exodus 34, God described Himself: merciful, gracious, long-suffering. And in Romans 2 we read of the riches of God's goodness, His forbearance, and His long-suffering.

God doesn't drive us like beasts. He leads, He draws, He allures with His eternal love. He is even willing to wait while we drag our reluctant feet. "And therefore will the LORD wait, that he may be gracious unto you" (Isaiah 30:18). Dare we ignore and despise such kind leadings?

"Or despisest thou the riches of his goodness and forbearance and longsuffering; not knowing that the goodness of God leadeth thee to repentance?" (Romans 2:4).

NOT YE, BUT THOU

DAILY BIBLE READING: EXODUS 20:1-7

"Thou shalt have no other gods before me" (Exodus 20:3).

Can we imagine the scene? All Israel stands trembling at the foot of Mount Sinai, while thunder crashes and lightning flashes from the peak. Then comes a voice like a trumpet, loud enough for the universe to hear: "I am the LORD thy God, which have brought thee out of the land of Egypt, out of the house of bondage."

Notice the Law was given to a people already saved from bondage. The Ten Commandments were not given as a means of salvation. They were given so that God's people could fulfill His will as a "kingdom of priests, and an holy nation" (Exodus 19:6).

In a sense we could say that the Law was given to govern a nation. But it's more personal than that. The Law was directed at individuals—at you and me. Where we speakers of English have only one second-person pronoun, *you,* the original Hebrew had two. Our *you* is both singular and plural. But the Hebrew had both a singular and a plural; the Ten Commandments use the singular.

The English of the King James Version preserves the two pronouns. *Thou* is singular and *ye* is plural. So even if we can't read the original Hebrew, we know the commandments are directed at individuals. They don't say, "*Ye* shall not kill," but "*Thou* shalt not kill."

The commandments are for everybody, yes; but specifically, they are for me. The only way a whole nation—or a whole church—can fulfill God's purpose is if the individuals live by the law.

"The law of the LORD is perfect, converting the soul" (Psalm 19:7).

ARE WE DOERS?

"But Jonah rose up to flee unto Tarshish from the presence of the LORD" (Jonah 1:3).

Have you noticed that everybody and everything in the story of Jonah obeyed God, *except* the man who claimed to be a follower of God?

God sent a mighty tempest to wreck the ship that carried the rebellious prophet. The wind obeyed.

The dice, or lots, cast by the sailors obeyed God, for they pointed to Jonah as the culprit.

The sailors, even though they hated to do it, obeyed God and threw Jonah into the sea. Not only that, but they "feared the LORD exceedingly, and offered a sacrifice unto the LORD, and made vows" (verse 16).

The fish obeyed God. "The LORD spake unto the fish, and it vomited out Jonah upon the dry land" (Jonah 2:10).

The Ninevites obeyed God. "So the people of Nineveh believed God, and proclaimed a fast, and put on sackcloth, from the greatest of them even to the least of them" (Jonah 3:5).

The gourd did exactly as God bade it; growing fast, it spread a welcome shade over the pouting prophet. And at the word of the Lord, a worm came to shrivel up the gourd.

But Jonah? He pouted. He ran. He rebelled. He had heard God's word, but he didn't do it. Christ had a sharp rebuke for people like that: "Why call ye me, Lord, Lord, and do not the things which I say?" (Luke 6:46).

"But whoso looketh into the perfect law of liberty, and continueth therein, he being not a forgetful hearer, but a doer of the work, this man shall be blessed in his deed" (James 1:25).

SEAWEED ROUND HIS HEAD

DAILY BIBLE READING: JONAH 2:1-6

"The weeds were wrapped about my head...yet hast thou brought up my life from corruption" (Jonah 2:5, 6).

This prayer of Jonah's from the whale's belly must be one of the most remarkable prayers ever. Its descriptive power alone makes it stand out. As Jonah prays, we can almost hear the crash and roar of the waves closing over his head! In fact, Jonah didn't just picture the waves going over his head. He describes them as reaching right into his soul.

Most picturesque of all is Jonah's description of the great depth to which he had fallen. Seaweed wraps around his head as he plunges down, down—right to the roots of the mountains. (Yes, a mountain's peak is impressive—but if we could see its roots, they would be impressive too.)

Finally, Jonah says that the "earth with her bars was about me for ever." Picture the huge iron-barred gate of a prison clanging shut.

But then came the whale! To Jonah, that was deliverance. From the whale's belly he praised God for delivering him.

Here is a powerful lesson for us. If I had been inside that whale, could I have praised God for saving me? Or would I have been frightened because the situation still looked extremely precarious? I'm afraid my prayer might have been a bargaining prayer. I might have told the Lord that if He gets me out of this, I'll always serve Him.

Not so Jonah. He neither pleaded nor bargained. He simply praised God for deliverance—right from the belly of the whale.

"Salvation is of the LORD" (Jonah 2:9).

Day 67

GOD'S TIMETABLE

DAILY BIBLE READING: GENESIS 37:23-28

"Then there passed by Midianites merchantmen" (Genesis 37:28).

Think back over your morning. You planned it, didn't you? Got out of bed at 6:30—ate breakfast at 7:30—arrived at work at 8:30. All according to schedule.

Those Midianites had followed a schedule too. From the northeast near the Sea of Galilee, they loaded their camels with merchandise. Then they plodded down the long road toward Egypt until one day they came upon a motley band of shepherds eating their lunch near Dothan. The Midianites thought they were following their own schedule—but unknown to them, God's timetable was in control.

Consider this: at a certain point in time, Joseph left his father's house in Hebron and traveled to Shechem, seeking his brothers. Not finding them, he continued to Dothan, a place right on the route used by merchants on their way to Egypt. At the exact hour when the Midianites came, Joseph lay at the bottom of that pit.

Mere coincidence? Hardly. Everything was going according to God's timetable! God wanted Joseph in Egypt; and under God's control, events took him there.

Isn't this a comfort for us? We may think we are following our own schedule, but our schedule is subject to God's timetable. His sovereign power governs all that happens on earth. We can gratefully pray with the psalmist, "My times are in thy hand" (Psalm 31:15).

"It is not for you to know the times or the seasons, which the Father has put in his own power" (Acts 1:7).

HE NOTICED THEIR SADNESS

DAILY BIBLE READING: GENESIS 40:2-7

"Wherefore look ye so sadly to day?" (Genesis 40:7).

Joseph had plenty of reason to be sad. Although he had the comfort of knowing he was trusted by the captain of the guard, he also faced the depressing possibility that he might never be released from prison—all because of Potiphar's wife.

But Joseph was not wallowing in his own misery. Apparently he had followed the advice of the psalmist: "Commit thy way unto the LORD; trust also in him; and he shall bring it to pass. And he shall bring forth thy righteousness as the light" (Psalm 37:5, 6).

Far from drowning in self-pity, Joseph was quick to notice the sadness on the faces of his fellow prisoners. The struggles he had endured gave him a keen sympathy toward others. His attitude was "What can I do to help you?"

Joseph is a classic example of what Paul wrote to the Corinthians: "The God of all comfort; who comforteth us in all our tribulation, that we may be able to comfort them which are in any trouble, by the comfort wherewith we ourselves are comforted of God" (2 Corinthians 1:3, 4).

"Look not every man on his own things, but every man also on the things of others" (Philippians 2:4).

HE FORGOT

DAILY BIBLE READING: GENESIS 40:18-23

"Yet did not the chief butler remember Joseph, but forgat him" (Genesis 40:23).

In Ecclesiastes 9:13-18 there is a little story you may have never heard. Once there was a little city (so goes the parable) with only a few inhabitants. Along came a great king with his army and besieged the little city. The outlook seemed hopeless.

Yet in that little city was one wise man, who by his wisdom delivered the city. Perhaps he thought up a crafty plan that outwitted the besiegers. "But," says Solomon, "no man remembered that poor man."

Doesn't that little parable remind us of what happened to Joseph? He certainly was a wise man—wise enough to ask God when a problem was too great for him. And when God revealed the meaning of his fellow prisoners' dreams to him, Joseph had just one request for the butler: "Think on me . . . and make mention of me unto Pharaoh, and bring me out of this house" (Genesis 40:14).

We can't help feeling indignant at the butler's forgetfulness. To think that Joseph had brought about his deliverance—yet the butler went his merry way and forgot him.

But are we so different? There is One who delivered us by His wisdom—nay, by His own lifeblood. He brought us up out of the miry pit of sin. Do we remember our Saviour enough? Are we fulfilling His requests?

"Bless the LORD, O my soul, and forget not all his benefits: who forgiveth all thine iniquities . . . who redeemeth thy life from destruction" (Psalm 103:2-4).

IT IS NOT IN ME

DAILY BIBLE READING: GENESIS 41:9-16

"And Joseph answered Pharaoh, saying, It is not in me: God shall give Pharaoh an answer of peace" (Genesis 41:16).

Joseph's life was adorned with humility. Human nature being what it is, Joseph could have been swollen with pride when Pharaoh's messenger summoned him. But no. When Pharaoh said, "I've heard you can interpret dreams." Joseph replied simply, "It is not in me."

Daniel was like that too. After God revealed Nebuchadnezzar's dream to him, he burst forth in a song of praise to the Lord: "He revealeth the deep and secret things." And to the king he said, "There is a God in heaven that revealeth secrets."

Most of all, though, Joseph reminds us of Jesus. Even He said, "The Son can do nothing of himself, but what he seeth the Father do" (John 5:19). When the Jews marveled at His teaching, Jesus told them, "My doctrine is not mine, but his that sent me" (John 7:16). And later when the Jews began to seriously challenge Jesus, He said, "I speak that which I have seen with my Father" (John 8:38).

Let us strive and pray for this humility in our lives. It doesn't come naturally. Perhaps Joseph learned humility through his trials. Think back to his early days, when he was the dreamer. There he didn't sound quite so humble, did he? There is hope for us too. We can learn humility, if we submit to our Father.

"He that speaketh of himself seeketh his own glory: but he that seeketh his glory that sent him, the same is true, and no unrighteousness is in him" (John 7:18).

A PICTURE OF JESUS

DAILY BIBLE READING: GENESIS 41:37-43

"Can we find such a one as this is, a man in whom the Spirit of God is?" (Genesis 41:38).

What a dramatic promotion—from dungeon to throne in a single day! And, like so much of Joseph's story, it reminds us keenly of Jesus. Let's count the similarities, starting back when Jacob sent Joseph to see how things were going with his brethren. Even so the Father sent Jesus for our welfare.

Joseph was the well-beloved son; Jesus was God's beloved and only begotten. Joseph's brethren rejected him; of Jesus we read that "he came unto his own, and his own received him not" (John 1:11).

The brothers' plotting against Joseph reminds us of the Jews' plotting against Jesus. Joseph was falsely accused and condemned; so was Jesus.

Thrown into a pit, and finally into prison—is not that a picture of Christ's crucifixion and death? Indeed, as Paul wrote to the Philippians, Christ was "found in fashion as a man . . . humbled himself, and became obedient unto death, even the death of the cross" (2:8).

Like Joseph brought rescue to a fellow prisoner, so Jesus gave salvation to one of the thieves crucified with Him.

But it's in his exaltation that Joseph portrays Jesus most vividly of all. God has set Jesus "at his own right hand . . . far above all principality, and power . . . and every name that is named . . . and hath put all things under his feet, and gave him to be the head over all things" (Ephesians 1:20-22).

"Wherefore God also hath highly exalted him, and given him a name which is above every name" (Philippians 2:9).

BREAD OF LIFE

DAILY BIBLE READING: GENESIS 41:53-57

"And all countries came into Egypt to Joseph for to buy corn" (Genesis 41:57).

Do we realize how valuable grain was in Bible times? Everybody ate grain. With no refrigeration, grain could be stored much longer than milk and vegetables. Indeed, grain was so important that some countries used it as money.

It didn't take much to induce famine in those days. Chemical fertilizers and pesticides didn't exist. Though Egypt had some irrigation, many countries did not, so they were at the mercy of rainfall. Variations in weather could cause desperate situations. When we consider all that, we realize how wonderful was God's provision through Joseph. Without that provision, whole nations might have crumbled.

And our comparison of Joseph with Jesus continues. In John 6, we find Jesus faced with five thousand hungry people. To the disciples the thing looked impossible! But for the God of the universe, this was another opportunity to show that nothing is impossible with Him. The five thousand were fed, and the leftovers were abundant.

Our world is in the grips of a terrible spiritual famine, alienated from God because of sin. But God has made provision for this famine too. He sent His Son to be the Bread of life for mankind. In the words of Isaiah 55:1, Jesus invites us all: "Ho, everyone that thirsteth, come ye to the waters, and he that hath no money; come ye, buy, and eat; yea, come, buy wine and milk without money and without price."

Freely Jesus offers His life as manna for us today. Without price, yes, but we have our part to do: We must come, we must hearken, we must seek, and we must call on God.

"Hearken diligently unto me, and eat ye that which is good, and let your soul delight itself in fatness" (Isaiah 55:2).

HARSH YET TENDER

DAILY BIBLE READING: GENESIS 42:7-24

Hereby ye shall be proved" (Genesis 42:15).

How it must have puzzled Joseph's brothers to have the Egyptian ruler speak so roughly to them. How they quailed beneath his harsh accusations, and how they trembled at the ultimatum to bring Benjamin to meet him.

And how their terrible secret sin must have weighted their hearts. We know it did, because they admitted their guilt to each other: "We are verily guilty concerning our brother" (verse 21). So effectively had they kept the secret all these years that their aged father still blamed himself for the death of his favorite son.

Secret sin is a hard companion. It haunts us with guilt, anxiety, and uncertainty.

But wait! Is there such a thing as secret sin? God knows everything that is in our hearts. And He wants to bring us to repentance. He allows trials and tribulations in our life. We feel we are being harshly dealt with—just like those frightened brethren, who trembled because of famine and because of this frowning governor who suspected them of being spies.

Yet behind all this was the tenderest love. Joseph was testing his brothers because he hoped for a restored relationship. Unknown to them, Joseph understood their words and had to leave the room because of his tears. He saw the beginnings of repentance—just as our loving God will see when we repent.

"I say unto you, that likewise joy shall be in heaven over one sinner that repenteth" *(Luke 15:7).*

ALL THESE THINGS

DAILY BIBLE READING: GENESIS 42:29-38

"Ye bring down my gray hairs with sorrow to the grave" (Genesis 42:38).

"All these things are against me!" To Jacob the load seemed more than he could bear. (A literal translation from the Hebrew would be "All these things are upon me.") We get the picture of a white-haired man stooped beneath a heavy burden.

Picture Jacob's sons telling all about their ill-fated trip to Egypt, adding one burden after the other to their father's shoulders. "Joseph is dead!" he cries. "Simeon is as good as dead. And you want to take Benjamin too!" Besides all that, Jacob was frightened by the account of that harsh Egyptian official. The mysteriously returned money also alarmed him. Jacob was a good man, but even good men can be overwhelmed with grief and fear. And so he cried, "All these things are against me!'

Can't we all identify with Jacob's desperate wail? Haven't we all had times when our load seemed too great to bear?

But what Jacob didn't know—and what we often forget—is that actually, "all these things" were for him. Under a sovereign God, all these trials would work out to the good of Jacob and his family. "All things work together for good to them that love God, to them who are the called according to his purpose" (Romans 8:28).

"Nay, in all these things we are more than conquerors through him that loved us" (Romans 8:37).

A PICTURE OF CONVERSION

DAILY BIBLE READING: GENESIS 43:11-17

"God Almighty give you mercy" (Genesis 43:14).

This part of Joseph's story could be used as an illustration of how it is when you come to conversion. Like Jacob's starving family, you are aware of a lack in your life. Jacob knew what he would have to do in order to be saved from starvation: send Benjamin to Egypt. You also know that if you want to be saved from sin, you must surrender all and come to Jesus.

Yet you fear the unknown. You compare your own feebleness with God's righteous greatness. You scrape together some "gifts" to bring Him—a few good works of your own, to find favor in His sight. Just so, Jacob assembled a present of honey and spices, and planned to send double the money.

In his heart, though, Jacob knew that it all depended on the mercy of that great man down in Egypt. So also, you come to the realization that you must throw yourself on the mercy of God. And so you come to Jesus, having surrendered your "Benjamin," and ask Him for spiritual food to give you life.

What a welcome awaits you! Love's arms enfold you—a love that asks not for presents, but only that you bring yourself. Did Joseph's brethren fear that he would cast them into prison? What a shock when they were invited to a feast instead! So, like the father of the prodigal son, Jesus has slain the fatted calf and waits to receive you with joy.

"Jesus saith unto them, Come and dine" (John 21:12).

WITH ME WHERE I AM

"And when he saw the wagons which Joseph had sent to carry him, the spirit of Jacob their father revived" (Genesis 45:27).

In his wildest dreams Jacob had not imagined receiving such news: "Joseph is yet alive, and he is governor over all the land of Egypt" (Genesis 45:26).

Not only that, but Joseph wanted his family to come and be with him. He made ample provisions for their journey: wagons for transportation; "meat for his father by the way"; "ten asses laden with the good things of Egypt"; "changes of raiment"; "three hundred pieces of silver"; and above all, a heartfelt invitation.

The disciples of Jesus, sorrowful after the Crucifixion, were also stunned to hear that Jesus lived. And today the resurrected Christ is in Heaven, inviting us to come! He has gone to prepare a place for us: "If I go and prepare a place for you, I will come again, and receive you unto myself; that where I am, there ye may be also" (John 14:3).

Think of the provisions Jesus has made for our journey. He Himself is the way—the transportation to get us to Heaven. He provides all the spiritual meat we may need. He paid the price of sin (far more than three hundred pieces of silver). For our raiment He gives us blood-washed robes of righteousness. And He fills our saddlebags with the riches of grace!

And Jesus warns us just as Joseph did his brethren, "See that ye fall not out by the way." Let the road to Heaven be traveled in love and unity.

"Father, I will that they also, whom thou hast given me, be with me where I am; that they may behold my glory, which thou hast given me" (John 17:24).

SHALL WE BE ASHAMED?

DAILY BIBLE READING: GENESIS 47:1-7

"Then Joseph came and told Pharaoh, and said, My father and my brethren . . . are come"
(Genesis 47:1).

From archaeological discoveries in ancient Egyptian tombs, we know that the court of Egypt's king was a very grand place. Joseph had been accustomed to that grandeur for years. Life for him was surrounded with ivory and bedecked with jewels.

Then down from the land of Canaan comes an old, stooped man with his descendants—all of them shepherds in work-stained garments. And behold, the prime minister of Egypt rushes out to greet them! Not only that, but he falls on the neck of the old patiarch and weeps for a "good while."

Joseph's father has come. Is he ashamed to bring this toil-worn man from the lowly pastures into the glittering court of the king? Not at all. Eagerly he presents Jacob to Pharaoh. And then a marvelous thing happens. Pharaoh in all his glory bends his head to receive a blessing from Jacob!

Our Saviour was a lowly man, and He calls His followers to lowliness as well. Are we ready to tear ourselves away from the world's glittering allurements? Are we ready to identify ourselves with mere shepherds, rather than clinging to the company of the rich?

Think of it! Jesus came from the courts of Heaven—yet He is not ashamed to call us brethren (Hebrews 2:11). Shall we be ashamed of Him?

"And now, little children, abide in him; that, when he shall appear, we may have confidence, and not be ashamed before him at his coming" (1 John 2:28).

DIMENSIONS OF LOVE

DAILY BIBLE READING: EPHESIANS 3:14-19

"What is the breadth, and length, and depth, and height" (Ephesians 3:18).

The dimensions of God's love! Can we grasp them? Only with the eyes of a spiritually enlightened heart. God's love is total, so vast that really there are no dimensions. Why then does Paul urge us to "know" God's love? Because he wants us to experience it; in experiencing it we learn to know it. Yet it is a kind of knowing that will always need to grow. The measurements of the dimensions just keep expanding.

The breadth (width) of God's love encircles the globe. It covers the whole vast mystery of salvation in Christ.

The length of God's love reaches throughout the ages, from eternity past to eternity future. It certainly covers the whole length of your life.

God's love can reach the depth of the lowest fallen, the deepest depravity of the human heart. And God's love can touch the deepest discouragement and despair.

The height of God's love reaches to the throne of Heaven. And wonder of wonders, His love brings us to that throne! He "that overcometh will I grant to sit with me in my throne, even as I also overcame, and am set down with my Father in his throne" (Revelation 3:21). God's love is so high that it is beyond the reach of any foe who may assail us.

"O the depth of the riches both of the wisdom and knowledge of God!" (Romans 11:33).

FULLNESS

DAILY BIBLE READING: COLOSSIANS 2:8-10

"For in him dwelleth all the fulness of the Godhead bodily" (Colossians 2:9).

Fullness is a curious word. According to the dictionary it simply means the quality or state of being full. Here in Colossians 2, Paul is saying that God's fullness—in other words, all of God Himself—dwelt in Christ.

Then in Ephesians 3, Paul brings the concept of fullness into our own experience. He prays in verse 19 that we may be filled with all the fullness of God. This doesn't mean that we can contain all of God. But it means we can be filled, in our little measure, from that great fullness. It means that we can be complete in Christ, as Paul says in Colossians 2:10.

How can this fullness, this completion, be ours? Love is the key. As we experience Christ's love, the way is opened for Him to infill us. His fullness is available—but we must reach for it through faith and prayer.

Then there's another point. The church can be filled with the fullness of Christ. He is so vast that He needs a whole body of believers to contain Him. Paul says it this way in Ephesians 1:22, 23:

"The church, which is his body, the fulness of him that filleth all in all" (Ephesians 1:22, 23).

ALL IN ALL

DAILY BIBLE READING: 1 CORINTHIANS 15:25-28

"That God may be all in all" (1 Corinthians 15:28).

"All in all": another phrase that gives us a feeling of awe because it's so vast and incomprehensible. We find the phrase four times in the New Testament. Here in 1 Corinthians 15, "all in all" is used to express the utter supremacy of God. He is supreme over all things everywhere. Sometimes it's hard for us to remember how very much God is our all. Let's learn to pray as the psalmist did in Psalm 73:25: "Whom have I in heaven but thee? and there is none upon earth that I desire beside thee."

The phrase is used in 1 Corinthians 12:6: "And there are diversities of operations, but it is the same God which worketh all in all." God does it all. He gives the gifts; He enables us to use them. He is the fountain of goodness and power.

We find the phrase in Colossians 3:11, in the context of different kinds of people: Jew, Greek, barbarian, slave, free. Paul wants us to see that such surface differences don't matter, because "Christ is all, and in all." God in Christ created all mankind; all are purchased by His blood. He is the Maker, Preserver, Saviour, and Judge of all men. Christ *is* all that matters, and He is *in* all who believe! Thus He is the Christian's all—all his hope and happiness.

And finally in Ephesians 1:23, we read that the church "is his body, the fulness of him that filleth all in all." Christ needs the church to fulfill Himself. He is the Head, the church is the body—altogether filled with Christ.

Let's praise Him, and daily pray that we may be filled more and more with Christ, the all in all.

"And the Lord shall be king over all the earth: in that day shall there be one Lord, and his name one" (Zechariah 14:9).

Day 81

SUPPLYING THE NEED

DAILY BIBLE READING: LUKE 8:43-48

"Thy faith hath made thee whole" (Luke 8:48).

For twelve years this woman had sought healing, spending any money she made in hope of a cure. But no doctor could help her. Did she pray during those twelve years? Did she daily bring her desperate need to the throne of God? We don't know. But surely this act of faith—reaching out to touch the hem of Christ's garment—could be called a prayer.

It's the kind of prayer we all should pray daily. Don't we all have needs? When we pray, we bring our needs to God and commit them by faith to Him. As for the results, we can safely leave them to God. He will supply all we truly need.

Indeed, God is able to supply more than we can imagine! In Philippians 4:19, Paul says, "God shall supply all your need according to his riches in glory by Christ Jesus." If God supplies "according to his riches," then it will be beyond what we expect—just as the woman experienced instant healing after the touch of faith.

So let us also ask in faith—the kind of faith that does not waver, even if it takes years before our prayers are answered.

"Now unto him that is able to do exceeding abundantly above all that we ask or think, according to the power that worketh in us, unto him be glory in the church by Christ Jesus throughout all ages, world without end. Amen" (Ephesians 3:20, 21).

Day 82

THE SON OF MAN

DAILY BIBLE READING: MATTHEW 26:62-66

"Hereafter shall ye see the Son of man sitting on the right hand of power, and coming in the clouds of heaven" (Matthew 26:64).

Why did Jesus call Himself the Son of man more often than any other name?

Son of man is first used in Daniel 7:13: "I saw in the night visions, and, behold, one like the Son of man came with the clouds of heaven, and came to the Ancient of days, and they brought him near before him." Already here in Daniel's vision, the "Son of man" is the Messiah. The clouds may represent the awesome presence of God, the Ancient of days. Years later when Jesus stood before the high priest, He referred to this passage in Daniel. The Jews knew instantly that He was calling Himself the Messiah—and to them it was blasphemy.

John 1:51 gives us the best hint as to why Jesus is called the Son of man. Jesus told Nathanael, "Hereafter ye shall see heaven open, and the angels of God ascending and descending upon the Son of man." Do you see what He meant? Jesus is the ladder, the link, between Heaven and earth.

He can be this link because He is both fully God and fully man. Because He is human, He has known every temptation common to man; but because He is God, He won victory over every temptation.

God became man so that He could die for us. That is why Daniel saw in his vision the Son of man brought near to God: in Jesus, all mankind is brought near.

"Forasmuch then as the children are partakers of flesh and blood, he also himself likewise took part of the same; that through death he might destroy him that had the power of death, that is, the devil" (Hebrews 2:14).

Day 83

DON'T FORGET

DAILY BIBLE READING: DEUTERONOMY 8:2-6

"Thou shalt remember all the way which the LORD thy God led thee" (Deuteronomy 8:2).

If you were given a present, surely you would always remember who gave it. Surely you wouldn't let the memory fade until you forgot it was a gift and started thinking that it was something you earned for yourself.

Unfortunately, in spiritual matters this is something we tend to do. Moses feared the children of Israel would do so once they were safely settled in Canaan. He feared they would forget that this land flowing with milk and honey was a great and precious gift from God. Instead, they might begin to feel that they had earned the right to live there because of their own accomplishments.

That is why, throughout Deuteronomy, Moses used the word *remember* over and over—thirteen times, to be exact! Remember how God led you. Remember how He fed you. Remember how He provided water for your thirst. And when you become prosperous in Canaan, remember that God is the One who gives power to get wealth (Deuteronomy 8:17, 18).

Above all, Moses told the people to "Remember, and forget not, how thou provokedst the LORD thy God to wrath in the wilderness . . . ye have been rebellious against the LORD."

You and I need to remember the same two things: that we have sinned, and that it is God who saves us through the gift of His Son. If we remember that, we will always remain grateful for God's great gift.

"And thou shalt remember that thou wast a bondman in the land of Egypt, and the LORD thy God redeemed thee" (Deuteronomy 15:15).

ARE YOU AN EXAMPLE?

DAILY BIBLE READING: PHILIPPIANS 2:19-23

"But ye know the proof of him, that, as a son with the father, he hath served with me in the gospel" (Philippians 2:22).

Paul didn't hesitate to use real people as examples when he wanted to illustrate a point. Here in Philippians 2 he used three different people to illustrate humility. Jesus, of course, was the foremost and greatest example. Verses 5-8 give the most sublime picture of humility to be found anywhere: the Son of God forsaking Heaven to die on a cross.

Then in verses 17-22, Paul presents Timothy as an example of caring humility. No one else cared and served as sincerely as Timothy did.

And finally, in verse 25, Paul describes Epaphroditus as a humble, steadfast fellow soldier.

Now here is the question for us: could Paul use you and me as examples of humility today? Could we serve as flesh-and-blood examples for others to emulate?

That makes us shrink, doesn't it? Oh, no, not me! But the truth is, you and I are being examples every day, whether we know it or not. The question is not "Are we examples"—but "Is our example good or bad?" Does my life exemplify humility and faith, or do others see arrogance and selfishness?

There is only one way we can be a good example, and that is to follow the humble example of the One who said, "For I have given you an example, that ye should do as I have done to you" (John 13:15).

"Be thou an example of the believers, in word, in conversation, in charity, in spirit, in faith, in purity" (1 Timothy 4:12).

THE VOICE OF THE LORD

DAILY BIBLE READING: PSALM 29:3-8

"The voice of the LORD is powerful; the voice of the LORD is full of majesty" (Psalm 29:4).

What a poem this is! The poet seems to describe a violent thunderstorm that starts over the Mediterranean Sea ("The voice of the LORD is upon many waters") and moves on to the highlands of Lebanon, where the thundering power of God's voice is so great that it splits the mighty cedars. I've read that some of Lebanon's cedars were 150 feet tall! Verse 6 pictures the forest trees waving under the onslaught of the wind: "He maketh them also to skip like a calf." Then the storm moves down to the wilderness of Kadesh, south of Judea. Beasts are terrified by the thunder and trees stripped of their leaves by the mighty wind.

Bible writers frequently used thunder to describe God's voice. Job, Isaiah, Moses, and John all spoke of God's voice thundering. What power! What majesty! Thunder, lightning, earthquakes—all are used to picture God's power, and yet none can fully demonstrate it. No man can fully comprehend the power of God.

Still, Paul urges us to grasp God's power: "That ye may know . . . what is the exceeding greatness of his power to us-ward who believe, according to the working of his mighty power" (Ephesians 1:18, 19). And to demonstrate that power, Paul uses something greater than thunder: "Which he wrought in Christ, when he raised him from the dead" (verse 20). The earth has seen no greater demonstration of power than the day the voice of the Lord raised Jesus from the grave.

"According to the gift of the grace of God given unto me by the effectual working of his power" (Ephesians 3:7).

HE SHALL BE THEIR SHEPHERD

DAILY BIBLE READING: EZEKIEL 34:22-28

"And I will set up one shepherd over them, and he shall feed them, even my servant David" (Ezekiel 34:23).

"My servant David" means the Messiah. Why is Jesus so often called a Shepherd? Perhaps it's because we humans are so very much like sheep. Did you know that sheep are easily frightened? The slightest disturbance will make them scatter in panic. Aren't we also easily frightened? But the Good Shepherd offers peace.

Another characteristic of sheep is that they're not very good at seeking out food and water. The shepherd must do it for them. Left to themselves, sheep will even eat poisonous weeds. Aren't we just as dependent on our Shepherd for spiritual sustenance?

And sheep are utterly defenseless. Most animals have something with which to protect themselves, whether it be tooth or claw or mighty growl. Sheep have nothing. The Shepherd is their only protection. We can certainly identify with that.

Sheep tend to get lost easily. It seems they have a poor sense of direction. Don't we get lost easily too? What a blessing that we may trust our Shepherd to be our guide!

"I will seek that which was lost, and bring again that which was driven away, and will bind up that which was broken, and will strengthen that which was sick" (Ezekiel 34:16).

NO ROOM FOR COMPLACENCY

DAILY BIBLE READING: PSALM 18:19-23

"For I have kept the ways of the LORD" (Psalm 18:21).

I have heard that there is no such thing as a complacent Christian. Why? To be complacent is to be self-satisfied. If we're complacent, we're not Christian. If we're Christian, we're not complacent.

To understand why that is so, let's look at Psalm 18. David wrote this hymn of praise after God delivered him from Saul. David declares that God is his strength, his rock, his fortress, his deliverer, buckler, and high tower. There was no question in David's mind that God had done the delivering.

David could have become complacent. He could have basked in the glow of past victories. He could have decided that since God was doing all the work and the fighting, there was nothing left for him to do.

But no! David is fully aware of the reason for God's deliverance. God fought for David because he "kept the ways of the LORD." God's deliverance was a reward for David's righteousness. That's why he said in verse 25, "With an upright man thou wilt shew thyself upright."

This doesn't mean that we must be perfect if we want God on our side. It simply means that we must seek Him, and seek to obey Him, with all our hearts. Does that leave any room for complacency?

"As for God, his way is perfect: the word of the LORD is tried: he is a buckler to all those that trust in him" (Psalm 18:30).

BEGINNING AND ENDING WITH A CUBE

DAILY BIBLE READING: REVELATION 21:14-16

"The length and the breadth and the height of it are equal" (Revelation 21:16).

A perfect cube! That's how the New Jerusalem is described. Can we imagine a cube that's 1,500 miles in every dimension?

In the Bible, a cube is symbolic of completeness and perfection. Think of the wilderness tabernacle. What were the dimensions of the holy of holies? My Bible dictionary says it was fifteen feet high by fifteen feet wide by fifteen feet long—a perfect cube.

Now let's look at Solomon's temple. What were the dimensions of the holy of holies there? Twenty cubits by twenty cubits by twenty cubits (1 Kings 6:20). Another cube.

What does this mean to us? Remember that the tabernacle, the temple, and the New Jerusalem all represent the dwelling place of God. Today, the church is God's house, the place where He dwells by His Spirit.

The story of the Bible is the story of the church—God's people whom He created, loved, and redeemed. So we could say that the story of the church begins with a perfect cube in the tabernacle, and ends with a perfect cube in the New Jerusalem. Perfect in Jesus! "Christ also loved the church, and gave himself for it; that he might present it to Himself a glorious church, not having spot, or wrinkle, or any such thing; but that it should be holy and without blemish" (Ephesians 5:25, 27).

Are we sometimes discouraged by the faults and weaknesses we see in our local church? Let's keep our focus on God's view of the church in Christ—complete and foursquare.

"Ye are complete in him" (Colossians 2:10).

A TRANSFORMING RELATIONSHIP

DAILY BIBLE READING: COLOSSIANS 3:18-23

"Servants, obey in all things your masters" (Colossians 3:22).

Are you a servant? And do you sometimes find it difficult to maintain a proper relationship with your employer? Perhaps she seems hard to please, and as a result you feel resentful. Relationships can be difficult. I know a woman who said in frustration, "Life would be a lot easier without relationships."

But life is full of them. Children need to relate to their parents, and vice versa. Husbands and wives must get along. Servants need to relate to their masters, and their masters to them. (Paul mentions the masters too, in the first verse of the next chapter.)

We could say that today's reading is about transformed relationships— relationships befitting the Christian life. Husbands love; wives submit; children obey; fathers provoke not to anger; servants obey. Those are the kind of relationships we want—full of love and peace.

But how? We are so human and make so many mistakes.

The way to have transformed relationships is to first have a transforming relationship with Christ. The first chapters of Colossians tell us about this supreme relationship—receiving Christ by faith, buried with Him in baptism, putting off the old man, putting on the new. Christ is all, and in all!

"Put on therefore, as the elect of God, holy and beloved, bowels of mercies, kindness, humbleness of mind, meekness, longsuffering" (Colossians 3:12).

Day 90

THE DEVIL HAS A DEADLINE

DAILY BIBLE READING: REVELATION 12:10-12

"The devil is come down unto you, having great wrath, because he knoweth that he hath but short time" (Revelation 12:12).

The devil is faced with a deadline. Revelation 10:5, 6 tells about the angel declaring that time shall be no more. Time is short! Yet the devil still has so much that he wants to do. We can understand why the deadline makes him panic; we know that sensation all too well.

Faced with an adversary whose panic makes him seethe with rage, what should we do? We certainly should be well armed. Ephesians 6 tells us how to do that. We must also be on the lookout for the devil's snares "lest Satan should get an advantage of us: for we are not ignorant of his devices" (2 Corinthians 2:11).

The devil uses three main devices: "For all that is in the world, the lust of the flesh, and the lust of the eyes, and the pride of life, is not of the Father, but is of the world" (1 John 2:16). The "lust of the flesh" is simply our old nature, which delights in doing things displeasing to God. The devil certainly knows how to use our fleshly desires to his advantage. Think of Eve in the Garden of Eden: she "saw that the tree was good for food."

The second device is the "lust of the eyes." Your eyes are the gate that lets the world in to your flesh. Eve saw that the fruit "was pleasant to the eyes." The devil wants our eyes focused on the world and on earthly things. Christian warrior, focus your eyes on God!

Then there's the "pride of life"—living for superiority, focused on outward appearances. Eve saw "a tree to be desired to make one wise." What vain emptiness! Let not the devil ensnare you here.

"That they may recover themselves out of the snare of the devil" (2 Timothy 2:26).

THREE WILD BEASTS

DAILY BIBLE READING: 1 JOHN 3:8-10

"The devil sinneth from the beginning" (1 John 3:8).

Can you think of three beasts that are used in the Bible to symbolize Satan?

First is the serpent. In the Garden of Eden, we find the devil disguised as a snake, slithering up to Eve and deceiving her. Think of it! The devil had been an angel in the presence of God before he rebelled and was thrown out of Heaven. Now he is reduced to crawling on his belly in the dust of earth—and resorting to the meanest, lowest tricks.

Peter's picture of the devil is somewhat different. A lion is a more kingly animal—but oh, so fierce! Doesn't Peter's description make you shiver? A roaring, prowling lion, seeking prey; we are no match for him. But if we trust in God, we may say as Paul did, "Notwithstanding the Lord stood with me, and strengthened me . . . and I was delivered out of the mouth of the lion" (2 Timothy 4:17).

In Revelation the devil is frequently called a dragon—and a fearsome one. But we are also given assurance of God's power over Satan. In Revelation 20:2 we see an angel coming down from heaven, bringing with him the key to the bottomless pit. "And he laid hold on the dragon, that old serpent, which is the Devil, and Satan, and bound him a thousand years." Whether serpent, or lion, or dragon—the mighty adversary is no match for Almighty God!

"And behold a great red dragon, having seven heads and ten horns, and seven crowns upon his heads" (Revelation 12:3).

THE SERPENT

DAILY BIBLE READING: GENESIS 3:13-15

"Upon thy belly shalt thou go, and dust shalt thou eat" (Genesis 3:14).

Again we are reminded that the devil had been an angel before his disobedience cast him out of heaven. Look where he is now! Under the curse pronounced by God, the devil is given a place among the lowest of the low.

But that does not prevent Satan from trying to persuade us to follow his evil path. He will stoop to the vilest tricks. For instance, consider how the devil repeatedly tried to defeat Jesus during His earthly life. Truly, Satan "bruised the heel" of Jesus—time and again.

And he bruises our heel too. Sin has polluted the whole world. Sin separates us from God. The story of Satan's work on earth is a sad tale.

But still, a bruise on the heel is not deadly. By contrast, our Saviour delivered a crushing, deadly blow to the serpent's head when He rose from the dead! And He can give us victory too.

Jesus lives today to deliver us from the serpent. He indwells the faithful to give them power. Truly, by His grace the serpent can be crushed beneath our feet.

"Behold, I give unto you power to tread on serpents and scorpions, and over all the power of the enemy: and nothing shall by any means hurt you" (Luke 10:19).

THE LION

DAILY BIBLE READING: 1 PETER 5:7-9

"Your adversary, the devil, as a roaring lion, walketh about, seeking whom he may devour" (1 Peter 5:8).

The picture is so vivid. Can you see it too? A fierce-looking lion with royal mane and blazing eyes, stalking the African plain in search of food. That's the devil and his work on earth. Doesn't it make you shiver?

However, I'm told that lions are essentially cowards. They won't attempt to bring down an animal that is with a group. Nor will they choose a physically fit animal as prey. Lions will attack the sick, the young, and the stragglers.

The devil is the same. He likes to catch us in our times of weakness. No wonder Peter warns us to beware and to watch out for Satan's attacks.

Suffering makes us vulnerable. Often when we suffer, we feel alone, helpless, and weak. Our imagination tells us we are cut off from our friends. Thus we become prime targets for that roaring lion who is walking about "seeking whom he may devour."

So let's recognize how vulnerable we are. Let's seek support from our fellow believers. Let's keep our eyes on Jesus instead of focusing on our troubles. Above all, let's follow the advice given in James 4:7, 8:

"Submit yourselves therefore to God. Resist the devil, and he will flee from you. Draw nigh to God, and he will draw nigh to you" (James 4:7, 8).

THE DRAGON

DAILY BIBLE READING: REVELATION 12:9-11

"And the great dragon was cast out" (Revelation 12:9).

Satan as a dragon: in a way it's the most fearsome picture of all. The dragon, cast out of Heaven, makes his last stand on the earth. Revelation 12 and 13 are not easy to understand, but they do give us some idea of what Satan is like.

He hates Jesus. He hates all of God's people and persecutes them maliciously. "And the dragon was wroth with the woman, and went to make war with the remnant of her seed, which keeps the commandments of God" (Revelation 12:17).

The dragon has some measure of authority and power. "The dragon gave him his power, and his seat, and great authority" (Revelation 13:2).

The dragon is popular among those who do not believe in God. "And they worshiped the dragon . . . saying, Who is like unto the beast? who is able to make war with him?" (Revelation 13:4).

The dragon freely blasphemes God. "And he opened his mouth in blasphemy against God, to blaspheme his name, and his tabernacle, and them that dwell in heaven" (Revelation 13:6).

The dragon is a master at deception. "And he deceiveth them that dwell on the earth" (Revelation 13:14).

The dragon is at war with believers. "And it was given unto him to make war with the saints, and to overcome them" (Revelation 13:7).

But let us take heart. We can be the overcomers, if we take shelter in the blood of the Lamb—and if we love not our life and are willing to lay it down for Christ's sake.

"And the God of peace shall bruise Satan under your feet shortly" (Romans 16:20).

WHAT IS THAT WOUNDED MAN TO ME?

DAILY BIBLE READING: LUKE 10:29-33

"But a certain Samaritan . . . had compassion on him" (Luke 10:33).

This is such a familiar story. Who has not heard the parable of the Good Samaritan? Today, let's look at it from a slightly different perspective.

First, let's list all the characters in the story. There's the wounded man, of course; the thieves, the priest, the Levite, the Samaritan, and the innkeeper. We could also include the lawyer who asked the question that caused Jesus to tell this parable.

Think about the attitude that each character had toward the wounded man. To the thieves, he was someone they could exploit and use for their own vile purposes. To the priest and the Levite, he was a problem they hoped to avoid at all cost; to the innkeeper, he was an opportunity to make some money. The Samaritan, bless his heart, looked upon him as a fellow human who desperately needed love and care. As for the lawyer—well, I guess to him the wounded man was a topic for discussion!

What is my attitude toward the weak, the needy, the wounded? Which of the above attitudes most nearly matches mine?

May we learn to be like Christ, whose attitude toward us is that we're worth dying for in order to save from sin!

"Go, and do thou likewise" (Luke 10:37).

BEFORE HE COULD ENTER

DAILY BIBLE READING: LEVITICUS 16:1-7

"That he come not at all times into the holy place within the vail ... that he die not"
(Leviticus 16:2).

I like reading Leviticus 16. You might wonder why; it seems rather tedious, with its lengthy description of all the preparations Aaron had to make before he could enter the holy of holies.

But before we read Leviticus 16, let's read Hebrews 4:16: "Let us therefore come boldly unto the throne of grace, that we may obtain mercy, and find grace to help in time of need." Today we are invited to come freely into God's presence. Let's keep that in mind for a comparison as we ponder Aaron's instructions in Leviticus 16.

First, Aaron couldn't go into the holy place whenever he chose. Only once a year—on the Day of Atonement—could he enter the sacred precincts where God's presence hovered in a cloud above the mercy seat.

On the Day of Atonement, elaborate preparations were necessary. Aaron had to bathe himself and don a certain set of garments. Then he had to offer a young bullock to atone for his own sins and those of his family. From the two goats brought by the congregation, one was chosen by lot to be sacrificed and the other to be sent away.

Finally it's time for Aaron to enter. He must fill an incense burner with coals from the altar of the Lord. As he steps into the holy place, he must throw the incense on the coals to produce a smoke screen that will hide God's presence— or else he will die.

How much easier is our access to God by Jesus Christ!

"For by one offering he hath perfected for ever them that are sanctified" (Hebrews 10:14).

THE YOUNG AND THE OLD

"But many of the priests . . . who were ancient men, that had seen the first house . . . wept with a loud voice" (Ezra 3:12).

To the young workers who had commenced the rebuilding of the temple, this was an occasion for rejoicing and celebration. They were surrounded with singers praising God as they laid the foundation. In fact, "all the people shouted with a great shout."

But wait! What is that other sound mingling with the songs of praise and the happy shouts? Why, someone is weeping. Down the cheeks of the "ancient men" run tears of memory. Sadness overwhelms them as they recall the magnificence of the former temple, contrasting it with this pitiful beginning among the ruins.

Don't you think God was more pleased with the praises of the vigorous young people than the lamentations of the pensive old ones? I'm afraid it's a weakness we older people have. We look back yearningly at past accomplishments, at the so-called "good old days." And sometimes we forget to be thankful for young workers who labor faithfully today for God.

Take care, older people! We should never discourage those who are willing to get down into the trenches and do the dirty work of digging sturdy foundations for the future.

Take courage, young people! If we older ones sometimes recall precious memories, I hope you don't feel as though we're making unfavorable comparisons. Keep on in faith that God will bless your efforts too.

"Say not thou, What is the cause that the former days were better than these?" (Ecclesiastes 7:10).

CREDENTIALS

DAILY BIBLE READING: PHILIPPIANS 3:4-7

"If any other man thinketh that he hath whereof he might trust in the flesh, I more" *(Philippians 3:4).*

In today's society, credentials are very important. A person seeking a job needs a résumé listing all his credentials: what universities he attended, what courses he took, what other jobs he has successfully tackled.

Reading Philippians 3, it appears at first that Paul is flaunting his credentials. From a Jewish viewpoint, his accomplishments are impressive. Paul came from the tribe of Benjamin. Only the tribes of Judah and Benjamin had returned to Israel after the exile. We can almost hear Paul saying, "So I'm a real Jew if there ever was one!" He also seems to brag about his strict upbringing and meticulous observance of the Law.

But actually, Paul is doing the opposite of boasting. He's showing that no human achievements, however impressive, can ever earn salvation. He saw his achievements as nothing but garbage compared to the priceless treasure of knowing Christ.

What about you and me? Are we sometimes tempted to depend on things like Christian parents, church affiliation, or plain good works to make us right with God?

Credentials, accomplishments, reputations—none of those can earn salvation. No amount of law-keeping, self-improvement, discipline, or religious effort can make us right with God. We are made righteous by trusting in Christ and by daily knowing and walking with Him.

"Thus saith the LORD, Let not the wise man glory in his wisdom, neither let the mighty man glory in his might . . . But let him that glorieth glory in this, that he understandeth and knoweth me" (Jeremiah 9:23, 24).

Day 99

THE FIRST STEP

DAILY BIBLE READING: MATTHEW 9:9-13

"I am not come to call the righteous, but sinners to repentance" (Matthew 9:13).

What is the first step we must take to be made right with God? Before we answer that question, let's examine the Pharisees' attitude. Were they taking that first step?

One of the biggest concerns of the Pharisees was to appear holy. They would never associate with the kind of people Jesus was befriending. Oh, no. How unholy that would look!

Criticism was foremost on the Pharisees' tongues. Their sharp eyes were always watching Jesus, their sharp tongues always ready to condemn His actions.

To the Pharisees, it was more important to look outwardly respectable than to help people. And so, occupied with these self-serving attitudes, the Pharisees missed that essential "first step" by a long, long shot.

Not so with Matthew! We see him sitting there at his job, collecting customs. Along comes Jesus and invites Matthew to follow Him. Instantly the tax collector is on his feet. He took that "first step" right away: *he saw that he needed Jesus.*

For us, the first step is the same. We must see how sinful we are and how desperately we need Jesus. Only a sinner can repent. Repentance is not possible for one who considers himself righteous.

Paul was a Pharisee, and his attitudes had once been like theirs. But listening to him in 1 Timothy 1:15, we know he took that first step:

"Christ Jesus came into the world to save sinners; of whom I am chief" (1 Timothy 1:15).

COUNTING THE COST

DAILY BIBLE READING: LUKE 14:25-29

"For which of you, intending to build a tower, sitteth not down first, and counteth the cost, whether he have sufficient to finish it?" (Luke 14:28).

Following Jesus is a major undertaking. Jesus never pretended otherwise. When fickle crowds ran after Him, He presented the raw facts. "If you truly want to be a follower, consider what you will face," He warned. Here are some of the things He warned them of in Matthew 10.

The government will oppose followers of Jesus: "And ye shall be brought before governors and kings for my sake" (v. 18). Religious people will cause opposition: "They will deliver you up to the councils, and they will scourge you in their synagogues" (v. 17). Our own families may be against us: "And the brother shall deliver up the brother to death" (v. 21).

Faced with such an array of opposition, who could blame us for drawing back and saying that the cost is too high?

But Jesus also gives us reassurances for everything that might befall. Threats? "Fear them not therefore: for there is nothing covered, that shall not be revealed" (v. 26).

Physical harm? "Fear not them which kill the body, but are not able to kill the soul" (v. 28).

Ridicule? "Whosoever therefore shall confess me before men, him will I confess also before my Father" (v. 32). If Jesus is confirming us, ridicule won't matter.

Rejection? "Fear ye not therefore, ye are of more value than many sparrows" (v. 31). What is rejection, if God's love is sustaining us?

So let's not fear the cost.

"But rather fear him which is able to destroy both soul and body in hell" (Matthew 10:28).

A FATHER'S REGRETS

DAILY BIBLE READING: 2 SAMUEL 18:28-33

"Would God I had died for thee, O Absalom, my son, my son!" (2 Samuel 18:33).

As a child, I wondered why David was so upset by Absalom's death. After all, the young upstart had stirred up a rebellion and taken the throne from his father. Shouldn't David have agreed with the messenger who declared, "All is well"?

But now that I'm at the age David may have been when Absalom was slain, I have some idea why David was so sad. He may have felt he was to blame for his son's death.

Does that surprise you? You see, the roots of Absalom's rebellion reach far back into his childhood. Had David disciplined Absalom when he was a handsome young teenager? Had he worked to curb the young man's ego and show him the way of humility? I'm afraid not. Absalom was a spoiled boy, accustomed to having his own way.

Later, when Amnon abused Absalom's sister, we can see how headstrong Absalom was. Instead of seeking wise council, he took matters into his own hands and killed Amnon. Did David discipline him for this rash act? No indeed. Absalom did live in exile for a time, but eventually David welcomed him back. "And the king kissed Absalom" (2 Samuel 14:33).

Next we see Absalom stealing the hearts of Israel with his charm. What a reaping for David, when his son stole the kingdom! And what a bitter harvest, when Absalom died in his sin!

What do we learn from this? Simply that we should appreciate when our parents or leaders discipline us and teach the way of humility. They don't want us on that one-way street called Pride, headed for ultimate disaster.

"But the king covered his face, and the king cried with a loud voice, O my son Absalom, O Absalom, my son, my son!" (2 Samuel 19:4).

WHAT DO YOU BRING?

DAILY BIBLE READING: ISAIAH 43:22-24

"Thou hast wearied me with thine iniquities" (Isaiah 43:24).

God had a complaint against Israel. "You're not asking for My help anymore," He seems to say in these verses. "You've grown tired of Me. You haven't brought Me your lambs as burnt offerings, to honor Me with sacrifices. You've begrudged spending your money for sweet incense for the altar.

"In fact," He concludes, "when you come to the altar, all you've brought Me is your sins!"

That does seem ironic. Israel was supposed to offer the best of their cattle; but instead they brought only their sins to the altar!

I wonder if we are sometimes guilty of the same thing. What do we bring to God's altar? Are we perhaps wearying Him with our iniquities too? In other words, are we continually bemoaning our sins but not fully repenting and therefore not receiving full pardon?

We, too, need to bring a sacrifice when we confess our sins—Jesus is our sacrifice. Our prayer for forgiveness must be in His name. Paul says that Christ "hath given himself for us an offering and a sacrifice to God for a sweetsmelling savour" (Ephesians 5:2).

So when we come before God, let's not bring unrepentant hearts and unconfessed sins. Oh, yes, we come as sinners—but we come trusting in the greatest sacrifice of all, Jesus the Lamb of God.

"For we are unto God a sweet savour of Christ" (2 Corinthians 2:15).

Day 103

JUSTICE, MERCY, AND GRACE

DAILY BIBLE READING: EZRA 9:10-15

"Behold, we are before thee in our trespasses: for we cannot stand before thee because of this" (Ezra 9:15).

Imagine how Ezra felt. He had led the second group of Jews from Babylon back to Palestine. How thankful he was that God in His love wished to restore His people! But shocking news awaited Ezra when he came to Jerusalem: the first group of returning Israelites, now well established in Jerusalem, had not remained faithful to God's commandments. The Jews were intermarrying with heathens and dabbling in idol worship.

Ezra was so appalled that he tore out his hair, rent his clothes, and lay prostrate all day. When evening came, he "arose up from heaviness" and "spread out [his] hands unto the LORD [his] God." The prayer Ezra prayed is full of three things: justice, mercy, and grace.

Those are words with deep meanings. Yet we can give a fairly simple definition for each:

Justice means giving people what they deserve.

Mercy means not giving people what they deserve.

Grace means giving people what they do not deserve.

You and I are no different from the people of Ezra's time. We have overstepped God's commands. If God were to deal with us according to His justice, we would be condemned. But God's mercy prevents that. He does not give us the condemnation we deserve. And His grace gives us many undeserved gifts to enable us to stand before Him.

"Justice and judgment are the habitation of thy throne: mercy and truth shall go before they face" (Psalm 89:14).

SEND HIM AWAY

DAILY BIBLE READING: MATTHEW 18:32-35

"And his lord was wroth, and delivered him to the tormentors" (Matthew 18:34).

People who lived in Bible times could get into serious trouble if they didn't pay their debts. As you can see here in Matthew 18, they were in danger of being thrown into prison until they'd paid the full amount.

If you're like me, you've wondered how a person stuck in prison could earn money to pay his debts. But that's beside the point. Today, we want to look at this question: what is the "torment" you and I face if we refuse to forgive our fellow man?

Ultimately, of course, it is the torment of Hell. If we are a child of God, saved by grace, we simply cannot cling permanently to an unforgiving spirit.

But supposing, in our weakness, we do harbor a grudge toward someone who hurt us. Isn't it true that carrying a grudge brings with it a certain kind of torment? As long as we refuse to forgive, aren't we stuck in bondage—the tormenting bondage of Satan himself?

Someone once told me that the Greek word *aphiemi*, usually translated as *forgive* in our New Testaments, means "send away" or "let go." Thus, when we forgive, we "send away" the devil so he can't torment us—and we "let go" of the past so that the hurt no longer has a hold on us.

Who wouldn't want to be free of the devil's torment? Then by the grace of God, let's forgive.

"I say not unto thee, Until seven times: but, Until seventy times seven" (Matthew 18:22).

ABUNDANCE

DAILY BIBLE READING: JOHN 10:9-11

"I am come that they might have life, and that they might have it more abundantly" *(John 10:10).*

Surely the early settlers in America must have been impressed by the sheer abundance: forests full of game, rivers teeming with fish, fertile soil that produced bountiful crops.

Jesus offers spiritual abundance beyond anything we have imagined. Why is the life He offers so abundant? Because it is His very own life, the life of God Himself! Jesus gave His earthly life to pass on abundant spiritual life to us.

Are we prepared to receive this abundance? We certainly need Paul's prayer in Ephesians 3:17-19, where he prayed that we may have the power to grasp the vast dimensions of Christ's love, which surpasses knowledge—so that we can be "filled with all the fullness of God." Talk about abundance!

Yes, that's what is meant by the abundant life: Christ dwelling in our hearts by faith. Is my heart big enough to contain this marvelous abundance? Is yours? Paul had a reason for pleading in 2 Corinthians 6:13, "Be ye also enlarged." Make room for Jesus! Make room for the abundant life.

"Enlarge the place of thy tent, and let them stretch forth the curtains of thine habitations: spare not, lengthen thy cords, and strengthen thy stakes" (Isaiah 54:2).

FOR WHOSE SAKE?

DAILY BIBLE READING: EZEKIEL 36:22, 23

"I do not this for your sakes, O house of Israel" (Ezekiel 36:22).

Why does God save us? Does He save me for my sake, because of anything I have done? No! Paul wrote to Titus, "Not by works of righteousness which we have done, but according to his mercy he saved us" (Titus 3:5).

God saves us for His own sake. "I, even I, am he that blotteth out thy transgressions for mine own sake, and will not remember thy sins" (Isaiah 43:25).

In the next verse God seems to challenge us: "Let's sit down together and review your case. If you have anything with which you can justify yourself, then declare it."

If you and I were to appear before God planning to justify ourselves, what would happen? We would discover that we are utterly bankrupt. We have absolutely nothing with which to justify ourselves. Paul wrote to the Romans, "So then it is not of him that willeth, nor of him that runneth, but of God that sheweth mercy" (9:16). Our salvation doesn't depend on our desire or effort, but on God's mercy.

What a comfort this is! If God were to save us for our own sakes, we could not be saved. But because He saves us for His own name's sake, we have a living hope.

"We do not present our supplications before thee for our righteousnesses, but for thy great mercies, O Lord, hear: O Lord, forgive . . . defer not, for thine own sake, O my God" (Daniel 9:18, 19).

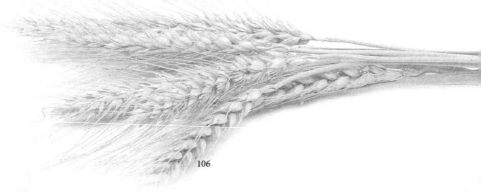

A NEW EXODUS

DAILY BIBLE READING: ISAIAH 43:15-21

"Behold, I will do a new thing" (Isaiah 43:19).

In this chapter Isaiah was prophesying to the Jews who were held captive in Babylon. He reminds the people about that first Exodus, when God made "a way in the sea, and a path in the mighty waters," and when He caused Pharaoh's army to be "extinct . . . quenched as tow."

Then Isaiah seems to say, "But forget all that. God is going to do something new—something even more marvelous than the first Exodus. We're going to take part in a new exodus! God will lead His people out of Babylon through the dry desert of the Syrian wilderness, and there He will cause rivers to flow for their sustenance."

Why did God bring about this new exodus? The explanation is in verse 21: "This people have I formed for myself; they shall shew forth my praise."

Today, you and I are the people whom God has formed for Himself. We can also take part in a new exodus—deliverance from the bondage of sin through the grace of Jesus Christ.

Today, the Holy Spirit flows as "waters in the wilderness, and rivers in the desert, to give drink to mine people, my chosen" (verse 20). Today, let us trust in God's delivering power. Let us step out into the unknown wilderness of life, assured that God is leading us.

"Go ye forth of Babylon, flee ye from the Chaldeans, with a voice of singing declare ye, tell this, utter it even to the end of the earth; say ye, the LORD hath redeemed his servant Jacob" (Isaiah 48:20).

AN HONEST PRAYER

DAILY BIBLE READING: JOSHUA 7:6-9

"Alas, O Lord God, wherefore hast thou at all brought this people over Jordan, to deliver us into the hand of the Amorites, to destroy us?" (Joshua 7:7).

Joshua's prayer reminds us of Exodus 14:12, where the despairing Israelites complained to Moses, "It had been better for us to serve the Egyptians, than that we should die in the wilderness."

But there is a difference. Joshua wasn't complaining. He was being honest with God. The defeat at Ai must have frightened and confused him. So when he prayed, his feelings came pouring out: "Lord, what am I to say? When the Canaanites hear of this, they'll surround us and wipe us of the face of the earth!"

God wants us to pray honestly. He doesn't want us to hide our feelings from Him; if we do, we spurn the only One who can really help. So when we pray, let's remember that God knows our every thought and feeling anyway; why try to hide them from Him? Let's also remember that His love never fails. That will encourage us to be honest.

Honest prayers, however, will receive honest answers. And honest answers from God can be painful. Notice how God answered Joshua's honest prayer: "Get thee up: wherefore liest thou upon thy face? Israel hath sinned."

If we pray honestly, and honestly listen to God's honest replies—what a blessing can be ours!

"Up, sanctify the people, and say, Sanctify yourselves against to morrow: for thus saith the Lord God of Israel, There is an accursed thing in the midst of thee" (Joshua 7:13).

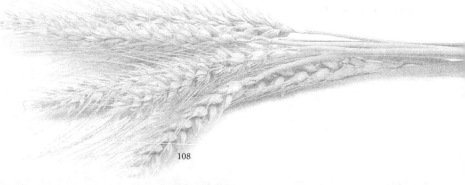

THE FIRST PLACE TO LOOK

DAILY BIBLE READING: JUDGES 6:7-13

"O my Lord, if the LORD be with us, why then is all this befallen us?" (Judges 6:13).

Gideon looked at all the problems facing Israel and wondered what was the cause. It actually sounds as though Gideon was trying to blame God for Israel's problems.

Gideon was just like we tend to be. We think others are accountable for our problems. If only this person would be kinder, or that person easier to get along with, then our problems would be solved.

But notice who really caused Israel's problems: the Israelites themselves. Chapter 6 begins with these words: "And the children of Israel did evil in the sight of the LORD: and the LORD delivered them into the hand of Midian seven years." Israel's problems were the consequences of their very own sins.

Blaming others never solves anything. When problems arise, the first place we should look for accountability is right in our own hearts. We are usually the main cause of our own problems. If we recognize that and confess our sins, we have taken a real step toward solving our problems.

Why are we so prone to think that someone else is at fault? We all need the Prophet Nathan to come and say to us as he did to King David, "Thou art the man!" And may our response then be like David's.

"And David said unto Nathan, I have sinned against the LORD" (2 Samuel 12:13).

WAS GIDEON AFRAID?

DAILY BIBLE READING: JUDGES 7:9-15

"But if thou fear to go down, go thou with Phurah thy servant down to the host" *(Judges 7:10).*

God had told Gideon to go down confidently with his tiny band of three hundred men to attack the host of Midian—which lay innumerable as grasshoppers in the valley. "I have delivered it into thine hand," God promised.

Gideon shouldn't have been afraid. Not with a clear promise like that to back him up.

You and I meet similar situations, don't we? We're confronted with something that looks simply overwhelming. We can't see through. Yes, we believe that God is with us; we know we shouldn't be afraid. But we are. Fear stalks us. We hesitate.

I think Gideon—mighty man of valor though he was—hesitated too. He'd never led an army before. When God had called him from his threshing to become the leader of Israel's army, Gideon had protested, "I am the least in my father's house." Gideon doesn't seem like someone who had a lot of self-confidence. I see him as somebody like me, who gets afraid.

God knew and understood Gideon's fear. But He didn't excuse him: instead, He helped him overcome his fear in a marvelous way. You know the story, how God told Gideon to sneak down to the enemy camp where he heard a conversation which showed him the Midianites feared Israel.

God provided a way for Gideon to regain courage. But notice, Gideon had to obey. He had to make a nighttime foray into the enemy camp. And out of that obedience, courage was born. From obedience to courage—that's the path we, too, must tread to leave fear behind.

"And what shall I more say? for the time would fail me to tell of Gedeon . . . Who through faith . . . out of weakness were made strong, waxed valiant in fight, turned to flight the army of the aliens" (Hebrews 11:32-34).

THE LOWLY TASKS

DAILY BIBLE READING: JUDGES 8:1-3

"Why hast thou served us thus, that thou calledst us not, when thou wentest to fight with the Midianites?" (Judges 8:1).

The men of Ephraim were angry because they felt Gideon had assigned them a lowly task—a mere "cleanup job." Meanwhile, Gideon's little army of three hundred had won a spectacular victory over the Midianites—the Ephraimites would have liked to share in that glory. At the end of Chapter 7 you can read what Gideon had asked Ephraim to do: they were to catch several Midianite princes as they fled.

Basically, we could say the Ephraimites weren't contented with the humble task assigned them. Are you and I sometimes like that? Do we sometimes wish God would not place us in such lowly positions? Do we long for a spot in life that would bring us more glory?

Oh, let us be content, no matter how menial our task may seem. Picture a tall building. Many lowly tasks need to be completed in order to construct that building. Yes, a highly educated engineer may plan the building, and a millionaire may finance it. But who really gets the job done? It's the carpenters, the stonemasons, the bricklayers, patiently performing their duties, who actually erect that building.

Gideon's reply to the Ephraimites is a classic example of a "soft answer" that "turneth away wrath." He asked, "What have I done now in comparison of you?" (verse 2). "Without your accomplishment," Gideon seems to say, "our campaign would have failed." May this be an encouragement to contentedly keep on in our assigned tasks, lowly though they are.

"God resisteth the proud, but giveth grace to the humble" (James 4:6).

 *Day* 112

WHO IS IN CONTROL?

DAILY BIBLE READING: JOSHUA 24:14-16

"Choose you this day whom ye will serve" (Joshua 24:15).

When asked, "Who is in control of your life?" one man replied, "I am! And that's the way I want it."

But he was believing a lie. God did not design us to be in control. He designed us to serve. You and I are always serving either God or the devil.

We might ask, what about self-serving? Aren't we mostly inclined to serve ourselves? Yes, indeed. We are very self-centered. We glorify self, justify self, and seek to please self. But the truth is, serving self is actually serving the world and the flesh—and therefore the devil.

This is a fact we must face: we are not in control of our life. The one whom we serve is the one who has control. There is only one aspect of our life over which we have control: we can control whom we choose to serve! The choice is ours. It's just like Joshua said to his people: "Choose you this day whom ye will serve." Will it be idols (the world, the flesh, the devil) or will it be the living God? Serving God means denying self. It means total surrender of one's life to God. We need to say no to ourselves and yes to God.

Great blessings will follow; we have such peace when God is Lord of our lives! And here is the paradox: it's only in complete surrender to God that we truly gain self-control.

"Let not sin therefore reign in your mortal body . . . but yield yourselves unto God . . . For sin shall not have dominion over you" (Romans 6:12-14).

Day 113

LIKE A BRAND ON THE FOREHEAD

DAILY BIBLE READING: EXODUS 13:6-10

"And it shall be for a sign unto thee upon thine hand, and a memorial between thine eyes" (Exodus 13:9).

When I was a third grader, we had a social studies project called "Children of many lands." We were given pictures to color; each showed a boy or girl wearing the national costume of a different country. The Japanese wore kimonos, the Scottish kilts, the Dutch wooden shoes, and so on.

At the time, I believed that these different nationalities really do wear such clothes. Today, of course, I realize that these costumes are mostly memories; if any still exist, they are only brought out of mothballs for special occasions.

When God instituted the Feast of Unleavened Bread, He wanted it to be a kind of "national brand" for His people. The feast marked the Hebrews as unique, almost as if they had been branded on the forehead. Year after year, the Feast of Unleavened Bread reminded Israel of God's great deliverance from Egypt.

As believers today, we also are a unique people. Our faith in Jesus sets us apart from the world. What "costume" do we wear? What brands us on the forehead? Jesus said in John 13:35, "By this shall all men know that ye are my disciples, if ye have love one to another." Our "costume" is the cloak of brotherly love.

"Put on therefore . . . kindness, humbleness of mind, meekness, longsuffering . . . And above all these things put on charity, which is the bond of perfectness" (Colossians 3:12, 14).

NO EARTHLY REASON

DAILY BIBLE READING: JOB 4:5-9

"Who ever perished being innocent?" (Job 4:7).

Why must we suffer? It's an age-old question—and Job's friend Eliphaz thought he had the answer. In fact, he claimed to have received the answer during a special nighttime vision (verses 12, 13).

Eliphaz reasoned that Job had to be guilty. He must have sinned, and these afflictions were God's chastisement for Job's guilt. To Eliphaz it was clear that Job could be relieved of his sufferings if he would repent.

But we know Eliphaz was wrong. God later rebuked him: "My wrath is kindled against thee . . . for ye have not spoken of me the thing that is right" (42:7).

It simply is not true that every time I suffer, it is because I have sinned. The disciples thought the man in John 9 was blind because he had sinned, but Jesus told them, "Neither hath this man sinned, nor his parents: but that the works of God should be made manifest in him" (verse 3).

The truth is that there may sometimes be no earthly reason for our suffering, other than the fact that we live in a fallen world. But there may be a heavenly reason! God often allows suffering so that He can show His strength in the midst of human weakness.

Sometimes, of course, we are the cause of our own suffering. Sometimes it really is our sin that brings affliction. So when we suffer, we should first check to make sure there is no earthly reason—then trust that God has a heavenly reason.

"But let none of you suffer as a murderer, or as a thief, or as an evildoer, or as a busybody in other men's matters. Yet if any man suffer as a Christian, let him not be ashamed; but let him glorify God on this behalf" (1 Peter 4:15, 16).

SOWING AND REAPING

"For he that soweth to his flesh shall of the flesh reap corruption; but he that soweth to the Spirit shall of the Spirit reap life everlasting" (Galatians 6:8).

We reap what we sow. That's a natural law. We'd be surprised, wouldn't we, if we planted corn kernels and tomato plants came up? In the spiritual realm, this law of reaping what we sow is very sobering. Who wants to harvest corruption? Who wouldn't want to harvest everlasting life? But it all depends on what we're planting here in our earthly life.

How do I know whether I'm planting to the flesh or to the Spirit? The Bible says, "By their fruits ye shall know them" (Matthew 7:20). If I am planting to please my wrong desires, the fruit will be evil; if I plant to please the Spirit, the fruit is good.

Wrong desires bring destructive results; the fruit of the Spirit is always constructive and productive.

The fruit of wrong desire is easy to ignite and inflame into hatred; the fruit of the Spirit is slow to anger, quick to love.

Always the fruits of the two are opposite to one another. The flesh is self-centered, the spirit self-giving. The flesh is oppressive and possessive; the Spirit liberates and nurtures. The flesh decays, the Spirit uplifts. Planting to the flesh brings sin; planting to the Spirit, holiness. In short, as Paul said here in Galatians 6:8, the fruit of the flesh is deadly, while the Spirit springs forth in abundant life.

"Sow to yourselves in righteousness, reap in mercy" (Hosea 10:12).

SIN SEPARATES

DAILY BIBLE READING: GENESIS 3:23, 24

"So he drove out the man" (Genesis 3:24).

Banished. Sent forth. Driven out. Those are hard words. Out from the Garden of Eden fled the man and his wife, while a flaming sword barred the way back.

Why? What separated man from God there in Eden? We all know the reason. Sin cannot stand before a righteous God. Because of sin, man's relationship with God was broken.

Let's look at the steps Adam and Eve took in breaking this relationship. First, they let the serpent convince them that their own thinking was better than God's way. Next, they tried to hide from God. And finally, they made excuses and tried to defend themselves before God. That is the recipe for breaking our relationship with God.

Now for the good news—how to get past that flaming sword and restore our relationship with God. It's a matter of reversing the sad series of steps taken by Adam and Eve. First, we must stop making excuses. Stop trying to defend ourselves and make ourselves believe we're all right!

Then we must stop trying to hide from God. Instead, we recognize that our sin is open and uncovered before Him. In repentance we must confess our sin.

And finally, we must be convinced that God's way is better—far better!—than our way. What is God's way? Jesus said, "I am the way." Through faith in Christ's sacrifice on the cross, our relationship with God is restored.

"But your iniquities have separated between you and your God, and your sins have hid his face from you, that he will not hear" (Isaiah 59:2).

SIN MUSHROOMS

DAILY BIBLE READING: GENESIS 4:8-10

"Cain rose up against Abel his brother, and slew him" (Genesis 4:8).

I shudder when I consider how quickly the sin of our forefathers mushroomed. Maybe Adam and Eve thought their disobedience was trivial. What could be so terrible about eating a little piece of fruit? But already in the very next generation, the sinful nature had developed to the point where one brother murdered the other.

Throughout the Bible we see the ugly mushrooming of sin. In Judges 9:5 we read how Abimelech killed all but one of his seventy half-brothers so he could rule over Israel. 1 Samuel 22 tells how King Saul murdered all the priests of Nob. In 1 Kings 21:13, Jezebel murdered Naboth because Ahab wanted his vineyard. In Matthew 2 we find King Herod killing all the babies; in Acts 7, the angry Jews murdered Stephen.

Why look at this chain of murders in the Bible? Surely we are not in danger of becoming murderers! No, but Jesus said that hating our brother is as bad as murdering him. And notice—each case started out with a "small" sin such as envy or ambition that mushroomed into murder.

God's word to Cain is still for us today: "If thou doest not well, sin lieth at the door . . . rule over him" (Genesis 4:7). May God help us to rule over the sin that lies at our very doorstep, ready to spring up and mushroom.

"Then when lust hath conceived, it bringeth forth sin: and sin, when it is finished, bringeth forth death" (James 1:15).

HE WILL NOT FORGET

DAILY BIBLE READING: AMOS 1:1-5

"For three transgressions . . . and for four, I will not turn away the punishment thereof" *(Amos 1:3).*

In the first two chapters of Amos, these words are repeated eight times: "For three transgressions, and for four, I will not turn away the punishment thereof." What does it mean? What is happening in these two chapters?

Amos was a shepherd of Judah whom the Lord called to prophesy to the Northern Kingdom of Israel. Amos boldly began his message by declaring that God is like a roaring lion ready to pounce. Upon city after city, he pronounced judgment, each time starting with those mysterious words about three plus four transgressions.

Perhaps at first as the people of Israel listened to Amos, they felt like cheering. They were only too happy to see God's judgment falling on places like Damascus, Gaza, Tyre, Edom—even Judah. But Amos did not stop there. Suddenly, starting in chapter 2:6, he pronounced judgment on Israel too.

Throughout those dire judgments, one message stands out stark and clear: God will not forget your transgressions! God does not overlook sin. What about my sins? I have committed far more than "three plus four" transgressions. If God never forgets, what will happen to me?

But wait. There is a difference, and that difference lies in the word *repentance.* The cities to whom Amos prophesied refused to repent. If we are God's repentant children, saved by the blood of His Son, we have His word that He will forget.

"I will forgive their iniquity, and I will remember their sin no more" (Jeremiah 31:34).

DO THINGS OWN YOU?

DAILY BIBLE READING: AMOS 6:3-6

"Woe to them that are at ease in Zion" (Amos 6:1).

Every now and then we ought to ask ourselves a few questions about "things"—the things we own, the things we enjoy, the things we wish we had. The way we feel about things is often an uncomfortable indication of whether or not our relationship with God is as it should be. Here are a few questions to consider:

Am I contented with what I have, or am I always wishing for things the neighbors have?

Do I love people, and use things to show that love? Or is it the other way around—am I loving things, and using people to satisfy my love of things?

Do I own things, or do things own me? Is my heart so attached to things that I barely have time for God? Then my things own me, and I am like the seed that fell among thorns in Jesus' parable, "choked with cares and riches and pleasures of this life" (Luke 8:14).

Jesus straightforwardly denounced the love of luxury and "things." So did the Prophet Amos. He warned the folks who lounged upon beds of ivory and gorged themselves on fatted calves that destruction would befall them.

The trouble with owning too many things is that it gives us a false sense of security. It isolates us from people who live in poverty and need. Let's use our things to help others—or else we will be like Joseph's brethren, who casually ate their lunch at the brink of the pit where Joseph lay in distress.

"But they are not grieved for the affliction of Joseph" (Amos 6:6).

IS SALVATION UNCONDITIONAL?

DAILY BIBLE READING: ROMANS 3:21-25

"Being justified freely by his grace" (Romans 3:24).

Is salvation free? Yes. Here in Romans 3, Paul speaks of being "justified freely." In the very last chapter of the Bible we read, "Whosoever will, let him take the water of life freely" (Revelation 22:17). And Isaiah gives us that all-inclusive offer for free salvation: "Ho, everyone that thirsteth, come ye to the waters, and he that hath no money; come ye, buy, and eat" (55:1).

But is salvation unconditional? No. Here are some conditions we must meet if we are to be saved.

First, we must be receptive to God's Word. James exhorts us, "Receive with meekness the engrafted word, which is able to save your souls" (1:21).

Faith and confession are two more conditions. "If thou shalt confess with thy mouth the Lord Jesus, and shalt believe in thine heart...thou shalt be saved" (Romans 10:9).

Having received the Word, we must allow it to cleanse us as we confess our sins. "He saved us by the washing of regeneration" (Titus 3:5).

All our lives, we need spiritual diligence if we are to be saved. "Give diligence to make your calling and election sure" (2 Peter 1:10).

Finally, we need endurance. Jesus said in Matthew 10:22, "He that endureth to the end shall be saved."

So there are the conditions for receiving the free gift of salvation: receiving, repenting, believing, confessing, cleansing, diligence, and endurance.

"Thanks be unto God for his unspeakable gift" (2 Corinthians 9:15).

IS IT FAIR?

DAILY BIBLE READING: ROMANS 5:15-19

"By one man's disobedience many were made sinners" (Romans 5:19).

Why are we declared guilty because of a sin Adam committed thousands of years ago? Is it fair that God judges us for Adam's sin?

That is not a good question to ask—but I will try to answer it anyway. The thing is, every person since Adam was born with a sinful nature. You and I prove every day that we have that nature by the sins we commit. So really, we're not being judged for Adam's sin, but for our own.

Do you see now why asking whether God is fair is not a good question? If God were to deal fairly with us, we would all be doomed. It's not fairness that we need, it's mercy!

Let me tell you what *is* a good question. Why did Jesus have to suffer as though He were guilty of our sins? That was not fair. Jesus wasn't guilty at all. Even though He was born as a man, Jesus didn't have a sinful nature.

In the very beginning, Adam was sinless too. So we could say that Jesus and Adam have something in common. Yet what a contrast between the two! Adam disobeyed; Jesus never did. Since Jesus always pleased God, He was able to make Himself the sacrifice for our sin and thus make us acceptable to God.

Why did Jesus have to suffer? Because God saw that we needed mercy, not fairness.

"For Christ also hath once suffered for sins, the just for the unjust, that he might bring us to God" (1 Peter 3:18).

ALL MY LIFE LONG

DAILY BIBLE READING: GENESIS 48:13-16

"The God which fed me all my life long unto this day" (Genesis 48:15).

"The LORD is my shepherd." We know David said that. But Jacob said it too, when he blessed Joseph's two sons: the phrase "which fed me" in the original Hebrew text is the same word translated *shepherd* in Psalm 23:1. Shepherding, feeding, tending, befriending, guarding—all those ideas are contained in that Hebrew word.

What word could better describe God our Saviour? What higher tribute could Jacob pay than to say that God had been his shepherd all his life long?

We know a few things about Jacob's life. We know that he saw a lot of hardships and suffering, not only because of Esau's hatred but also when his sons deceived him and brought him years of grief.

Furthermore, he was not always a good man. In his youth we see him as a schemer and a liar who selfishly grasped for the things he desired. Yet in his old age, Jacob could testify that God had been faithfully shepherding him all his life, teaching and leading him in the ways of uprightness.

So take heart. If you are like me, you sometimes get discouraged by your weaknesses and faults. God is your shepherd! He is guiding you into His truth. The more you trust His unfailing provision, the more you can overcome those human weaknesses. By the grace of God, you and I may also testify that God has shepherded us all our lives.

"Therefore will I save my flock . . . and I will set up one shepherd over them, and he shall feed them" (Ezekiel 34:22, 23).

SEVEN EDITIONS

DAILY BIBLE READING: 1 TIMOTHY 1:5-8

"But we know that the law is good" (1 Timothy 1:8).

When a book remains in print for many years, it may be published in several editions. Though the actual content of the book will not change, there may be changes from one edition to the next. For instance, the second edition might get a new cover, or a new foreword might be added to the third edition.

Even so it is with God's divine law. The law itself has never changed throughout history—but God's way of publishing it was not always the same. We could say that the world has seen seven "editions" of God's law.

From the beginning, God's law was written on *nature* itself. "The heavens declare the glory of God; and the firmament sheweth his handywork" (Psalm 19:1).

In creating humans, God incorporated His law into the *conscience of man.* "The work of the law written in their hearts, their conscience also bearing witness" (Romans 2:15).

In the time of Moses, God wrote the law on *tablets of stone.* "I will give thee tablets of stone, and a law" (Exodus 24:12).

Then came *Jesus,* the Living Word! "The Word was made flesh, and dwelt among us" (John 1:14).

Eventually God gave us the entire *Scriptures* as we know them today. "That we through patience and comfort of the Scriptures might have hope" (Romans 15:4).

Now God's Word becomes written in our *hearts.* "I will put my laws into their mind, and write them in their hearts" (Hebrews 8:10).

And finally, *your life* is a living letter to show forth God's law to those around you.

"Ye are our epistle . . . the epistle of Christ ministered by us, written not with ink, but with the Spirit of the living God" (2 Corinthians 3:2, 3).

A NEW CREATION

DAILY BIBLE READING: 2 CORINTHIANS 5:17

"Therefore if any man be in Christ, he is a new creature" (2 Corinthians 5:17).

Once a man boasted, "I'm turning over a new leaf. My life was going in the wrong direction, but I'm turning myself in a new direction."

The idea sounds commendable enough. Certainly we need to recognize our sinfulness. But if there is to be a real change, we need more than just a "new leaf" or a "new direction." We need to become brand-new people! We need the Holy Spirit to give us a new life.

Merely becoming reformed, rehabilitated, or reeducated is not enough. Jesus said, "Ye must be born again." We must be re-created—a new creation.

Why? Because in the depth of our being, something has died. Man's spirit is dead because of sin. It is useless to reform or reeducate something that is dead. New life is the only solution.

This new life comes at first to our spirit, but as we surrender ourselves more and more to the Holy Spirit, the new life can spread throughout our being. That's why Paul wrote in Romans 8:11, "He that raised up Christ from the dead shall also quicken your mortal bodies by his Spirit that dwelleth in you."

When we receive new life, God writes upon us His new name (Revelation 3:12). And on our lips will be a new song—the song of redemption. "He hath put a new song in my mouth" (Psalm 40:3).

"It is the spirit that quickeneth; the flesh profiteth nothing: the words that I speak unto you, they are spirit, and they are life" (John 6:63).

AN UNEVEN TRADE

DAILY BIBLE READING: ISAIAH 53:3-5

"For he hath made him to be sin for us, who knew no sin; that we might be made the righteousness of God in him" (2 Corinthians 5:21).

In ancient times, people did a lot of bartering. A woman might go to market and exchange some butter and cheese she had made for oranges or lotion. A man might exchange a bag of grain for an iron tool he needed. Such bartering worked only if two people had goods of nearly equal value so that there could be an even trade.

But think of the uneven "trade" that takes place between us and God when we trust in Jesus! What we bring as barter is absolutely worthless—in fact, worse than useless. Yet in return God gives us something of immeasurable worth.

The exchange we are talking about is this: we bring our sin, and He gives us the righteousness of God instead. Yes, God offers to trade His righteousness for our sins if we confess them!

Consider Isaiah 53:5. Jesus took the wounds, the bruises, the chastisement of our transgressions—we receive peace in exchange. Jesus got the stripes—we got the healing. Throughout Isaiah 53, the story is the same. Jesus took our sorrows and our griefs; He was stricken and smitten; He took our iniquities. He was oppressed. He was afflicted.

And what do we get in exchange? Eternal life in Jesus Christ our Lord.

"Who his own self bare our sins in his own body on the tree, that we, being dead to sins, should live unto righteousness" (1 Peter 2:24).

DOWNWARD SPIRAL

DAILY BIBLE READING: LUKE 15:11-16

"He would fain have filled his belly with the husks that the swine did eat" (Luke 15:16).

Yearning for a few husks—surely that was the bottom. Could you paint a picture that shows more graphically the utter debasement of sin? Jesus was certainly a master of human language. He was able to get across His message in a vivid way.

The prodigal son's story can be shown as two stairways, one downward, one upward. On each step is a describing word. All the words on the downward stairs begin with *S:*

We start at the top with *self-will.* "Father, give me the portion of goods that falleth to me" (verse 12).

The next step downward is *selfishness.* "The younger son gathered all together" (verse 13).

Separation. He "took his journey into a far country" (verse 13).

Then comes *sensuality:* "wasted his substance with riotous living" (verse 13).

All that leads to *spiritual destruction.* "And when he had spent all, there arose a mighty famine in that land; and he began to be in want" (verse 14).

Now we see *self-abasement.* In his desperation, the son was ready to do anything, even to the point of becoming a swineherd (verse 15). In his hunger, even pig feed was denied him (verse 16).

Do we see ourselves in this sad downward spiral of sin? Do we recognize in our own life the evidence of self-will and selfishness, resulting in spiritual death and abject poverty?

"And knowest not that thou art wretched, and miserable, and poor, and blind, and naked" (Revelation 3:17).

THE UPWARD WAY

DAILY BIBLE READING: LUKE 15:17-24

"And when he came to himself, he said . . . I will arise, and go to my father" (Luke 15:17, 18).

Again, that is the bottom. But it is the bottom step of an upward stairway! The first step toward making things right is recognizing how wrong we are—coming to our senses. On this upward staircase, each describing word begins with *R*:

First, *realization*. "How many hired servants of my father's have bread enough and to spare, and I perish with hunger!" (verse 17).

Next, *resolution*—acting upon our realization. "I will arise and go to my father" (verse 18).

Repentance. "I have sinned against heaven, and before thee" (verse 18).

This brings the *return*. "And he arose, and came to his father" (verse 20).

Oh, the beauty of the *reconciliation* on the next step upward. "His father saw him, and had compassion, and ran, and fell on his neck, and kissed him" (verse 20).

Nor does the Father stop there. We now come to the *reclothing*. "Bring forth the best robe, and put it on him; and put a ring on his hand" (verse 22). The royal robe of righteousness, washed in the blood of the Lamb.

Finally we reach the stairway's pinnacle of *rejoicing*: "For this my son was dead, and is alive again; he was lost, and is found. And they began to be merry" (verse 24).

"We all had our conversation in times past in the lusts of our flesh, fulfilling the desires of the flesh . . . But God . . . even when we were dead in sins, hath quickened us together with Christ" (Ephesians 2:3-5).

THE RING OF RECONCILIATION

DAILY BIBLE READING: ROMANS 5:1-5

"And put a ring on his hand" (Luke 15:22).

We could call the ring bestowed by the father upon his prodigal son the *ring of reconciliation*. Romans 5 gives a description of this beautiful ring, which we all receive as proof of our justification in Christ.

Picture a golden band topped with eight sparkling jewels. The first few verses of Romans 5 give us the identity of each jewel. All eight of the jewels are gifts from Christ, and they all help to complete the "ring of reconciliation."

The first jewel is *peace*. "We have peace with God through our Lord Jesus Christ" (Romans 5:1). This is not to say that we will always feel peaceful, but deep in our spirits there remains a "peace that passeth all understanding."

Then there is the jewel of *access*. Wonder of wonders, through Jesus we can have constant access to God the Father. "By whom also we have access by faith into this grace wherein we stand" (verse 2).

Jesus also gives us the jewel of *joy in hope:* "and rejoice in hope of the glory of God" (verse 2).

One jewel has a mysterious, darker sparkle: *joy in suffering.* "We glory in tribulations also" (verse 3).

That jewel leads us to the jewel of *patience,* or perseverance: "knowing that tribulation worketh patience [produces perseverance]" (verse 3).

All this brings the jewel of *experience,* or godly character: "and patience, experience" (verse 4).

Two more shining jewels complete the ring of reconciliation: *hope* and *love.* (verses 4, 5).

"And hope maketh not ashamed; because the love of God is shed abroad in our hearts" (Romans 5:5).

ALL OVER THE MAP

DAILY BIBLE READING: LUKE 23:1-6

"And the whole multitude of them arose, and led him unto Pilate" (Luke 23:1).

Have you ever studied a map showing the route Jesus traveled on the night of His betrayal? Jesus entered Jerusalem at the eastern gate. He would have followed the winding streets to a house somewhere in the southern part of the city, where He took supper with His disciples.

Next, He and His disciples must have retraced their steps back to the eastern gate and out to the Garden of Gethsemane. Later, after being captured by the officials, the maps show Him being led along the Kidron Valley outside the city and entering through a less-used gate at the southeastern corner near the high priest's palace.

From there the arrows point back up the full length of the city to Pilate's judgment hall. But as we know, Jesus also took a side trip from there over to the western edge of the city where Herod had his palace—then back again to the judgment hall. Finally, after the sentencing, Jesus toiled northward to Golgotha.

Christ's travels that night took Him all over Jerusalem. Just looking at a map barely helps us realize this brutal fact: Jesus took that winding journey *one weary step at a time.* As He crisscrossed Jerusalem that night, He may have traveled more than twenty miles.

Let's remember this, the next time we are in the midst of tribulations that seem to drag on and on while our feet grow ever more weary and sore.

"Consider him that endured such contradiction of sinners against himself, lest ye be wearied and faint in your minds" (Hebrews 12:3).

WRONG DESIRES

DAILY BIBLE READING: JAMES 4:1-3

"Ye lust, and have not: ye kill, and desire to have" (James 4:2).

Two key words in this passage are *lust* and *desire*, both meaning "wrong desire." Much havoc is played in our lives by wrong desire. Our flesh lusts for more money, more possessions, or more recognition from others. Then, in order to fulfill those evil desires, we quarrel and fight and trample on the rights of others.

Surely pride is at the root of wrong desires. Pride makes us self-centered. It makes us think we deserve to have whatever we want. Pride gives us a greedy appetite for more than we need.

James provides the cure for pride in this same chapter: "Humble yourselves in the sight of the Lord" (verse 10). "Submit yourselves therefore to God" (verse 7). Humility releases us from our self-centered desires.

Bowing humbly before God, we realize we don't need man's approval—only God's. His Spirit in our hearts assures us that we don't need the things of this world. They are nothing but cheap substitutions for the real joys God offers. There at the foot of the cross, we can leave our sorry little pile of wrong desires and receive instead the abundant life.

"Better it is to be of an humble spirit with the lowly, than to divide the spoil with the proud" (Proverbs 16:19).

MY WILL BE DONE

DAILY BIBLE READING: ISAIAH 14:12-15

"I will exalt my throne above the stars of God" (Isaiah 14:13).

Of whom is Isaiah speaking in this passage? He mentions *Lucifer,* a name given to Satan. Yet the rest of the chapter speaks of the king of Babylon. We really don't need to know the answer to that question. Whether it was Satan or a king who made these boastful statements, you and I can learn an important lesson by reading them.

Notice how often Lucifer says "I will" in these verses. Five times! And the last claim is the most preposterous of all: "I will be like the most High."

I see pride in those five "I wills," the very same kind of pride you and I struggle with. Pride clings to its own ideas. If pride rules me, then I want my ideas to be fulfilled. "I will" do this, "I will" do that—all in my own power, my own way, to please no one but myself.

But look what happened to Lucifer. All those "I wills" ended in utter defeat for him. He was "brought down to hell, to the sides of the pit." In Hell are those who said, "My will be done." In Heaven are those who said, "Thy will be done."

What if Jesus had come to earth with the intention of doing His own will? Yes, He was human; He had a will of His own, and Satan tried to get Him to follow that will and achieve earthly success. But in the end, He said, "Nevertheless, not as I will, but as thou wilt." And that is how He won absolute victory over Satan, the one who says, "My will be done."

"Thy wisdom and thy knowledge, it hath perverted thee; and thou hast said in thine heart, I am, and none else beside me" (Isaiah 47:10).

A DOOR WHERE SATAN ENTERS

DAILY BIBLE READING: LUKE 22:31-34

"Satan hath desired to have you" (Luke 22:31).

I find those words a little scary. Does Satan ask to have me too? And if so, will the Lord give him permission to sift me like wheat? One thing is quite sure however: Satan can have no power in my life unless I leave a door open that allows him to reach inside.

Unfortunately, there is a door that we leave ajar far too often: a door marked *Pride.* Nothing gives Satan greater access to our lives than our own pride. We can see that in the story of Peter here in Luke 22. Not long before Christ's startling statement about sifting, we find Peter and the other disciples indulging in pride: "And there was also a strife among then, which of them should be accounted the greatest" (verse 24). Nothing but pride could have started a quarrel like that!

So Peter left the door of pride open, and look how utterly he was defeated. Though he had the best of intentions—"Lord, I am ready to go with thee, both into prison, and to death" (verse 33)—because of pride, Peter lost any ability to carry out those good intentions. He ended up denying his Lord with an oath.

Pride is nothing less than an open invitation to the god of this world. Self-exaltation, self-righteousness, self-centeredness—all prevent us from humbly admitting our need for the righteousness and strength of Christ. Praise Him! He won't give up on us as we struggle with pride, but instead He does for us what He did for Peter:

"But I have prayed for thee, that thy faith fail not: and when thou art converted, strengthen thy brethren" (Luke 22:32).

THE SIN THAT GREW

DAILY BIBLE READING: LUKE 22:54-60

"Man, I know not what thou sayest" (Luke 22:60).

Sin has sometimes been compared to cancer. Like cancer, it will grow and spread if left unchecked.

Look at the way Peter's sin grew. First he simply denied that he knew Jesus (verse 57). We can imagine how his heart beat faster and his hands became clammy when he realized that the servant girl had recognized him. Unless he managed to convince this sharp-eyed maiden otherwise, he was in deep trouble!

Oh, Peter, if you had only turned to God in prayer at that moment. He could have rescued you in a better way. "He delivereth and rescueth, and worketh signs and wonders in heaven and in earth" (Daniel 6:27).

But Peter tried to rescue himself from his folly. And so his sin grew. Someone else looked at Peter and insisted, "You must be one of them!" Peter's retort dug him even deeper into the mire: "I am not a follower of Jesus."

As sin grows, the cover-up grows too. An hour later, still another person voiced suspicions: "You must be one of His followers; you're a Galilean." And Peter spat out the biggest lie of all. "I don't even know what you're talking about!"

Let's learn to deal with sin before its poison gets a major grip on us. Covering up sin only makes it worse. We need to confess our sins and our desire to sin, so the Deliverer can rescue us before the cancer spreads too far.

"He that covereth his sins shall not prosper: but whoso confesseth and forsaketh them shall have mercy" (Proverbs 28:13).

A PREDECIDED VERDICT

DAILY BIBLE READING: MATTHEW 26:62-67

"And they that had laid hold on Jesus led him away to Caiaphas the high priest, where the scribes and the elders were assembled" (Matthew 26:57).

Some things about the trial of Jesus simply boggle the mind. The verdict, for one: it was predecided. The Jewish leaders had made up their minds that Jesus must die. In no way would this be a fair trial to find out whether Jesus was guilty or not.

What a lot of thought and effort the Jews must have put into this so-called "trial"! Three different hearings were arranged, all with only one aim: somehow gaining enough false witness to condemn Jesus. And it had to happen overnight. The Sabbath was only twenty-four hours away; Jesus had to be dead before Friday evening.

So, in a space of less than eighteen hours, this is what the Jews managed to do. First they took Jesus to Annas, the former high priest. From there He was taken to Caiaphas, the legal high priest. How relieved the Jews must have been when Caiaphas found grounds to hand out a death sentence. Then, in the predawn darkness, Jesus was brought before the Jewish high council to plan the finishing touches.

Of course, the Jews had no power to carry out a death verdict. That is why Jesus endured three more hearings—twice before Pilate and once before Herod.

How consumed with hatred those Jews must have been, to go to such extraordinary lengths to get this Man killed! The devil still hates us like that today. He has a predecided verdict for us too: he wants to drag us with him down into Hell. Is it any wonder that the followers of Jesus face so many temptations?

"Be sober, be vigilant; because your adversary the devil, as a roaring lion, walketh about, seeking whom he may devour" (1 Peter 5:8).

Day 135

ONE NEGATIVE OPINION

DAILY BIBLE READING: NUMBERS 13:31-33

"And they brought up an evil report" (Numbers 13:32).

Are you like me—quick to express your opinions? How careful we should be not to give negative opinions! Just think what happened in Numbers 13 and 14 because of the negative opinion brought back by the ten scouts after their tour of the promised land.

"The land is full of giants!" they wailed. "We felt like mere grasshoppers, and no doubt we looked like grasshoppers to those huge people. Their cities are walled and fortified."

Why were the people of Israel so quick to believe that negative opinion? I don't know. Is it human nature to believe a negative report rather than a positive one? Why didn't they believe the cheerful, optimistic report brought by Joshua and Caleb who urged, "We can surely conquer the land; let's go at once and take it"?

But no. Israel latched onto the negative opinion. They cried all night, complaining against Moses and Aaron, moaning that they should have stayed in Egypt. They even spoke of choosing a new leader and hurrying back to the false security of the slavery from which God had delivered them.

We all know what happened as a result. God vowed that this unbelieving generation would not enter the promised land. How sobering it is to consider the terrible, far-reaching effects of one negative opinion given by a group of discouraged men! How much rather we should seek to be like Joshua and Caleb, offering encouragement born of faith!

"Only rebel not ye against the LORD, rather fear ye the people of the land . . . the LORD is with us: fear than not" (Numbers 14:9).

FULL SONSHIP

DAILY BIBLE READING: GALATIANS 4:5-7.

"That we might receive the adoption of sons" (Galatians 4:5).

After years of living in assorted foster homes, a twelve-year-old girl was over-joyed when a family decided to adopt her. What privileges would now be hers! By becoming someone's legal daughter, she would enjoy all the things that many girls took for granted. No longer would she need to feel like a "second-class cit-izen" with no rights of her own.

As time went on, however, this newly adopted girl realized that along with privileges came accountability, and also tremendous responsibilities. Yes, she had been given the rights of a daughter—but that included obedience and sub-mission. Unless she submitted to every aspect of her adoption, the full benefits would never be hers.

We, too, have received the privileges of adoption into God's family. No longer are we cowering and fearful slaves. Christ has bought our freedom from sin with His lifeblood. Thus we gain the rights of full sonship.

Can we grasp what a wonderful privilege this is? Do we realize what marvel-ous treasures are ours, as coheirs with Jesus? God the Father has given us price-less gifts: His Son, forgiveness, eternal life, the inward witness of the Holy Spirit. And beyond those initial gifts, God encourages us to keep on asking for all we need, because we are His children.

Yet for us too these great privileges bring responsibilities and accountability. In order to live out the Christ-life God has given us, we must give up our own rights, serve others, and say no to the world, the flesh, and the devil. But no suffering can compare with the price Jesus paid to secure our adoption into God's family!

"And if children, then heirs; heirs of God, and joint-heirs with Christ; if so be that we suffer with him, that we may be also glorified together" (Romans 8:17).

HE STANDS IN THE GAP

DAILY BIBLE READING: 2 CORINTHIANS 5:18-20

"God was in Christ, reconciling the world unto himself" (2 Corinthians 5:19).

What causes earthquakes? When God created the earth, He created different plates of rock, with fault lines that tend to move. It is this movement that causes earthquakes.

Similarly, when God created the human soul, He did not fix it into an immovable relationship with Himself. Instead, He created man with the ability to choose—the ability to move his allegiance away from God if he so desired.

Man chose. He chose his own way instead of God's. He chose disobedience over obedience. Immediately, the "earthquake" of sin created a huge chasm between man and the solid Rock that was God.

What has God done about this sad situation? Has he taken away the "fault lines" that make us prone to sin and therefore separate us from God?

No. The fault lines of our human weakness are still there. We are still prone to "earthquakes." But the wonderful truth is that God sent His Son to stand in the gap. Jesus bridged the chasm of sin with His own lifeblood. God reconciles us to Himself through Jesus, and thus He closes the horrible chasm opened up by the "earthquake" of sin.

"And that he might reconcile both unto God in one body by the cross, having slain the enmity thereby" (Ephesians 2:16).

THE TOUCH OF CHRIST

DAILY BIBLE READING: LUKE 6:17-19

"The whole multitude sought to touch him" (Luke 6:19).

Great wonders were wrought for those who touched Jesus or were touched by Him. Matthew 14:36 tells how people jostled and pleaded for that touch, "and as many as touched were made perfectly whole."

His touch held cleansing too. When the leper bowed before Him, "Jesus put forth his hand, and touched him, saying, I will; be thou clean. And immediately his leprosy was cleansed" (Matthew 8:3).

Christ's touch brought light to the blind. "Then touched he their eyes . . . and their eyes were opened" (Matthew 9:29, 30).

In the hour of fear, Christ's touch brought reassurance. His disciples were struck down and sore afraid when a voice spoke from Heaven, but "Jesus came and touched them, and said, Arise, and be not afraid" (Matthew 17:7).

What liberating power there was in Christ's touch! A man's ears and tongue were bound; but Jesus touched him, "and straightway his ears were opened, and the string of his tongue was loosed" (Mark 7:35).

Peter's mother was sick when Jesus came to her house; "he touched her hand, and the fever left her" (Matthew 8:15).

Does this make you yearn to still have Jesus among us with His marvelous touch? Yearn no more, for His Spirit *is* here today: His healing, cleansing, illuminating, reassuring, liberating Spirit! Yield to His touch and the feverish cares of life will flee, leaving a heart calmed and purified by contact with Christ.

"For he had healed many; insomuch that they pressed upon him for to touch him" (Mark 3:10).

GOD BREATHED

DAILY BIBLE READING: 2 TIMOTHY 3:14-17

"All scripture is given by inspiration of God" (2 Timothy 3:16).

Shelves and shelves of books. All shapes and sizes and colors of books. That's often what you see when you walk into a secondhand store.

Occasionally, tucked in with the other books, you will find a Bible. Somehow it doesn't seem right to see this Book of books in there with the motley assortment. The Bible is special. It deserves better treatment than that.

What makes the Bible different from all other books?

It is "given by inspiration of God." The Greek wording used here is sometimes translated as "all Scripture is God-breathed." The breath of God—our very life! That is God's Word.

The Bible isn't a mere collection of stories, fables, or human ideas. In fact, the Bible is not a human book at all. Yes, humans did write the different books of the Bible—but they wrote by inspiration of the Holy Spirit, the "breath of God." The Bible is varied because each writer used his own mind, his own talents, his own language—but the inspiration came from God.

The Bible is completely trustworthy, completely true. It is our standard for testing anything else that claims to be true.

And notice, in verse 17, the different ways that these God-breathed Scriptures are profitable for us. They teach us the truth, they tell us when we do wrong, and they show us the right way to live. Praise God, if we look to His Word, we are thoroughly equipped to live as He commands!

"For the prophecy came not in old time by the will of man: but holy men of God spake as they were moved by the Holy Ghost" (2 Peter 1:21).

MARY LEARNED TO SERVE

DAILY BIBLE READING: LUKE 10:38-42

"Martha, Martha, thou art careful and troubled about many things" (Luke 10:41).

Reading this little story, we tend to see Martha as the person who had the most to learn. But I think Mary needed to learn a few things as well.

Think about it. Jesus was not telling Martha that it's wrong to be hospitable. He wasn't rebuking her for her devoted service, or for always having a meal and a bed ready when He came.

Hospitality is a necessary virtue. We needn't think Jesus doesn't want us to clean our houses or prepare food for family and visitors. He's definitely not saying we should never do anything but sit and listen, the way Mary was doing.

I think Jesus was speaking against Martha's needless worries. The trouble with Martha was not her serving—but the way she did it. I can imagine her fretting over the appearance of her home, perhaps bringing herself to the point of exhaustion because she felt every little corner had to be clean. All that fretting and fussing would have made those around her uncomfortable too.

"There's really only one thing worthy of our concern," Jesus seems to tell Martha, "and Mary has discovered that one thing." However, we know how much emphasis Jesus places on obedience, and acting upon the truths of His Word. Perhaps Mary needed a nudge in that direction.

Both women may have had something to learn: Martha to serve in a calm way out of a loving heart; and Mary, to translate her devotion into practical service. We have evidence that Mary did indeed learn how to turn worship into action. In the Bible's final glimpse of her, we see Mary anointing Christ's feet with perfume and wiping them with her hair.

"Whatsoever ye do, do it heartily, as to the Lord" (Colossians 3:23).

HE CAME TO DISTURB US

DAILY BIBLE READING: MATTHEW 2:1-6

"When Herod the king had heard these things, he was troubled, and all Jerusalem with him" (Matthew 2:3).

Jesus came to earth to disturb people. Right from His earliest days, that's what His birth did. Not only was Herod deeply disturbed when the wise men from the East inquired about a new king, but all Jerusalem was troubled right along with Herod.

Why was Herod disturbed? He may have known about the prophecies of Scripture. But he probably hoped those prophecies were mere fables; he didn't want anybody challenging his right to the throne. Then along came these so-called wise men, who had traveled many miles because of a star that portended a new king! Calling Herod troubled was probably an understatement.

And why would all Jerusalem have been troubled with him? The people may have feared change. Like you and me, they preferred a comfortable status quo to an unknown, volatile event.

But Jesus had come to disturb the world. His birth caused people to react. For some, the reaction was spiritual longing. In others, it caused fear and uncertainty. A big question stared everyone in the face: was Jesus really the King, the Son of God?

Today, Jesus still disturbs the carnal man. The word of Christ pressures us to make choices. Will we draw back, fearing the revolution that must take place in our souls if we dethrone self and choose the rule of Christ? Do we prefer the slavery of sin to the glorious liberty of the children of God?

"Think not that I am come to send peace on earth: I came not to send peace, but a sword" (Matthew 10:34).

HE WOULDN'T GO FIVE MILES

DAILY BIBLE READING: MATTHEW 2:7-12

"When they saw the star, they rejoiced with exceeding great joy" (Matthew 2:10).

How should we respond to the challenge of Christ? What a beautiful example the wise men gave us! When they saw the star, they could have thought, "Oh well, if a new prince actually arises, we'll find out soon enough"—and stayed at home.

But no! So eager were they to meet the new King, they traveled hundreds of miles to seek Him. And when they found Him, their response was humble adoration. They furnished us with an example of joy, worship, and freely giving.

Contrast that with Herod's example. He, too, heard of a new king—and how did he react? With consternation and rebellion. Seek out Jesus? No indeed! Bethlehem was only five miles from Jerusalem, but Herod wouldn't even travel that distance. True, he said he wanted to worship the child—but in reality he only wanted to murder the new king.

So once again comes the question—how will we respond to God? Do we expect Him to come looking for us and give us gifts? Do we pretend to be religious, when in reality we have not allowed Jesus into our hearts? Instead of opening our hearts to Jesus, do we in effect kill Him with our rebellious attitudes?

Or are we wise enough to diligently seek Him—fall down in joy to worship Him—and surrender our whole lives to Him?

"There shall come a Star out of Jacob, and a Scepter shall rise out of Israel" (Numbers 24:17).

SUPREME OVER NATURE

DAILY BIBLE READING: 1 KINGS 16:29-33

"And Ahab the son of Omri . . . went and served Baal, and worshipped him" (1 Kings 16:30, 31).

Who was Baal? Supposedly, Baal was the god of things like water and fire and farm crops. Ancient people often did that—dividing the realm of nature into categories, they would parcel it out to their different gods. How tragic, that Israel was forsaking the God who ruled the universe and turning instead to false gods!

But God kept sending miracles that demonstrated who really controls nature. Nearly all of the miracles in the days of Elijah and Elisha clearly demonstrated God's power over the elements that idol worshippers attributed to Baal's control.

Today and tomorrow as we take a quick look at the miracles of Elijah and Elisha, let's keep this in mind: we, too, are tempted to set our affection on earthly things and neglect the God of the universe. If perchance He allows some cherished earthly thing to be taken from us, it may be because we need to restore our trust in Almighty God.

First, God sent food to Elijah by means of ravens. Can you see how that was an indication of God's sovereignty over Baal? Supposedly, Baal controlled crops and food—but God could provide food anywhere and by any means.

Again, God's sovereign provision of food is evident when He multiplied the destitute widow's flour and oil (1 Kings 17:12-16).

To use a Hebrew expression, God is *Yahweh Yireh:* "The Lord provides."

"And Abraham called the name of that place Jehovahjireh: as it is said to this day, In the mount of the LORD it shall be seen [provided]" (Genesis 22:14).

PROVIDER OF LIFE AND FOOD

DAILY BIBLE READING: 1 KINGS 17:17-24

"Now by this I know that thou art a man of God, and that the word of the LORD in thy mouth is truth" (1 Kings 17:24).

You might wonder how this miracle demonstrates God's sovereignty over Baal. But sometimes people sacrificed their children to Baal. So we can see that here, and as well as the time when Elisha raised a dead boy to life, God was declaring that the lives of children belong to Him.

Next we look at the consummate miracle on Mount Carmel (1 Kings 18:16-46). What a demonstration of God's power over fire and water! Baal could not provide so much as a spark—whereas the flames from God consumed even the water.

In 2 Kings 1:9-14, God sent more fire from Heaven, twice destroying a group of fifty Baal-worshipping soldiers. Later when Elijah parted the Jordan, we see God's power over water; and when Elijah was transported to Heaven, we again see God using fire and wind for His purpose.

Four times in Elisha's life we see him demonstrating God's power over water: when he, too, parted the Jordan; when he purified a spring at Jericho (2 Kings 2:19); when the axe head floated; and when Naaman was healed of leprosy by washing in the river.

Three times Elisha demonstrated power in the realm of food or crops. We all know the story of how that widow's oil was multiplied until she could not find another jug to fill. Then in 2 Kings 4:38-44 we see two miracles concerning food for the prophets who followed Elisha: a handful of flour cleansed poison from a stew, and a donated sack of grain miraculously fed a hundred people. How manifest is God's power over crops and food—indeed over the whole realm of nature!

"Therefore I say unto you, Take no thought for your life, what ye shall eat, or what ye shall drink" (Matthew 6:25).

POUTER

DAILY BIBLE READING: 1 KINGS 21:1-4

"And Ahab came into his house heavy and displeased" (1 Kings 21:4).

One mother, when a child pouted because something had not gone his way, would say, "Let's read the story of Ahab the pouter!" And she would get a Bible storybook and read the account of Ahab turning his face to the wall and refusing to eat. That tended to curve pouting lips into smiles. Even a child can see how ridiculous it was that Ahab literally made himself sick with pouting.

When we consider what started Ahab's fit of pouting, it becomes even more ridiculous. Ahab already owned ten-twelfths of Israel. Yet as long as this coveted vineyard was forbidden him, all his other possessions couldn't make Ahab happy.

Let's face it. Pouting is a tendency of human nature. If we're honest we'll admit we've all had times when we pouted because things didn't go our way. But, oh, how important it is not to indulge in pouting!

Think what a great sin sprang out of Ahab's pouting. Naboth, an innocent man, was murdered. True, Jezebel was the one who engineered that sin. But we must not forget how it all started: with two "small" sins on Ahab's part. The sin of selfishness, and the sin of pouting.

"But every man is tempted, when he is drawn away of his own lust, and enticed. Then when lust hath conceived, it bringeth forth sin: and sin, when it is finished, bringeth forth death" (James 1:14, 15).

A CYCLE THAT STRENGTHENS

DAILY BIBLE READING: JOSHUA 8:1-8

"And the LORD said unto Joshua, Fear not, neither be thou dismayed" (Joshua 8:1).

When we hear the name Ai, we automatically think, "That's where Joshua lost the battle because of Achan's sin." But did Joshua really lose?

It's true that Achan's sin brought failure. The army of Israel was put to rout. Joshua was so dismayed that he tore his clothes, put dust on his head, and fell on his face before the Lord.

It has been said, however, that the only way to lose is to give up. Supposing Joshua and the elders had stayed lying there with their faces in the dirt—then yes, Ai would have been a disastrous defeat.

But that's not how God wanted this failure to affect Israel. God said to Joshua, "Get thee up; wherefore liest thou thus upon thy face?" And God proceeded to tell Joshua how to receive cleansing and forgiveness through confession and true repentance.

In Chapter 8, God assured Joshua that Israel could be victorious. So Joshua got busy and devised a shrewd attack strategy. Then he gave the people instructions, and this time they were ready to truly obey.

Do you see what happened? The initial failure actually strengthened Israel for ultimate victory.

We all know what it's like to go through that cycle of failure, confession, and forgiveness. It's not a cycle that has to weaken us. On the contrary, it can strengthen us—as long as we don't give up. (And providing we are ready to obey.)

"According to the commandment of the LORD shall ye do" (Joshua 8:8).

HE LOOKED TO ASSYRIA

DAILY BIBLE READING: 2 KINGS 16:1-9

"Come up, and save me out of the hand of the king of Syria, and out of the hand of the king of Israel" (2 Kings 16:7).

King Ahaz was in big trouble: the armies of Israel and Syria were besieging Jerusalem, the capital of his nation, Judah. What an opportunity this would have been to seek divine aid! Surely God would have gladly delivered His holy city from the besieging armies—if only Ahaz had asked.

But Ahaz had a lot of things he needed to make right with God. He was worshipping idols—even sacrificing his own children to pagan gods. He was not ready to pay the price for God's help. Instead he turned to the one whom he should have considered his mortal enemy: the king of Assyria. Ahaz was willing to sell his nation as slaves to Assyria. He even took money and silver from the temple of God to use as a bribe. What a tragic mistake!

But perhaps I am too often like King Ahaz. When burdened by failures and trials, where do I look for help? To whom do I turn? God is the only one who can truly help. But will I allow the spotlight of His righteousness to scan my failings? Will I repent and submit?

Or am I like Ahaz, turning for help to anything but God? Do I try to fill my emptiness with money, or possessions, or harmful habits? If I do, I will become a slave to those things, just as Judah became enslaved to Assyria.

"Save us, O LORD our God, and gather us from among the heathen, to give thanks unto thy holy name, and to triumph in thy praise" (Psalm 106:47).

AMBITION: RIGHT OR WRONG

DAILY BIBLE READING: MARK 9:33-37

"By the way they had disputed among themselves, who should be the greatest" (Mark 9:34).

Ambition can be so destructive. It destroys peace and harmony and love among brethren. Might we not say that this quarrel among the disciples was about ambition? Arguing about who would be the most important in the kingdom of Heaven surely did nothing to promote good feelings.

How embarrassed the disciples must have been when, after they entered the house, Jesus leveled His discerning gaze at them and asked, "What were you arguing about out there on the road?" They were like schoolboys who hadn't realized that their teacher was listening. In their shame they refused to answer. Having walked with Jesus for several years, surely they had some idea what He thought about ambition.

As an earnest desire to achieve something, ambition is not necessarily wrong in itself. It depends on what we earnestly desire!

Jesus sat down to explain to His disciples that there is also a right kind of ambition. What is it that we should "earnestly desire"? Not our own greatness—but the furtherance of Christ's kingdom. We pray for it daily when we say "Thy kingdom come." Our ambition should be to do all we can for Jesus and His kingdom.

That kingdom is not one where people hold positions or lord it over each other. Christ's kingdom is one where the greatest people are those who humbly serve—and the greatest ambition is to help others and bring them into that kingdom.

"But he that is greatest among you shall be your servant" (Matthew 23:11).

A BITTERSWEET RAIN

DAILY BIBLE READING: HOSEA 6:3, 4

"He shall come unto us as the rain" (Hosea 6:3).

What is this "rain" that God brings into our lives if we "follow on to know the LORD"? We can take falling rain as symbolic of repentant tears. We know how important rain is to the natural world. Gentle spring rains cause new green things to grow. Summer rains swell crops to abundance.

Do we realize how important repentance is to our spiritual lives? Modern religion promotes a "faith" devoid of the repentance that brings true righteousness. Yet the very first sermon of Jesus bade the world to repent. Just as crops cannot grow without rain, so our spiritual life cannot grow without repentance.

You see, repentance is not just a one-time thing, a single burst of emotion that will turn us once and for all in the right direction. Repentance needs to be a constant part of the believer's life. Bittersweet tears of repentance need to fall like a continual, gentle rain.

Why? Notice what Hosea says in verse 4. "Your goodness is as a morning cloud, and as the early dew it goeth away." We fail. We make mistakes. Our spiritual life would soon grow barren and dry if it were not for the soft rain of our repentant tears.

But even though repentance is a form of sorrow, we need not despair. It is a sorrow that constantly reminds us of God's wonderful mercy and grace.

"The rebellious dwell in a dry land" (Psalm 68:6).

NOT BY WORKS OF RIGHTEOUSNESS

DAILY BIBLE READING: DEUTERONOMY 9:4-6

"Understand therefore, that the LORD thy God giveth thee not this good land to possess it for thy righteousness" (Deuteronomy 9:6).

Did the children of Israel actually think God was giving them the promised land because they deserved it? Did they reason that they must be pretty good people if God was giving them such a marvelous gift?

We don't know whether the Israelites had such thoughts. But Moses must have suspected it, for he told them in no uncertain terms that they did not deserve this bonus. This whole chapter of Deuteronomy is filled with Moses' reminders to Israel of their past rebelliousness. Moses ended his outburst with this rather exasperated remark: "Ye have been rebellious against the LORD from the day that I knew you" (Deuteronomy 9:24).

Are we ever tempted to think we deserve God's wonderful gift of salvation? Such folly! We are no different from Israel. Rebellion has been part of our nature from the day we were born.

We need to say with Job, "If I justify myself, mine own mouth shall condemn me: if I say, I am perfect, it shall also prove me perverse" (Job 9:20). There is no way we can say we have merited God's gift because of our own righteousness. "If we say that we have no sin, we deceive ourselves, and the truth is not in us" (1 John 1:8).

Titus 3:5 puts it this way: "Not by works of righteousness which we have done, but according to his mercy he saved us." And to the Ephesians, Paul wrote, "By grace are ye saved through faith; and that not of yourselves: it is the gift of God: not of works, lest any man should boast" (2:8, 9).

So in the end we must all say with Paul:

"By the grace of God I am what I am" (1 Corinthians 15:10).

THREE ASPECTS OF THE SPIRITUAL LIFE

DAILY BIBLE READING: JOHN 5:37, 38

"That ye might have life" (John 5:40).

Do not those words express the deepest yearning of our souls? "Lord, that we might have life—everlasting life, spiritual life!"

There are three aspects to this spiritual life for which we long. First, there must be *appropriation*. To *appropriate* is simply to take, or to receive. Like rich food on a platter, God holds out to us salvation through His Son. Will we receive it? We who are lost and dying, do we not gladly reach for this new life offered to us? The offer is universal: "Whosoever will, let him take the water of life freely" (Revelation 22:17). In the words of the psalmist, let us "take the cup of salvation, and call upon the name of the LORD" (Psalm 116:13).

Then there is *formation*. The spiritual life must be formed in us. This is a life-long process. Jesus set us the example of the holy life—but how can such a holy life be formed in the weakness of humanity? Transformation is the answer. "Be ye transformed by the renewing of your mind" (Romans 12:2). Look to the Lord, that His life may be formed in you. Paul says, "But we all, with open face beholding as in a glass the glory of the Lord, are changed [are being transformed] into the same image" (2 Corinthians 3:18).

And finally, there must be *donation*. If we truly receive spiritual life, we will give of that life to others. "Freely ye have received, freely give" (Matthew 10:8). Indeed, we are ready to give away our whole lives for the sake of this rich life in Christ. "Whosoever will lose his life for my sake shall find it" (Matthew 16:25).

Appropriation, formation, donation—the building blocks of spiritual life. And they are all tied together in these words of Peter:

"As every man hath received the gift, even so minister the same one to another, as good stewards of the manifold grace of God" (1 Peter 4:10).

Day 152

SECOND LAW

DAILY BIBLE READING: DEUTERONOMY 4:35-39

"Thou heardest his words out of the midst of the fire" (Deuteronomy 4:36).

If I asked you where the Ten Commandments are found, you would probably answer "Exodus 20," which is quite true. But they are repeated in Deuteronomy 5.

Why were the Ten Commandments given twice? In Deuteronomy, Moses was speaking to a new generation. Besides his 120-year-old self, only Joshua and Caleb remained of those who had left Egypt. So it was quite needful that the Law be repeated. That's basically what Deuteronomy consists of—three great sermons by Moses, each reminding the new generation of all that God had wrought and taught. *Deuteronomy* is a word that means "second law."

In our Christian life, we, too, get two different encounters with the law. Our first encounter is like Israel's at Sinai. There at the base of that fiery mountain, the people felt overwhelmed by God's holiness. They were condemned! To Moses they said, "Who is there of all flesh, that hath heard the voice of the living God speaking out of the midst of the fire, as we have, and lived?" (Deuteronomy 5:26).

But with the new generation on the banks of Jordan, it was different. Israel had experienced deliverance and victory. Ready to possess the land of grace, they could now receive God's law into their hearts, where it would impart life and strength.

Do you see the symbolism? We, too, stand condemned before God's righteous law. But when we have repented, and our old man is on the cross with Christ, God's law becomes part of our very life.

"I will put my law in their inward parts, and write it in their hearts; and will be their God, and they shall be my people" (Jeremiah 31:33).

FOUR-FOLD DAY OF REST

DAILY BIBLE READING: DEUTERONOMY 5:12-15

"And remember... that the LORD *thy God brought thee out thence through a mighty hand and by a stretched out arm" (Deuteronomy 5:15).*

The two "editions" of the Ten Commandments are basically the same. However, you may have noticed that they have different wordings for the fourth commandment. By reading both "editions," and also the New Testament teaching on the Sabbath, we discover four major reasons for a day of rest.

In Exodus 20 we find the original reason: the Sabbath reminds us of God's own day of rest, after He had created the world. Thus, down through the ages, the Sabbath is a memorial to Creation.

In Deuteronomy 5, however, the emphasis is on deliverance. The meaning appears to be, "Remember that you were once a slave in Egypt, where you had to work seven days a week. Keep the Sabbath to commemorate how God delivered you from that harsh slavery." So there we see that the Sabbath, for Israel, commemorated deliverance from Egypt.

Jesus Christ gave us a fresh emphasis on that deliverance and rest. He Himself is the spiritual fulfillment of the Sabbath. Through Him the believer is delivered from the bondage of sin into the "rest" of justification by faith. That's why Christians celebrate Sunday, because it was on the first day of the week that Jesus arose from the dead to accomplish His great deliverance.

And the Sabbath is a reminder to us of the eternal rest yet awaiting. So we see that the Sabbath portrays the whole spectrum of God's wonderful works: Creation, deliverance from Egypt, deliverance from sin through the resurrection, and everlasting heavenly rest.

"There remaineth therefore a rest to the people of God" (Hebrews 4:9).

WHOLEHEARTED

DAILY BIBLE READING: PSALM 119:10-15

"With my whole heart have I sought thee" (Psalm 119:10).

Psalm 119 is such a wholehearted psalm! Six times in those 176 verses, the psalmist declares his devotion, using the words "with all my heart" or "with my whole heart." Isn't that the kind of devotion we all want? Don't we long to serve God wholeheartedly?

But in our weakness we wonder—how can we do it? How does one give one's whole heart to God?

Let's take a look at what this "whole heart" must be like. First of all, it must be a praying, seeking heart. That's what the psalmist says, and Jeremiah said it too: "Ye shall seek me, and find me, when ye shall search for me with all your heart" (29:13).

The whole heart must be filled with repentance for sin. "Therefore also now, saith the LORD, turn ye even to me with all your heart, and with fasting, and with weeping, and with mourning" (Joel 2:12).

Also it must be a heart full of love. In Deuteronomy 6:5 we read those words so often repeated in the Gospels: "Thou shalt love the LORD thy God with all thine heart." Why should we not love the Lord when He has accepted our repentant hearts and extended His grace to save us?

Seeking, repenting, loving—all these build up to a sublime trust. Oh, the simple, childlike trust in the heart that wholly turns to God! "Trust in the LORD with all thine heart; and lean not unto thine own understanding" (Proverbs 3:5).

And finally, this "whole heart" that we give to God is a heart full of obedience. "Give me understanding, and I shall keep thy law; yea, I shall observe it with my whole heart" (Psalm 119:145).

"I cried with my whole heart; hear me, O LORD: I will keep thy statutes" (Psalm 119:45).

ANANIAS ASSUMED

DAILY BIBLE READING: ACTS 9:10-19

"Lord, I have heard by many of this man, how much evil he hath done to thy saints at Jerusalem" (Acts 9:13).

Ananias assumed that Saul of Tarsus must be an evil man who could never become a Christian. We can understand why Ananias felt that way. Saul had hounded many Christians to death. It's no wonder Ananias protested when God asked him to go help Saul.

But the assumption Ananias made was completely wrong. Just as you and I are apt to do, Ananias looked at things from a human perspective. The human perspective often protests, "But that's impossible."

Why do we limit God? Why do we think that anything is impossible for the Creator of the universe? Really, we are being ridiculous. The One who created mountains, seas, skies, and prairies can certainly create a new heart in a sinful man who repents.

Often when we protest that something is impossible, it's because we recoil from doing what God asks us to do. Maybe, like Ananias, we are asked to meet someone whom we fear or dislike.

Then let's take the example of Ananias. He obeyed God. He went to the street called Straight and laid his hands on Saul, just as God had told him to. Ananias even called him "Brother Saul," which goes to show that Ananias had completely laid down his earlier false assumption. Instead, he believed that God could do anything.

"But Jesus beheld them, and said unto them, With men this is impossible; but with God all things are possible" (Matthew 19:26).

I'LL GIVE IT ALL TO YOU

DAILY BIBLE READING: MATTHEW 4:8-11

"All these things will I give thee, if thou wilt fall down and worship me" (Matthew 4:9).

When you think about it, this offer of the devil's was quite ridiculous. Jesus Himself is the Creator of the world—and therefore its owner. Yet the devil dared to insinuate that the world was his to give, and that Jesus could have it all if He only bowed to Satan.

In a way, it's true that the kingdoms of the world belong to Satan. Mankind fell into sin, and therefore came under the devil's power. Still, what arrogance for the devil to suggest that he, on his own terms, could give the world to Jesus.

Jesus did indeed plan to win the world away from Satan's grip. And Jesus knew exactly how He could do that: by suffering and dying, and thus becoming a sacrifice for sin. He said in John 12:32, "I, if I be lifted up from the earth, will draw all men unto me." That "lifting up" meant the cross. Not the temple's pinnacle, not a high mountain selected by the devil, but a lowly, painful cross.

Today, the devil still pretends to offer what is not his to give. He entices us with worldly things, hoping to win our allegiance. He tempts us with worldly pinnacles, with carnal success. But we, like our Saviour before us, must turn away and choose the cross instead.

When the devil comes with such wily temptations, what should we do? How can we flee from his power? We must speak the very words that our Lord spoke during His temptation:

"Get thee hence, Satan: for it is written, Thou shalt worship the Lord thy God, and him only shalt thou serve" (Matthew 4:10).

THE DANGER OF ABUNDANCE

DAILY BIBLE READING: MARK 10:21-25

"Children, how hard it is for them that trust in riches to enter into the kingdom of God!"
(Mark 10:24).

By nature, we crave abundance. But does earthly abundance truly satisfy? Isn't it true that abundant material possessions only make us crave more and more? There are two hard facts about earthly abundance that we all must learn: material abundance can never satisfy, and an abundance of earthly possessions is actually dangerous for our spiritual life.

Why? For one thing, if all our physical needs are always met, we tend to become self-reliant. Whenever we sense an emptiness, we reach for our wallets and buy something to fill that emptiness. But that's folly! We're trying to fill with earthly things a void that only God can fill.

Can you think of anything more tragic than a person who has everything earth can offer—yet he lacks eternal life?

Let us seek the true abundance, the abundant life of Jesus dwelling in our hearts and filling our lives to overflowing.

"If I have made gold my hope, or have said to the fine gold, Thou art my confidence; if I rejoiced because my wealth was great, and because mine hand had gotten much; this also were an iniquity to be punished by the judge: for I should have denied the God that is above" (Job 31:24, 25, 28).

CONSIDER YOUR WAYS

DAILY BIBLE READING: HAGGAI 1:7-9

"Consider your ways . . . and build the house" (Haggai 1:7, 8).

Three times in the Book of Haggai, God repeats those words: "Consider your ways." Another translation says, "Give careful thought" (NIV).

Why did the people of Haggai's time need this admonition to "consider their ways"? They did not have their priorities straight. Everybody was busy building his own house, while the house of the Lord lay in ruins. They should have been expending every effort to build the temple, because it was the focal point of their relationship with God.

You and I can easily be caught in the same folly. No, it's not necessary to build actual temples anymore. But remember, the New Testament tells us that we are temples. Are we focused on building lives that glorify God? Is it our desire to be fitting stones for the building of the church, the dwelling place of God?

Notice what happened to the people Haggai was addressing. Their houses, their jobs were first priority—but the people weren't satisfied. Those priorities didn't bring contentment.

Let us "consider our ways." Let us keep God first. As we seek to build lives that glorify Him, Jesus will provide inspiration and help for the building. After all, He is the Master Carpenter.

"Ye are God's building . . . for other foundation can no man lay than that is laid, which is Jesus Christ" (1 Corinthians 3:9, 11).

Day 159

THEY THOUGHT THEY WERE FULL

DAILY BIBLE READING: 1 CORINTHIANS 4:6-8

"What hast thou that thou didst not receive?" (1 Corinthians 4:7).

The Corinthian believers had a problem, but they didn't know it. I wonder if you and I are sometimes like that too. We might have a problem that we're not recognizing.

Let's take a long look at the Corinthians. Maybe it will help us uncover our own hidden problems. First, what were the symptoms Paul saw? He describes them in 1 Corinthians 3:3: "Envying, and strife, and divisions." Some of the Corinthians were saying they preferred one leader over another. Ugly symptoms, indeed.

If even the symptoms were ugly, what would the root cause look like? Uglier still. The root was pride. Pride in their own ideas, opinions, and judgments. What else but pride could have made them prefer one leader over another?

In addressing their problem, Paul used a bit of irony. "You think you are full—you think you are rich—you imagine your spiritual attainments are so high that you don't have to hunger and thirst anymore."

But then Paul cuts to the heart of the matter. What do we have that we did not receive from God? That question is a thrust into our own inflated pride as well. Anything we have, whether physical or spiritual, is a gift from God. How ridiculous to pride ourselves in our own attainments! There is simply no room for pride in any shape or form—and the sooner we recognize this, the better.

"A man can receive nothing, except it be given him from heaven" (John 3:27).

BEING AN EXAMPLE

DAILY BIBLE READING: PHILIPPIANS 3:17-21

"Brethren, be followers together of me . . . ye have us for an ensample" (Philippians 3:17).

The church is the body of Christ. That brings with it a sobering realization: we are Christ's hands, His feet, His eyes, meant to do His work on earth. Our lives are to show an example of Jesus to those around us.

How can we, as poor humans, be such an example? In three different letters, Paul urges us to follow his example. The word *ensample* in the daily reading could also be translated "pattern." Paul seems to say, "Pattern your lives after mine."

In 1 Thessalonians 1:6, 7, Paul commends the Thessalonians for being good examples. We gather that they became followers of Paul (and of the Lord) even though it meant much affliction. And thus, through joy in suffering, they became examples to others.

To Timothy, Paul wrote that God used him as a pattern in a rather humbling way. "In me first Jesus Christ might shew forth all longsuffering, for a pattern" (1 Timothy 1:16). Paul was the "chief of sinners," yet God had mercy upon him. Thus he could be an example of God's mighty grace.

If we really want to *be* an example, however, we must above all *follow* the example of Christ. "Take my yoke upon you, and learn of me," Jesus says in Matthew 11:29, "for I am meek and lowly in heart." The meekness of Jesus is the greatest example of all.

"Wherefore I beseech you, be ye followers of me" (1 Corinthians 4:16).

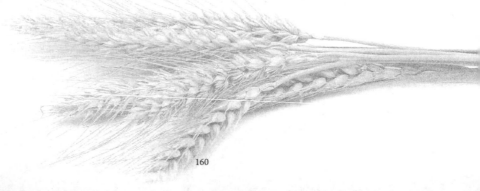

WHOSE JUDGMENT COUNTS?

DAILY BIBLE READING: 1 CORINTHIANS 4:1-5

"But with me it is a very small thing that I should be judged of you, or of man's judgment" (*1 Corinthians 4:3*).

This passage searches my heart and finds me guilty in more than one way. Five times over, Paul uses a variation of the word *judge*. Am I like Paul, not caring about others' judgment?

Paul isn't saying that we should be unconcerned and tactless toward our fellow man. But if we seek above all the approval of men, we are on a dangerous path. There is only One about whose judgment we should truly care, and that is God. Our whole lives should be trained on winning His approval. His praise—not the praise of men.

In another sense, these words of Paul's strike even deeper for me. He warns in verse 5, "Therefore judge nothing before the time." How often do I scrutinize my fellow Christians, perhaps even judging whether or not they are true followers of Christ? How often do I criticize others' actions or voice my opinion on others' motives?

Such things are folly. It is sin to judge others. Whether we realize it or not, if we judge others, we are implying that we are better than they, and that is wrong.

But there is a still deeper reason why we should not judge others. God alone is the Judge. We see only the outward acts, but God searches the hearts. To judge others is His job and His alone. On that great and glorious day of His return, God will overturn many a rash and harsh judgment that we have made.

"Who both will bring to light the hidden things of darkness, and will make manifest the counsels of the hearts" (1 Corinthians 4:5).

CROSSPIECES

DAILY BIBLE READING: LUKE 23:32-34

"There they crucified him" (Luke 23:33).

Such stark, simple words. "There they crucified him." Hidden in those words are pain and suffering such as we cannot imagine! It has been said that the cross is the place where the worst thing that could happen, did happen. At the same time, the cross is the place where the world's most wonderful thing happened.

We could take those two contradictory statements and compare them to the two pieces that formed the Lord's cross. First, the main post, driven deep into the earth: it represents the terrible pain and suffering of the world—all because of sin. The problem of sin and suffering was so great that it seemed insurmountable.

But God had an answer for this universal problem. Horizontally across the post of the world's agony He placed a bar, a crosspiece—and there He allowed the world to hang His Son. There, the full tide of God's love was shed abroad in the blood that flowed from the hands of Christ.

Do you see in those two crosspieces the mystery of the Christian faith? The path of joy runs straight through the heart of pain and suffering. Those crosspieces represent ultimate suffering and ultimate love. By the death of Jesus, suffering and love were brought into harmony.

That is why we do not run from suffering. By faith we see that the path to Heaven is through suffering. By faith we know that God has for us a river of joy to heal any suffering we endure.

"Jesus the author and finisher of our faith; who for the joy that was set before him endured the cross" (Hebrews 12:2).

THE COMFORT OF GOD

DAILY BIBLE READING: 2 CORINTHIANS 1:1-4

"Who comforteth us in all our tribulation" (2 Corinthians 1:4).

A little girl stubs her toe and runs crying to her mother. Mother's hands caress the wounded foot. She blows on the sore toe and wipes the child's tears. Soon the tears are replaced by a smile.

Yet think about it. The toe probably still hurts. Mother's caresses did not take away the pain. To comfort is not to remove the pain. To comfort is to provide whatever is needed to endure the pain.

Isn't that exactly the way God works with us? He is the "God of all comfort," yes, but that doesn't mean He removes our pain when we cry to Him for help. If He did—if His means of comforting were to always make our troubles go away—then we would start looking to God for the wrong reason. God would merely be our "pain reliever." Instead, we come to God because we love Him. Through His love, He give us the strength and encouragement to endure the pain. And this is the marvelous result: the comfort God gives us can then flow out as gifts of comfort to others. Through it all, God is training us to be like Joses in Acts 4:36, whose surname meant "son of consolation."

Think of it! My trials and yours can bring great gain in the form of comfort and consolation—not only for us, but also for others, because we are learning how to comfort.

"Wherefore comfort yourselves together" (1 Thessalonians 5:11).

THE COMFORT OF CHRIST

DAILY BIBLE READING: 2 CORINTHIANS 1:5-7

"As the sufferings . . . so our consolation" (2 Corinthians 1:5).

We can't really separate the comfort of God and the comfort of Christ; for as God and Christ are one, so also is the comfort. God and Christ are one with the great Comforter Himself, the Holy Spirit sent for our consolation. For just a few minutes, however, let's look at the comfort Christ offers. Immediately this fact strikes us: the comfort and the suffering are equal. As sufferings abound, so does the comfort. Paul seems to say, "We can stand as surely in the heaviest trial as in the lightest, because Christ metes out the comfort in proportion to the trial."

Then too, we realize that Jesus identifies Himself with our suffering. Remember how He spoke to Saul at Damascus? "Saul, Saul, why persecutest thou me?" (Acts 9:4). Jesus was one with the suffering of His church. Remember also, how He bids us, "Take my yoke upon you." A yoke brings two into one. What one bears, the other bears also.

This gives us a glimpse of how Jesus comforts us. We can rejoice in sufferings because they help us to become more like Jesus. What is more, suffering lets us experience—even if only in a small way—what Jesus suffered on our behalf. Suffering draws us to Jesus as nothing else does. Through suffering we can learn to know Him. What a comfort!

"That I may know him . . . and the fellowship of his sufferings" (Philippians 3:10).

THRESHING

DAILY BIBLE READING: MATTHEW 5:10-12

"Blessed are ye, when men shall revile you, and persecute you" (Matthew 5:11).

Another word for this persecution Jesus spoke of is *tribulation*. Jesus is saying that tribulations bring blessing. It's a little hard for the human mind to grasp. Paul even tells us to rejoice in tribulations.

The Greek word for tribulation has roots in terms like *bruising, wounding—* even *threshing*. That could help us get an inkling of where the blessings come from. We know how necessary threshing is. If we want the nutritious kernels, threshing must come into play to separate them from the chaff.

Picture threshing the way it was done in Bible times. Picture a man wielding a flail, thumping it down on the pile of wheat, bruising the plants over and over again. If the wheat were human, it might complain that threshing is unpleasant. Yet look at the reward: plump kernels, ready to provide food for many.

Tribulations can do that for us. They can strip away the superficial, the unnecessary, the lighthearted—leaving only the gold. As we endure, our faith can be strengthened. We can learn to lift our eyes to heavenly rewards rather than mere earthly rewards. And we can take comfort in this thought: would a man bother to thresh wheat that has borne no promising kernels?

"And ye shall be hated of all men for my name's sake: but he that endureth to the end shall be saved" (Matthew 10:22).

NOT IN CHAINS

DAILY BIBLE READING: 2 TIMOTHY 2:7-11

"The word of God is not bound" (2 Timothy 2:9).

The catacombs of Rome are the underground cemeteries used by ancient pagans, Christians, and Jews. Originally, Christians used the catacombs were merely burial places. During the persecutions of the third century, they used the catacombs as places of temporary refuge.

Those early Christians often carved or painted verses and symbols on the walls of the catacombs in order to express their faith without openly drawing attention to themselves. Picture a Christian down there in the darkness, feeling compelled to leave a message, a witness. Working by the light of flickering torches, he carves his testimony into the rock wall.

This triumphant verse has been found inscribed on the wall of the catacombs beneath Rome: *The word of God is not bound.*

When Paul wrote these words to Timothy, he faced much opposition. The Gospel of Jesus Christ was an offense to many. Because Paul proclaimed the Gospel, he was hated by Jews, Greeks, and Romans. He wrote these words from prison, where he was bound.

But the Word of God cannot be bound. In spite of the chains Paul bore—perhaps even because of them—many people were coming to Christ. What an encouragement this can be to us. Do we have days when opposition stares at us? Do we feel restricted, fettered? But God's Word is never bound. It shall triumph in the end.

"For the hope of Israel I am bound with this chain" (Acts 28:20).

THE CHRISTIAN LIFE IN A NUTSHELL

DAILY BIBLE READING: 2 THESSALONIANS 1:11, 12

"That our God would . . . fulfil the work of faith . . . that . . . Jesus . . . may be glorified"
(2 Thessalonians 1:11, 12).

What is the purpose of the Christian life? Here in this little prayer, Paul seems to put the answer into a nutshell: our lives must glorify Christ.

Susanna Wesley once prayed for help to accomplish the things her faith was prompting her to do. Here is an excerpt from her "Prayer for Diligence": "Help me . . . to be industrious without covetousness; diligent without anxiety; exact in each detail of action."

Such a prayer almost scares me. True, faith prompts the same things in my heart. I, too, long for purity and diligence. But I am a failing human.

The concluding words of the "Prayer for Diligence" contain the answer to our dilemma. "And yet help me to be so resigned as to leave all events to Thee, and still attributing to Thee the praise of every good work."

It sounds paradoxical. How can we be on the one hand diligent and exact and striving, yet on the other hand resigned and relaxed and trusting only in God?

It's this way. Our faith prompts us to the good—but God supplies the power to accomplish those promptings. Paul's prayer says the same thing. It is God who fulfills the goodness in us. Only by the grace of God can Jesus be glorified, thus fulfilling the purpose of the Christian life.

"For it is God which worketh in you both to will and to do of his good pleasure"
(Philippians 2:13).

WORTHY OF THE CALLING

DAILY BIBLE READING: 1 THESSALONIANS 2:10-12

"That ye would walk worthy of God, who hath called you unto his kingdom and glory"
(1 Thessalonians 2:12).

It is a weighty charge to "walk worthy of God." Yet we feel very unworthy. Instead of focusing on our own unworthiness, let's look at the calling for which we are to be worthy. It is a *high calling:* "the prize of the high calling of God" (Philippians 3:14). It is a *holy calling:* "called us with an holy calling" (2 Timothy 1:9). It is a *heavenly calling:* "partakers of the heavenly calling" (Hebrews 3:1).

It is a *call to light:* "him who hath called you out of darkness into his marvellous light" (1 Peter 2:9). It is a *call to holiness:* "as he which hath called you is holy, so be ye holy" (1 Peter 1:15). It is a *call to follow Jesus:* "For even hereunto were ye called . . . that ye should follow his steps" (1 Peter 2:21).

Our calling brings *hope:* "that ye may know what is the hope of his calling" (Ephesians 1:18). It brings a *blessing:* "ye are thereunto called, that ye should inherit a blessing" (1 Peter 3:9).

What a calling! And of such a calling we are asked to walk worthily. That looks daunting indeed.

But in another place where Paul mentions being worthy of our calling, he uses a different word: *count.* "We pray always for you, that our God would count you worthy of this calling" (2 Thessalonians 1:11). God counts us worthy through Jesus. The original Greek gives the sense of enabling, of deeming, of making us meet. Praise be to the Lord, who not only gives us a high calling, but also enables us to walk worthy of it!

"Giving thanks unto the Father, which hath made us meet to be partakers of the inheritance of the saints in light" (Colossians 1:12).

THE BLESSEDS OF THE PSALMS

DAILY BIBLE READING: PSALM 1:1-6

"Blessed is the man that walketh not in the counsel of the ungodly" (Psalm 1:1).

When we hear the word *beatitudes*, we usually think of Matthew 5, where Jesus tells us what brings true happiness, or blessedness. But did you know that there are also many beatitudes in the Psalms?

The very first psalm starts with a blessing. As you read it, picture yourself at a fork in the road. The path on your right leads into the temple of praise; the path on your left into the company of the ungodly, the mockers, the sinners. On your right is the path of obedience; on your left the path of rebellion. Which shall it be?

As you make your choice, consider also the end of each path. On the left, we see the ungodly being blown away like chaff, sinners who will not be able to stand before the judgment seat of God. In short, as verse 6 says, "the way of the ungodly shall perish."

How different is the end of the path on the right! Upon the doorpost of the temple of praise is inscribed a beautiful promise of blessing. Within, we are seated with those who love the law. And—in contrast to that dry, weightless chaff—we become like trees soaking up nourishment from the river of water of life.

"Whatsoever he doeth shall prosper" is the promise of verse 3. That's not a guarantee of wealth and health on earth. It means simply that the more we delight in the law, the more spiritual fruit we can bear. Truly that is a blessed state.

"This book of the law shall not depart out of thy mouth ... then thou shalt make thy way prosperous" (Joshua 1:8).

OH, THE BLESSEDNESS!

DAILY BIBLE READING: PSALM 2

"Blessed are all they that put their trust in him" (Psalm 2:12).

The first psalm begins with a beatitude; the second ends with one. In both cases, the original Hebrew could be translated as an exclamation: "O, the blessedness!'

This second psalm has a vast scope. Read it in four parts.

Verses 1-3 give us a picture of worldly, ungodly folk who hate God's people. In the time of the Book of Acts, the apostles quoted these words as they sought strength to stand during persecution (Acts 4:25, 26).

The second part, verses 4-6, shifts from earth to Heaven, from fear to confidence. God is on His throne. He alone is reality; with Him is true tranquility, regardless of heathen rage.

The third part, verses 7-9, crashes upon us like a roll of thunder. The curtains of the heavens are parted to reveal the Son, the Saviour, the Christ. Jesus is victor. Those raging heathen—the powers of sin—are dashed to pieces like an earthen pot thrown down upon a rock. Portions of these verses are quoted many times in the New Testament. Paul quoted verse 7 in Acts 13:33. Hebrews 1:5 echoes the same words. In Revelation 2:26 we see the fulfillment of verse 8, where Jesus was given "power over the nations."

The last part of Psalm 2 tells us what we must do to embrace all this. Gladly we will "be wise"—we will "serve the Lord"—we will "kiss the Son." No wonder the psalm ends with this sublime thought, "O the blessedness of them that put their trust in him!"

"Let all those that put their trust in thee rejoice; let them ever shout for joy" (Psalm 5:11).

THE BLESSING OF SALVATION

DAILY BIBLE READING: PSALM 3

"Salvation belongeth unto the LORD: thy blessing is upon thy people" (Psalm 3:8).

The most vivid picture in this psalm is in verse 5: "I laid me down and slept; I awaked; for the LORD sustained me." David was able to do that, even though ten thousand foes were after him, and many scoffed that God could not help him.

That reminds me of Jesus, sound asleep while the boat tossed upon high waves; and of Peter, sleeping peacefully though chained between two soldiers and knowing that Herod planned to kill him.

We may not have enemies of the kind that beset David, Peter, and Jesus. The enemy that so often keeps us from peaceful rest is our own sin. In despair we feel like crying, "There is no help for me in God."

There is only one place to turn for salvation from sin. "I, even I, am the LORD," we read in Isaiah 43:11, "and beside me there is no saviour."

The longer we live, the more we realize how true that is. None but the Lord can save us from sin. I certainly cannot. Only God can "break the teeth" of sin. What a blessing is salvation, and what a sweet pillow for our sleep!

"Thou shalt call his name JESUS: for he shall save his people from their sins" *(Matthew 1:21).*

BLESSED ARE THE PURE IN HEART

DAILY BIBLE READING: PSALM 24:1-6

"He that hath clean hands, and a pure heart...he shall receive the blessing from the LORD*" (Psalm 24:4, 5).*

We could say that this psalm is just a longer version of Christ's words in Matthew 5: "Blessed are the pure in heart." David asks, "Who shall stand in his holy place?" Who can stand before the Lord? Who can be part of His kingdom? And the answer is, he that has a pure heart.

How can we have a pure heart? Surely that answer lies in the last part of verse 5, where David speaks of the God of his salvation. Only through cleansing by the blood of the crucified Son can our hearts be pure. David mentions clean hands as well. But heart-purity must come first. Without the inner cleansing, we cannot be clean outwardly.

Remember that Jesus condemned the Pharisees for being more concerned about the outward than the inward. "Thou blind Pharisee, cleanse first that which is within the cup and platter, that the outside of them may be clean also" (Matthew 23:26).

I'm told that the priests of David's time used to sing this psalm every Sabbath morning as they led worshippers up to the temple. If I were to compose a tune for this psalm, I would have the notes soaring up and up. The final words, "The LORD of hosts, he is the King of glory" would touch the highest scale!

May this be the psalm of our hearts, made pure by the blood of the Lamb, as we travel our earthly path upward to the eternal, heavenly Temple.

"Cleanse your hands, ye sinners; and purify your hearts, ye double minded" (James 4:8).

THE BLESSING OF FORGIVENESS

DAILY BIBLE READING: PSALM 32:1, 3-5

"Blessed is he whose transgression is forgiven" (Psalm 32:1).

Oh, the joy of a repentant sinner whom God has forgiven! Is forgiveness not one of the greatest blessings, the greatest source of happiness? Many years after David's time, the Apostle Paul referred to these words in his epistle of justification by grace to the Romans.

But notice: David does not devote the entire psalm to describing the joy of forgiveness. He also points out the sheer misery of being unrepentant and therefore unforgiven (verses 3, 4). David had experience with that. After he had sinned with Bathsheba, he did not immediately confess his sin. The result was horrible mental suffering.

Verse 3 describes that suffering. The language may sound strange; we could reword it thus: "as long as I refused to acknowledge my sin, I felt sick and I groaned all day." Elsewhere, David gives more descriptions of how it is when a sinner doesn't confess. "For mine iniquities are gone over mine head," he wrote in Psalm 38:4, 5, "as an heavy burden they are too heavy for me. My wounds stink and are corrupt because of my foolishness."

It's like a child who has managed to get a sliver into his finger. Terrified of the pain that might result from extraction, he tries to keep the injury hidden. But the wound festers and fills with pus until it becomes unbearable.

What a relief when he finally asks for help! Just so, we find enormous heart-relief when we acknowledge our sin and receive the undeserved blessing of Christ's forgiveness.

"If we confess our sins, he is faithful and just to forgive us our sins, and to cleanse us from all unrighteousness" (1 John 1:9).

THE BLESSING OF SIN NOT IMPUTED

DAILY BIBLE READING: PSALM 32:2, 6-11

"Blessed is the man unto whom the LORD imputeth not iniquity" (Psalm 32:2).

Perhaps you wondered why we skipped verse 2 in yesterday's reading. It's because verse 2 contains still another of the beatitudes we are digging from the treasure chest of the Psalms.

Does this blessing seem like the same as yesterday's, on forgiveness of sin? Yes, in a way it is the same. But the subject of God's mercy is a mulitfaceted diamond. If we hold it up to the light and turn it this way and that way, new beams of brightness will reflect from its brilliant surface.

Yesterday's blessing was of sin forgiven. Today we look at sin not imputed. Imagine you are a businessman who has fallen into debt. The lord who keeps record has a page where he daily writes down more debts that keep accruing. You hate to even think about that record, let alone read those columns of red ink.

Like the desperate servant in Matthew 18, you fall before the Lord and plead, "Have patience with me, and I will pay thee all." Such a futile promise—one that we can never keep!

But the Lord surprises you. With one stroke of His pen, He cancels all the heavy debts that stood against you. "This debt is no longer imputed to you," He declares.

Again, what joy. You feel like one who has been saved from the "floods of great waters" (verse 6). And you have learned firsthand the truth of David's words in verse 10:

"He that trusteth in the LORD, mercy shall compass him about" (Psalm 32:10).

A BEATITUDE FOR THE NATIONS

DAILY BIBLE READING: PSALM 33:8-13

*"Blessed is the nation whose God is the L*ORD*" (Psalm 33:12).*

God is sovereign. Do you know what that means? The Psalms give us a ring-ing reply to that question. "The LORD reigneth" (Psalm 93:1). "That men may know that thou, whose name alone is JEHOVAH, art the most high over all the earth" (Psalm 83:18). "Whatsoever the LORD pleased, that did he in heaven, and in earth" (Psalm 135:6). "He shall subdue...the nations under our feet" (Psalm 47:3).

To say that God is sovereign is to acknowledge that He is fully in control of His entire creation. We sometimes find that hard to believe. Do we wonder whether God is in control when daily newspapers are filled with the evil committed by governments and nations? Yes, God is in control—but He allows men to choose whether or not they will be under His lordship. Untold evil has resulted from the fact that so many do not have God as their Lord. What blessings they forfeit!

In Acts 17, Paul told the Athenians who really is God. Among their idols the Athenians had an altar designated "to the unknown god." Paul declared to those educated men, "God made the world. He doesn't live in man-made temples. He rules over the nations. He doesn't need anything from you. The one thing He desires is that we all should seek the Lord" (Acts 17:24-27, paraphrased).

Let's not be like the Athenians. Although they acknowledged that there is a God, they did not know Him and certainly did not submit to His sovereignty. We, like the nations, can be truly blessed when "God is our Lord."

*"For the L*ORD *most high is terrible; he is a great King over all the earth" (Psalm 47:2).*

THE BLESSING OF FEARING THE LORD

DAILY BIBLE READING: PSALM 34:4-9

"Blessed is the man that trusteth in him. O fear the LORD, ye his saints" (Psalm 34:8, 9).

At first glance, you might think that this beatitude is the same as an earlier one, concerning trust in the Lord. But notice that here the psalmist also speaks of fearing the Lord. Our focus today is not only on trusting the Lord but also on fearing Him.

Fearing? Maybe it doesn't sound like a very blessed thing to do. Who wants to fear someone? But remember, to fear the Lord means to reverence and honor Him deeply.

"O taste and see that the LORD is good!" Imagine that someone is offering you a piece of cake. "Is it good?" you ask doubtfully; it doesn't look very appetizing. The other person doesn't try to describe the cake; she simply urges, "Taste it and you'll see."

God's ways are like that. They have to be experienced—tasted—in order to be appreciated. Before you can enjoy the blessings, you must actually obey and fear the Lord.

"O taste and see that the LORD is good!" What a warm invitation! It's an invitation especially to young people. In our youth we still lack experience of the Lord's ways. Our knowledge is incomplete. Not that older ones have learned everything either, but we have learned enough that we know the value of tasting the Lord daily by trusting and fearing.

Merely professing that we belong to the Lord is not enough. If we want His blessings, we must go farther and obey Him in fear. Then we will know. We will know that He is good!

"Let us have grace, whereby we may serve God acceptably with reverence and godly fear" (Hebrews 12:28).

THE BLESSING OF INHERITANCE

DAILY BIBLE READING: PSALM 37:18-22

"For such as be blessed of him shall inherit the earth" (Psalm 37:22).

This passage begins and ends with the idea of inheritance. To be blessed is to inherit the earth. Jesus said much the same thing in Matthew 5:5: "Blessed are the meek: for they shall inherit the earth."

The question is, who wants to inherit the earth? It might be all right to inherit a little piece of the earth from our parents. But the whole earth? That sounds like an inheritance we wouldn't know what to do with.

We must understand that both here in Psalm 37 and in Matthew 5, the original word had the idea of *land* rather than *earth*. That makes us think of the promised land. When the Bible speaks of inheriting the land, it's a promise that we can inherit the many blessings of God's land, God's kingdom. Faith in Christ brings us into that inheritance.

Let's look at some of the Bible's inheritance promises. First, Psalm 15:5: "The LORD is the portion of mine inheritance." What a blessing! Christ Himself is our inheritance through faith.

If we thus "inherit the Lord," we may one day hear these blessed words: "Come, ye blessed of my Father, inherit the kingdom prepared for you" (Matthew 25:34).

We find another inheritance promise in Hebrews 9:15: "They which are called might receive the promise of eternal inheritance." This is surely worth far more than any earthly inheritance.

But we must not forget what sort of people receive these blessings of inheritance. It is the meek ones. Jesus said so, and the psalmist said it too, right here in this same psalm: "But the meek shall inherit the earth; and shall delight themselves in the abundance of peace" (11). Not those who rely on their own righteousness, not the bold and brash, but the meek—they shall have this inheritance of peace.

"Know ye not that the unrighteous shall not inherit the kingdom of God?" (1 Corinthians 6:9).

RESPECT NOT THE PROUD

"Blessed is that man that maketh the LORD his trust, and respecteth not the proud" *(Psalm 40:4).*

Is this beatitude any different from others? Haven't we already studied the blessing of trusting in the Lord?

Yes, we have; but we never really get finished studying that blessing. There are so many facets to trusting the Lord. Here, the emphasis is trusting God rather than "respecting not the proud." Who are the proud? There is no pride that more surely bars us from God than the pride of trusting in our own righteousness.

We can think of this beatitude as urging us to trust solely in the righteousness of Jesus Christ. He alone saves! We dare not trust our own righteousness. Nor dare we trust in people who rely on their own righteousness. Our eyes must stay on Jesus. If we do anything less, we are "turning aside to lies."

What is the outcome of such single-minded trusting? It is praise. Look at all the praises crammed into verse 5. The psalmist doesn't even itemize the praises. He simply says that God's wonderful works can't be counted. They are too many to enumerate.

In these two verses, then, we see how the blessing of trust and the blessing of praise go hand in hand. The more we trust, the more we realize how wonderful are God's "thoughts which are to us-ward."

"Though the LORD be high, yet hath he respect unto the lowly: but the proud he knoweth afar off" *(Psalm 138:6).*

CARING FOR THE POOR

DAILY BIBLE READING: PSALM 41:1-3

"Blessed is he that considereth the poor" (Psalm 41:1).

God's Word places a great deal of emphasis on caring for the poor. Verse after verse in Exodus and Leviticus speak of man's duty to the poor. Psalms and Proverbs encourage us again and again to help the poor. In the teachings of Jesus, we have the memorable story of the beggar named Lazarus who ended up in Heaven while the man who refused to succor him ended up in Hell.

Why is it so important to help the poor? There's more than one reason, of course, but Jeremiah touches the main one when he delivers a sharp message against King Jehoiakim, reminding him of his father's good example, which he failed to follow: "He judged the cause of the poor and needy; then it was well with him: was not this to know me? saith the LORD. But thine eyes and thine heart are not but for thy covetousness" (22:16, 17).

Opening one's heart to the needy and poor—that's what it means to know the Lord. In caring for others, we learn to know the heart of God.

This makes us think of more words from Jeremiah: "Let not the rich man glory in his riches: but let him that glorieth glory in this, that he understandeth and knoweth me, that I am the LORD which exercise lovingkindness" (9:23, 24). Again, the blessing and the glory lie in knowing God—and He is a God of loving and caring.

Because God cares for the poor, His children do too. It's as simple as that. What's more, Jesus says that the care we give to the poor is actually given to Him. "Inasmuch as ye have done it unto one of the least of these my brethren, ye have done it unto me" (Matthew 25:40).

A heart for the poor is a heart for the Lord.

"Whoso hath this world's good, and seeth his brother have need, and shutteth up his bowels of compassion from him, how dwelleth the love of God in him?" (1 John 3:17).

THE BLESSING OF BEING CHOSEN

DAILY BIBLE READING: PSALM 65:1-4

"Blessed is the man whom thou choosest" (Psalm 65:4).

In these four verses I see a picture of how God draws us to Himself. I hear an echo of Christ's beautiful words in John 12:32: "I, if I be lifted up from the earth, will draw all men unto me." David said it this way: "O thou that hearest prayer, unto thee shall all flesh come" (verse 2). And in verse 4, "Blessed is the man whom thou . . . causest to approach unto thee."

How does God draw us? Through Jesus. When we are overwhelmed and remorseful about our sin—or, as David says in verse 3, "iniquities prevail against me"—God has a marvelous gift for us. He purges our transgressions by His grace. Jesus was lifted on the cross to accomplish that forgiveness, and thus He draws us unto Himself.

But what about the choosing? Whom does God choose to draw to Himself? Why, those who believe in Jesus. Paul wrote to the Ephesians about that divine choosing: "According as he hath chosen us in him . . . that we should be holy and without blame before him in love" (1:4). We are chosen in Christ. The choosing and the faith go hand in hand.

When David wrote this psalm, he was probably thinking of the Levites, who had the privilege of being chosen by God to enter the holy place as priests. "Blessed is the man whom thou choosest . . . that he may dwell in thy courts." Today every believer is a priest; every believer is chosen to "draw nigh to God" and to "come boldly to the throne of grace."

"But ye are a chosen generation, a royal priesthood . . . that ye should shew forth the praises of him who hath called you out of darkness into his marvellous light" (1 Peter 2:9).

DWELLING IN GOD'S HOUSE

DAILY BIBLE READING: PSALM 84:4

"Blessed are they that dwell in thy house" (Psalm 84:4).

When David penned these words, he was an exile, hiding from his rebellious son Absalom. Can we imagine how David longed to return to the tabernacle of God and once again take part in worship there? It seems David even envied the little sparrows who made their nests in the eaves of the tabernacle. If only he could dwell in God's house again!

You might wonder what connection this beatitude has with us. After all, we do not long to live in a church house. But let's take this in a spiritual sense. David's greatest longing, I'm sure, was to dwell with God. That is our longing too.

Jesus made this very thing possible. He says in John 14 that His Father's house has many mansions, or dwellings; and He is preparing a place for us. Often we think of the heavenly home when we read John 14. But we may take it also for our daily "dwelling in God" right here on earth. By going to the cross and dying there, Jesus prepared a dwelling for us in the heart of God. Daily we may rest there, as secure as a sparrow in her nest.

It may seem very mysterious to speak of dwelling in God. Yet Jesus said that for the believer, this truly is so. In John 14:20 He declares, "Ye shall know that I am in my Father, and ye in me, and I in you." He dwells in us—and therefore we dwell in Him. An unfathomable blessing!

"Abide in me, and I in you" (John 15:4).

Day 182

DEPENDING ON GOD'S STRENGTH

DAILY BIBLE READING: PSALM 84:5-8

"Blessed is the man whose strength is in thee" (Psalm 84:5).

In these verses we may picture pilgrims traveling up to Jerusalem. The way has been long. The pilgrims have trudged through many a dry valley. The word *Baca* denotes weeping.

Is not our journey through this life also at times a "vale of tears"? The way seems long, the path rough and hard; our strength wanes until it seems we cannot go on.

But we can reach out for a strength much greater than our own. Our strength is in God Himself. "The LORD is my strength and song," the psalmist exclaims in Psalm 118:14, echoing words sung by Moses many years before, when he and all Israel praised God for their passage through the Red Sea (Exodus 15:2).

"They go from strength to strength," we read in the seventh verse of today's passage. Such beautiful words! God does not supply all the strength we need in one big lump. A little at a time in proportion to our trials—from strength to strength He leads us.

Then lo! The valley of tears is transformed. Instead of a dry desert we see living springs. The low spots in our lives become pools of water beneath the refreshing rain of God's grace.

The barren places in our life, the times of adversity—are not those the times when we grow stronger in the Lord? Our strength is in Him.

"He giveth power to the faint; and to them that have no might he increaseth strength" (Isaiah 40:29).

SUN AND SHIELD

DAILY BIBLE READING: PSALM 84:9-12

"For the LORD God is a sun and shield...blessed is the man that trusteth in thee" *(Psalm 84:11, 12).*

Here is another facet of the blessing of trusting in the Lord: He is to us both a sun and a shield. When the way is dark, He is our light; when we are oppressed by the heat of trials, He is like a cloud that gives us shade.

Doesn't that make us think of the way God protected the children of Israel? He was both a pillar of cloud (a shield) and a pillar of fire (bright light for direction).

"The LORD shall be unto thee an everlasting light, and thy God thy glory," says Isaiah in 60:19. In the same verse he tells us that we need no longer depend on the natural sun for light, because we have One greater than the sun to shine upon us.

This God who is our sun and shield gives us two things: grace and glory. We could say that His grace corresponds to the shield. What but grace can remove our sins and shield us from God's righteous wrath?

And the glory corresponds with God as our sun. "Holy, holy, holy is the LORD of hosts: the whole earth is full of his glory!" Thus cried the angels in Isaiah 6:3. The more we stand in the light of God's glory, the more we can be changed into His likeness.

"But we all, with open face beholding as in a glass the glory of the Lord, are changed into the same image from glory to glory, even as by the Spirit of the Lord" (2 Corinthians 3:18).

Day 184

THE JOYFUL SOUND

DAILY BIBLE READING: PSALM 89:11-18

"Blessed is the people that know the joyful sound" (Psalm 89:15).

What is this "joyful sound" that blesses us? Surely the psalmist is referring to praise. If you start reading at verse 1 of this psalm, you will find line after line of praise to God.

"I will sing of the mercies of the LORD for ever. The heavens shall praise thy wonders, O LORD"—it seems the psalmist can't stop praising all of God's attributes. All nature praises Him: the raging sea, the skies above, the mountains and hills. The entire universe is filled with a song of praise!

Do we know that joyful sound? Are we part of it? We certainly can be; Psalm 98 gives the reason why we, too, can praise the Lord: "The LORD hath made known his salvation...all the ends of the earth have seen the salvation of our God. Make a joyful noise unto the LORD, all the earth" (Psalm 98:2-4).

There we see our greatest reason for joy and praise: God's salvation. Jesus Christ. He came to bring us joy—to give us a part in the "joyful noise" resounding from angels round the throne. Jesus Himself told us, "These things have I spoken unto you, that my joy might remain in you, and that your joy might be full" (John 15:11). Did not the angels declare at Christ's birth, "Behold, I bring you good tidings of great joy"?

It's up to us to believe it. Jesus came to bring us fullness of joy. He endured suffering and death to accomplish that joy. And so, regardless what suffering we face, we can always rest in the knowledge of this abiding joy.

"Ask, and ye shall receive, that your joy may be full" (John 16:24).

THE MAN WHOM THOU CHASTENEST

DAILY BIBLE READING: PSALM 94:8-13

"Blessed is the man whom thou chastenest, O LORD" (Psalm 94:12).

Chastening. Discipline. They are not the most pleasant words. What child does not dread chastisement, even when it is lovingly administered? We all know those words in Hebrews 12:11, "No chastening for the present seemeth to be joyous, but grievous."

Yet chastening is so necessary. Why? Today's passage supplies some reasons. For one thing, it's because God knows us so well. Do we realize just how well He knows us? The psalmist tries to get that across in verses 8 and 9. He seems to ask, "When will you finally catch on? If God created our ears, won't He hear everything we say—or even think? If He created our eyes, won't He see everything we do?"

In short, God knows absolutely everything about us, even our innermost thoughts. "The LORD knoweth the thoughts of man, that they are vanity." There is the clincher—the reason why we need chastening. Even our thoughts are worthless, and God knows it.

Chastening, however, opens the way to correction and teaching. Notice that right after the psalmist pronounces his blessing on the man who is chastened, he reminds us that God teaches us out of His love. That's the great blessing of chastisement—all the teaching that comes with it.

What shall we do when God's chastening is so heavy that our hearts are sore? Let's pour it all out to Him in prayer.

"LORD, in trouble have they visited thee, they poured out a prayer when thy chastening was upon them" (Isaiah 26:16).

 *Day 186*

DEALING JUSTLY

DAILY BIBLE READING: PSALM 106:1-5

"Blessed are they that keep judgment" (Psalm 106:3).

Another way to read this would be "Blessed are they who deal justly with their fellow men." For the Biblical view of "dealing justly," let's look at Psalm 82:3, "Defend the poor and fatherless: do justice to the afflicted and needy." Or we could read Romans 13:7, "Render therefore to all their dues: tribute to whom tribute is due . . . fear to whom fear; honour to whom honour."

Justice is based on righteousness and truth. Zephaniah says, "The just LORD is in the midst thereof; he will not do iniquity: every morning doth he bring his judgment to light, he faileth not" (3:5).

God's justice is high and holy. But we are weak humans. Can we deal as justly with our neighbor as God does with us? We need to depend on God. Even Jesus said, "I can of mine own self do nothing: as I hear, I judge: and my judgment is just; because I seek not mine own will, but the will of the Father which hath sent me" (John 5:30).

Above all, we need to remember that with God, "mercy and truth are met together" (Psalm 85:10). God is altogether true and just, but He is also altogether merciful. Praise God for His mercy, which saves us from His righteous judgment. We could never stand before a perfectly just God if it were not for His mercy and grace.

In Jesus, therefore, we have a pattern for dealing justly with our fellow man. Love and mercy must go hand in hand with justice and truth.

"What doth the LORD require of thee, but to do justly, and to love mercy, and to walk humbly with thy God?" (Micah 6:8).

DELIGHT IN HIS COMMANDMENTS

DAILY BIBLE READING: PSALM 112:1-8

Blessed is the man that . . . delighteth greatly in his commandments" (Psalm 112:1).

True fear and love toward God will lead to obedience—delight in His commandments. And what a list of blessings the psalmist promises for the one who does that!

Let's focus on the blessing we see in both verse 7 and verse 8: "he shall not be afraid." Isn't this an interesting paradox? When we fear the Lord, we will not be afraid. Other fears will fade into the background.

Why? Because our hearts are fixed. Our hearts are established; we trust in God, and Him alone.

It's not that no fears lurk around us. One writer said that in this psalm, he pictures a lone traveler pausing for rest in the depth of the forest. Wild beasts prowl in the darkness around him. But the traveler is not afraid, because he rests in the ring of light cast by the fire of God—the light that ariseth "in the darkness" (verse 4).

Does it seem that this psalm promises material prosperity to the man who delights in God's commandments? Perhaps. But above all, the righteous man will have spiritual wealth—the true riches. Grace is better than gold. Why? Because grace will last into eternity. Some parents may leave to their children an inheritance of gold. But the best inheritance is if the children are taught to delight in God's commandments.

"The fear of the LORD is the beginning of wisdom: a good understanding have all they that do his commandments" (Psalm 111:10).

IN THE NAME OF THE LORD

DAILY BIBLE READING: PSALM 118:24-29

"Blessed be he that cometh in the name of the LORD" (Psalm 118:26).

Why would there be a blessing upon the one who "cometh in the name of the LORD"? Let's look at it this way. At the beginning of today's reading, verse 24 admonishes us to remember that "this is the day which the LORD hath made" and we ought to "rejoice and be glad in it."

But what if we don't feel like rejoicing? What if our mood is down and our situation is out of control? What if the darkness presses in on every side? How can we rejoice?

Go to verse 26. Remind yourself that you are one who "comes in the name of the LORD," because you believe in Jesus as Saviour. "Who is among you that walketh in darkness, and hath no light? let him trust in the name of the LORD, and stay upon his God" (Isaiah 50:10). The truth is, if we are "in the name of the LORD," we are in Him.

And the psalmist says in 113:3, "From the rising of the sun unto the going down of the same the LORD's name is to be praised." If we occupy our thoughts with trust and praise for the name of the Lord, doesn't that give us all we need to make this a day of rejoicing? Can we say any longer that we "walk in darkness" and "have no light" when we are busy praising and trusting in the name of the Lord? Surely not, for now our song is that of verse 27: "God is the LORD, which hath shewed us light."

"Our Father which art in heaven, Hallowed be thy name" (Matthew 6:9).

INTEGRITY

DAILY BIBLE READING: PSALM 119:1; 26:1-6

"Blessed are the undefiled in the way" (Psalm 119:1).

There are no less than three beatitudes in the first two verses of Psalm 119. That's why we are also reading part of Psalm 26, because its topic ties in directly with today's: integrity.

What is integrity? Here are some synonyms and describing words: undefiled, blameless, honest, without deceit. In Psalm 26, David pleads vigorously for recognition of his integrity. "Judge me, try me, prove me—I'm innocent!" he cries. Is David claiming to be absolutely sinless? No. This psalm was probably written during Absalom's rebellion. David is simply saying that his son's charges against him are false.

What about my integrity and yours? Can we claim the blessings promised to the undefiled, the blameless, the honest? We certainly would like to. But when we look into our hearts, we see deceitful and dishonest tendencies. We feel we cannot stand before God and boldly say, "Judge me, O LORD . . . I have walked in thy truth."

Yet there is a way for us to wash our hands in innocency. We truly can stand in integrity before God. Jesus made this possible. His blood washes whiter than snow. Believing in Him, we stand innocent in the eyes of God. What a blessing!

Now I want you to notice something in Psalm 26. Read it all, and you will see that David, in spite of his protestations of blamelessness, still felt his need for God's mercy. In verse 11, even while declaring that he walks in integrity, David humbly pleads, "Redeem me, and be merciful unto me."

"And as for me, thou upholdest me in mine integrity, and settest me before thy face for ever" (Psalm 41:12).

KEEPING THE TESTIMONIES

DAILY BIBLE READING: PSALM 119:2-8

"Blessed are they that keep his testimonies" (Psalm 119:2).

As you know, nearly all 176 verses of Psalm 119 mention God's law, using no fewer than ten synonyms for *law*. They include terms such as *statutes, precepts, word, way, judgment,* and *path*. In today's beatitude the word is *testimonies*.

Do we realize just how significant God's law is? Practically all of Leviticus and Deuteronomy, and much of Exodus and Numbers, are concerned with the commandments of the Lord. God's law shows His absolute righteousness. It also shows what stringent requirements for righteousness are placed on us.

That makes us cringe. We belong to a fallen human race, lacking the ability to perfectly follow God's law. In the words of the Apostle Paul, "In me...dwelleth no good thing...how to perform that which is good I find not" (Romans 7:18).

Verse 4 of today's reading reminds us, "Thou hast commanded us to keep thy precepts diligently." Yet we can identify so well with the despairing cry of verse 5: "O that my ways were directed to keep thy statutes!"

Verse 8 makes us think of the king's servant in Matthew 18. He had a huge unpayable debt, yet he made this desperate plea, "Lord, have patience with me, and I will pay thee all." The psalmist also seems to plead, "I'll try to keep your law—don't give up on me."

But such pleas are futile. At least they would be if it were not for Jesus. He came. He justified us in the sight of a righteous God, and He sent the Holy Spirit. Through Him, God's law is no longer an impossible outward requirement, but a testimony written in our hearts. Now our lives can be a constant hymn of praise to God, who teaches us to keep His testimonies.

"I will praise thee with uprightness of heart, when I shall have learned thy righteous judgments" (Psalm 119:7).

Day 191

SEEK HIM WHOLEHEARTEDLY

DAILY BIBLE READING: ISAIAH 55:1-9

"Blessed are they that . . . seek him with the whole heart" (Psalm 119:2).

Seek God! Great blessings are ours if we seek Him with our whole hearts. It takes endurance and commitment and sheer hard work to seek God with our whole hearts. Notice all the imperative verbs in this little passage from Isaiah 55. Come. Buy. Eat. Hearken diligently. Incline your ear. Come. Hear. And in verse 6—Seek.

Jesus once told a parable to illustrate how diligently and persistently we must seek God. Remember the widow who kept pestering the judge until he finally fulfilled her needs? She refused to give up, even though the judge seemed to turn a deaf ear to her pleas (Luke 18:1-8).

Sometimes it seems to us that God turns a deaf ear. Perhaps we are seeking help to overcome a weakness. Perhaps we seek guidance for a certain circumstance. Or we seek strength for a hard trial. Yet God does not seem to be replying.

Why does it seem that way to us? Verses 8 and 9 of today's reading supply the answer. God's thoughts are not like ours, and His ways are vastly higher. In His own timing, in His own way, He responds.

That is why we keep on seeking Him. Jesus gave a precious promise to those who seek: "I say unto you, Ask, and it shall be given you; seek, and ye shall find" (Luke 11:9).

Remember: It's not that God is insensitive to our needs. But He knows what a blessing it is for us to be persistent—to seek Him with our whole hearts.

"And ye shall seek me, and find me, when ye shall search for me with all your heart. And I will be found of you, saith the Lord" (Jeremiah 29:13, 14).

CORNERSTONE DAUGHTERS

DAILY BIBLE READING: PSALM 144:9-15

"Happy is that people, whose God is the LORD" (Psalm 144:15).

As you may know, the words *happy* and *blessed* in the Scriptures are interchangeable. So we could say, "Blessed is that people whose God is the Lord."

Such a simple blessing, yet so profound. Do we truly obey God as Lord of our life? We gladly acknowledge Him as Saviour, just as the psalmist did in this passage. The "new song" in verse 9 is the song of redemption, the song of salvation. I daresay it is the same new song we read of in Revelation 15:3, the "song of the Lamb," praising the crucified One.

We know, however, that Jesus the Saviour and Jesus the Lord are one and the same. This beautiful picture of happiness in Psalm 144 is describing those people whose God is the Lord. Many of the blessings seem to be material: strong oxen, full barns, prolific herds, freedom from crime and complaint. But that can be taken figuratively as the "fruit of the Spirit" borne by people whose God is the Lord.

Let's focus on just one of the blessings: "that our daughters may be as corner stones, polished after the similitude of a palace." How could a maiden be called a "corner stone" unless she were linked by faith to the Chief Cornerstone, Jesus Christ? How could a girl be likened to a pillar in a palace unless she had yielded her life to be a temple for the Holy Spirit? Such will be the blessed state of the young generation in a church "whose God is the LORD."

"Behold, I lay in Zion for a foundation a stone, a tried stone, a precious corner stone, a sure foundation: he that believeth shall not make haste" (Isaiah 28:16).

THE BLESSING OF HOPE

DAILY BIBLE READING: PSALM 146

"Happy is he . . . whose hope is in the LORD his God" (Psalm 146:5).

Hope is such a necessary component of earthly life. Like the steel girders of a tall building, hope provides a framework. From earliest childhood we learn what it means to hope. We hoped for a nice day, we hoped we could visit grandparents, we hoped for good grades on a test, we hoped to have good friends.

But the best and most important hope far surpasses such material wishes. The hope of the Christian casts an anchor beyond earthly shores into the realm of eternity: "Which hope we have as an anchor of the soul, both sure and stedfast, and which entereth into that within the veil" (Hebrews 6:19).

How shall we describe the believers' hope? In a way it is a present hope, real in our hearts every day. Peter speaks of "the hope that is in you" (1 Peter 3:15). It is a hope based on mercy and grace: "Our Father, which hath . . . given us . . . good hope through grace" (2 Thessalonians 2:16). This hope came about through the resurrection of Christ: "a lively hope by the resurrection of Jesus Christ" (1 Peter 1:3) So you see, our hope is not just for the present, but also for the eternal future.

"The hope which is laid up for you in heaven" (Colossians 1:5).

BLESSED IN HIM

DAILY BIBLE READING: PSALM 72:17-19

"Men shall be blessed in him" (Psalm 72:17).

This beatitude is the capstone of them all. Or, conversely, we could call it the foundation of all the beatitudes—because if our blessings are not "in Christ," they are not really blessings at all.

Is there a psalm anywhere that speaks more abundantly of Christ's reign than Psalm 72? Verse after verse mentions Christ's glory, might, and marvelous love. "Abundance of peace...dominion from sea to sea...all kings shall fall down before him...he shall deliver...he shall redeem...he shall live."

Originally, this psalm was written about Solomon. He was such a good king that people pinned their hopes on him, anticipating a glorious reign. But Solomon disappointed them. He was only human. He sinned. He failed. His glory certainly did not endure forever.

Can't we see ourselves in that? We tend to pin our hopes on our own strength, our own goodness. But before true blessedness can be ours, all we have—or think we have—must go to the cross.

In Christ, and in Him alone, are we blessed. Those two little words "in him" have so much meaning. Writing to the Ephesians and the Colossians, Paul used these words many times to show us what we have and what we are in Christ. We are chosen in Him—rooted in Him—built up in Him—complete in Him—alive in Him—hidden in Him—redeemed in Him—quickened in Him—reconciled in Him—accepted in Him.

But before we can have all those blessings, we must be dead with Him, buried with Him, and risen with Him. Christ is all in all!

"And, having made peace through the blood of his cross, by him to reconcile all things unto himself" (Colossians 1:20).

DRAW BACK THE CURTAINS

DAILY BIBLE READING: REVELATION 21:22-25

"The city had no need of the sun . . . for the glory of God did lighten it" (Revelation 21:23).

Imagine a girl who owns a lamp that she really admires. The lamp itself is so beautifully colored that she can't stop admiring its artistic value, but what she appreciates most is its soft, mellow light. She spends hours basking in its glow.

"Well, what is wrong with that?" you wonder.

Just this: that girl has never been out in the sun. She always keeps her curtains pulled. She is so busy idolizing her lamp's dim light that the brilliance of real sunlight is unknown to her.

What a shame! You rush into that dim room and wrench the curtains wide. In floods the pure, clear sunlight. The brilliance is almost more than the girl can bear. Will she cover her eyes, shrink from the blazing light, and beg to have the curtains drawn? Or will she turn from her pitiful lamp to embrace this new enlightenment?

Here in Revelation 21, God is pulling back the curtains of Heaven. He knows we need a glimpse of the sublime light that surpasses even the sun. He knows we are far too engrossed with the meager things of this earth.

Like Saul at the Damascus gate, what we desperately need is a flash of heavenly light to blind us to earth's allurements. We should appreciate the earth's beauties. God created them for our enjoyment. But we need to remember that He has more in store for us. Infinitely more! Most important of all, it's those glimpses of heavenly light that give us strength for earth's rugged pathway.

"The sun shall be no more thy light by day . . . but the LORD shall be unto thee an everlasting light" (Isaiah 60:19).

AWAKE, AWAKE!

DAILY BIBLE READING: ISAIAH 52:1, 2

"Awake, awake . . . shake thyself from the dust" (Isaiah 52:1, 2).

This chapter was originally a call for Israel to rouse and be freed from the captivity of Babylon. What vigorous descriptive terms Isaiah uses! Israel was called to wake up, to put on clothes, to rise from the dust and sit erect, and to break off their chains—because God was setting them free.

For us today, these words are a vivid picture of a sinner escaping from sin's captivity. The first call is to awake: to recognize our sin and repent. Next we are called to dress ourselves. God has prepared two sets of "clothing" for the awakened sinner. One is the strength of God—His power and grace. The other set is here called the "beautiful garments," making us think of the Christian's attire Paul describes in Colossians: "Put on . . . bowels of mercies, kindness, humbleness of mind, meekness" (3:12).

Third is the call to be purified: "no more . . . unclean." The church is purified by the blood of Christ through the grace of God.

Fourth, we are called to "shake ourselves from the dust." Job's friends, when they came to mourn with him, sat on the ground and sprinkled their heads with dust. God calls us out of mourning to His comfort!

Fifth, we may arise, and sit up. God in His love "hath raised us up . . . and made us sit together in heavenly places in Christ Jesus" (Ephesians 2:6).

Sixth, we may "loose ourselves from the bands" of sin's captivity. Let us lay hold upon "the glorious liberty of the children of God" (Romans 8:21)!

"Deliver thyself, O Zion, that dwellest with the daughter of Babylon" (Zechariah 2:7).

DEPART, DEPART!

DAILY BIBLE READING: ISAIAH 52:11, 12

"And the God of Israel will be your rereward [rear guard]" (Isaiah 52:12).

The first part of this chapter spoke of waking up, of breaking free. Now the last part urges us to get out—depart—flee!

The word *flee* makes us think of haste, of fearful glances backward to see whether the foe is pursuing us. (Were you ever a little girl who used to run out of a dark cellar, feeling sure that monsters nipped at your heels?) But God promised the Jews of Babylon that their journey back to Jerusalem would not be "with haste." The Lord Himself would go before them; and best of all, He would also guard behind them. (That's what *rereward* means.)

We, too, may claim this promise that God will guard us both before and behind. Because you see, we, too, must depart—must flee—from the world's defilement. Perhaps we have developed a sense of false security in this world, just like the Jews had in Babylon. They had good homes and good jobs there. Would they be willing to forsake that ease and make the long trek back to a devastated homeland where rugged pioneering awaited them?

Let us be roused by God's command to "go ye out of the midst of her; be ye clean, that bear the vessels of the Lord" (verse 11). Just as Israel bore the temple vessels on their return to Zion, so God calls the church to hold aloft the Gospel of Jesus Christ. But we cannot do that unless we depart from the world and are cleansed by Christ's blood.

"And the angel of God, which went before the camp of Israel, removed and went behind them; and the pillar of the cloud went from before their face, and stood behind them" (Exodus 14:19).

BE DILIGENT TO REST

DAILY BIBLE READING: HEBREWS 4:9-11

"Let us labour therefore to enter into that rest" (Hebrews 4:11).

Suppose you were a hired girl. One day your employer issues this strange order: "Get busy and lie down." Wouldn't that be confusing? Verse 11 of Hebrews 4 appears to give a similarly confusing command: "Let us labour [be diligent] therefore to enter into that rest." Why would we need to be diligent in order to rest?

Let's ask a few other questions before we answer that one. What does the word *rest* mean? The definition that best fits Hebrews 4:11 is "to be firmly based or grounded; to become fixed."

The Scriptures contain at least four instances of rest.

1. God rested on the seventh day of Creation and later instituted the Sabbath in commemoration of that rest.

2. The promised land of Canaan was a rest for God's people.

3. Today, we can have rest when we repent of our sins, believe in Jesus as Saviour, and live a life of obedience to Him.

4. Life in Heaven is the ultimate rest that awaits us.

For the answer to our question, we look at the third kind of rest. That certainly requires diligence on our part! It is true that we can have rest when we are firmly based on Jesus and grounded in His grace. But that means ceasing from our own work, as it says in verse 10. We must stop thinking that we can earn God's favor through good works, and instead trust in Christ to fulfill His purpose in us. That will take great diligence on our part—the diligence of repentance, faith, and obedience.

"Come unto me, all ye that labour and are heavy laden, and I will give you rest" (Matthew 11:28).

GOD HAS NOT CHANGED

DAILY BIBLE READING: ACTS 5:7-11

"And great fear came upon all the church" (Acts 5:11).

Does this story trouble you? Does it seem that God dealt very harshly with Ananias and Sapphira? Striking people dead because of sin—that sounds rather like Old Testament times. Yet in Acts 5, the new dispensation had begun. Where was God's love and grace when this couple received such a swift punishment?

It is not for us to question God's ways. He always knows best. And He does not change. "For I am the Lord, I change not," He declares in Malachi 3:6. Neither His love nor His holiness changed one bit in the shift from the Old Testament to the New.

So we do not question whether God's dealing with Ananias and Sapphira was right. However, we do want to learn something from this event. Could it be that some people in the early church had become too relaxed? Had they started to think that they can do as they pleased in this new dispensation of grace?

If so, the death of Ananias and Sapphira was a vivid testimony to God's unchangeableness. God's holiness is still in effect. He hates lies and sins as much as ever. The fear that came upon the church was surely a godly fear, the kind that can produce much good.

Just think what a purifying effect it must have had on the church. Had some folks been joining the church merely to get free meals, even money? God's swift judgment upon Ananias and Sapphira would have put a stop to that.

When something happens that increases our fear of God, we can be sure of this: our unchangeable God has a perfect purpose in mind.

"Sanctify the Lord of hosts himself; and let him be your fear, and let him be your dread"
(Isaiah 8:13).

SHE FAILED TO TRUST AND WAIT

DAILY BIBLE READING: GENESIS 27:1-10

"Bread of deceit is sweet to a man; but afterwards his mouth shall be filled with gravel" *(Proverbs 20:17).*

Why did Rebekah do it? Why did she tell her son to practice such deceit and tell so many lies? After all, the Lord Himself had promised her that the "elder would serve the younger" (Genesis 25:23). Why did she devise a deceitful plan to accomplish a promise God had already given?

We could think of various reasons why Rebekah did it. Perhaps she no longer trusted her husband. Isaac was getting old. She may have felt the need to override his judgment by tricking him into doing what she thought was right. It seems too that Rebekah wasn't free of partiality where her children were concerned. She loved Jacob so much more that the very thought of Esau getting the blessing sent her into a panic.

But Rebekah's biggest problem may have been this: she didn't trust God. Why else would she have taken matters into her own hands?

What a reaping there was for this sowing of deceit! Rebekah and Jacob never saw each other again. Esau sought Jacob's life. Strife tore the family apart. Later, Esau founded an enemy nation that caused centuries of hardship for Israel.

Let us trust the Lord to carry out His will in His own good time. We will only bring sorrow upon ourselves if we take matters into our own hands instead of trusting and waiting.

"Commit thy way unto the Lord; trust also in him; and he shall bring it to pass" *(Psalm 37:5).*

THE WRONG REASON

DAILY BIBLE READING: GENESIS 27:11-17

"Behold, Esau my brother is a hairy man, and I am a smooth man" (Genesis 27:11).

Jacob didn't yield to his mother's deceitful plan without protest. In these verses we see him hesitating and bringing up an objection.

But the question is, why did Jacob object? Was it because his mother's deceit horrified him? Did he hate to trick his elderly father like that? Was there enough righteousness in him that he abhorred the thought of doing this treacherous thing?

I'm afraid not. As far as we can see, there was only one reason Jacob objected—he was afraid of getting caught.

Aren't we often like that too? When we're faced with something questionable, we may decide to turn away. But are we concerned with doing right, or are we motivated by the fear of getting caught?

Let's be wary of this tendency in our fallen human nature. If we catch ourselves worrying that people will find something out, that should raise a red flag. It's a sign that our motives are wrong; dishonesty is lurking somewhere.

Saying no to temptation is good. But saying no for the wrong reason is as bad as saying yes.

What are the right reasons for saying no? Read again how the devil tempted Jesus in the wilderness. Jesus said no—for all the right reasons.

"Get thee hence, Satan: for it is written, Thou shalt worship the Lord thy God, and him only shalt thou serve" (Matthew 4:10).

THE EVIL OF ANGER

DAILY BIBLE READING: GENESIS 27:34-41

"Then will I slay my brother Jacob" (Genesis 27:41).

This passage from Genesis 27 is full of violent feelings. I think the main emotion can be expressed in one word: anger. With all the force of his being, Esau was angry at his brother because Jacob had stolen his blessing. But Esau's immense anger blinded him to the facts. The truth was that Esau himself had given away his birthright years before.

It's sobering to consider what Esau's anger did to him. He was so upset that he no longer saw the good he still had. His whole view got distorted. All he could think of was what had been taken from him. Worst of all, he decided to kill Jacob.

We must learn to control our anger. Anger can do terrible things to us and cause us to do terrible things to others. If we become angry over a situation, we no longer see things clearly.

How can anger be controlled? First, we must recognize our anger for what it is. If we won't admit that our anger is out of control, nothing will change.

Second, we must turn to God for help. His grace is sufficient. His power is far greater than our anger. He can help us to see what good may come from the situation. When the flames of our anger have died down, God can cause beauty to rise from the ashes.

"Cease from anger, and forsake wrath: fret not thyself in any wise to do evil" (Psalm 37:8).

A CAMPAIGN AGAINST SIN

DAILY BIBLE READING: MATTHEW 4:23-25

"Teaching in their synagogues, and preaching the gospel of the kingdom, and healing all manner of sickness" (Matthew 4:23).

You look around and declare, "This kitchen is a mess. Something must change in here. Boys, pick up your toys! Girls, put away your things!"

You have started a campaign against dirt and disorder. Your weapons are a broom and some stern commands. At the end of the war, you eye with satisfaction the well-cleared battlefield.

Such a "kitchen campaign," of course, is no comparison to the campaign Jesus waged when He began His earthly ministry. His was an all-out campaign against sin. Here at the end of Matthew 4 are a few verses that nearly take our breath away. Can we imagine the tremendous energy of the Son of man as He entered the battlefield of Galilee?

His weapons were three: teaching, preaching, and healing. Everywhere in the synagogues He stood to teach God's word, God's purpose. Jesus wanted the people to understand God's plan for mankind, the plan for victory over sin.

Volley after volley of preaching He unleashed against sin. At every opportunity—whether from mountainsides or fishing boats—Jesus proclaimed the Gospel, the Good News. God's kingdom had come, and He was the bearer.

Wherever Jesus went, He healed—all manner of disease, even people possessed by devils. Sickness in all its forms is a result of sin. Sin had to flee in the face of this divine campaign. No wonder multitudes joined His army!

My life and yours are battlefields too. Let's yield to the One who has such power over sin, that He may cleanse us as He once cleansed the villages of Galilee.

"For the weapons of our warfare are not carnal, but mighty through God to the pulling down of strong holds" (2 Corinthians 10:4).

PLEASE HURRY, LORD

DAILY BIBLE READING: PSALM 27:11-14

"Wait, I say, on the LORD" (Psalm 27:14).

Have you ever said to someone, "Please hurry! We haven't got all day!"

There may be times when we feel like saying that to God. Maybe we're in trouble, and we want to call out as David did here: Deliver me! Please hurry! I can't stand this much longer.

In John 11, when Mary and Martha urgently asked Jesus to come because their brother was sick, we can almost hear them plead, "Please hurry. Lazarus might die if you don't come quickly." In other words, "We haven't got all day."

But that is not how we should speak to God. He does have all day. He has all the time in the world. In fact, He has eternity! God cannot be hurried. A thousand years are like a day to Him, and a day like a thousand years.

Jesus didn't hurry either when Mary and Martha beckoned. He waited four days before starting off. And in that waiting, great blessings were realized. Jesus demonstrated His resurrection power! Jeremiah says in Lamentations 3:26, "It is good that a man should both hope and quietly wait for the salvation of the LORD."

David had lots of experience in waiting. The Bible doesn't tell us how old he was when Samuel anointed him, but it seems likely that he was no older than fifteen. Yet David didn't become king till he was thirty. In those waiting years, he experienced all sorts of trials from his foes. But David also learned how to wait in faith. He learned the truth of what he expresses here: "Wait on the LORD: be of good courage, and he shall strengthen thine heart."

"This is the LORD; we have waited for him, we will be glad and rejoice in his salvation" (Isaiah 25:9).

TO FEAR IS TO OBEY

DAILY BIBLE READING: PSALM 34:11-15

"I will teach you the fear of the LORD" (Psalm 34:11).

What does it mean to fear the Lord? We have explored this question before and seen that it means to respect, honor, and reverence Him.

Reverence. That word makes us think of folding our hands and sitting quietly in church as we listen to God's Word.

But of course, there is more to reverence than that. The Bible makes it plain that fearing God and obeying God are intimately connected. To fear is to obey. "Let us hear the conclusion of the whole matter," Solomon says in Ecclesiastes 12:13, "fear God, and keep his commandments."

Our reading in Psalm 34 says the same thing in greater detail. "Come, children, while I teach you to fear the Lord," urges David. Then David goes on to explain that a person who fears the Lord will be careful how she speaks; she will not tell lies; she will avoid evil and seek to do good; she will actively search for and pursue peace.

Isn't that a fairly thorough description of obedience to God? At the same time, it's a description of the person who fears God. So again we conclude that to fear God is to obey Him.

What a blessing we reap from fearing and obeying! Many years later, Peter quoted this whole passage from Psalm 34 in his first letter, and he said it the same way: "For the eyes of the Lord are over the righteous, and his ears are open unto their prayers" (1 Peter 3:12).

"If a man love me, he will keep my words" (John 14:23).

THE EVERLASTING COVENANT

DAILY BIBLE READING: PSALM 105:5-10

"And confirmed the same unto Jacob for a law, and to Israel for an everlasting covenant"
(Psalm 105:10).

God's covenant with Israel was everlasting. In His view, the covenant was not meant to be broken. "He hath remembered his covenant for ever, the word which he commanded to a thousand generations."

But we know what happened. Israel broke their side of the covenant. They sinned, they wandered away from God. Indeed, through their idol worship they utterly rejected Him.

God's judgment on Israel was severe. Divine righteousness could not do otherwise. Many places in the Bible we can read of God's righteous wrath toward covenant-breakers. "Therefore, behold, I, even I, will utterly forget you, and I will forsake you . . . and cast you out of my presence: and I will bring an everlasting reproach upon you, and a perpetual shame, which shall not be forgotten" (Jeremiah 23:39, 40).

What terrible words! They make us shudder. We, too, have broken the covenant. We have fallen short of the glory of God. We have sinned. Is there any hope for us in the face of divine wrath?

Yes, oh yes, there is! God has renewed His covenant through Jesus Christ. Read Isaiah 61 to get the sweet taste of the salvation God offers to repentant sinners, who of themselves would be absolutely unworthy. In Christ God gives us "beauty for ashes, the oil of joy for mourning, the garment of praise for the spirit of heaviness" (Isaiah 61:3).

"I will greatly rejoice in the LORD . . . for he hath clothed me with the garments of salvation, he hath covered me with the robe of righteousness" (Isaiah 61:10).

THE OXYGEN OF HEAVEN

DAILY BIBLE READING: REVELATION 4:6-9

"They rest not day and night, saying, Holy, holy, holy, Lord God Almighty" (Revelation 4:8).

I have never climbed a high mountain, but I have heard from others how the atmosphere changes as you climb higher up the slopes. The oxygen that is so vital to life on earth becomes less and less. Once up in the clouds, a person will gasp like a fish out of water.

The atmosphere of Heaven is different from the atmosphere of earth. The atmosphere of Heaven is pure holiness.

In today's reading, we are not concerned with figuring out who those strange "beasts" are; we want to focus on what they are doing. They have an eternal unrest! The atmosphere of Heaven is so rarefied by holiness that these heavenly beings must constantly declare the holiness of the Lord.

Now we think again of mountain climbing. That's our earthly pilgrimage—climbing toward Heaven. Will we be ready for the holy atmosphere of Heaven? We won't be able to breathe Heaven's oxygen unless God's holiness has begun to permeate us here. No wonder Peter urges, "But as he which hath called you is holy, so be ye holy" (1 Peter 1:15).

Still, while we live on earth we continue to struggle with the downward pull of sin. But let's not despair. In Hebrews 10:14, the words could be translated thus: "For by that one offering he forever made perfect those who are being made holy" (NLT). Through Christ's sacrifice we are made perfect in God's eyes—but at the same time we are still "being made holy." We are still climbing the mountain, still learning to breathe the oxygen of Heaven.

"Holiness becometh thine house, O LORD, for ever" (Psalm 93:5).

WHAT CAUSED THE DISTRESS?

DAILY BIBLE READING: PSALM 77:1-20

"I complained ... my spirit was overwhelmed ... I am so troubled that I cannot speak"
(Psalm 77:3, 4).

Asaph certainly is troubled! His prayer brims with distress. In verse 1 we hear him moaning and wailing. In verse 2 we see him stretching his hands in supplication to God. Verse 3 has Asaph complaining out of an overwhelmed heart. Verse 4 shows him lying sleepless because of his trouble. What caused all this deep distress?

I wonder if the answer lies in verses 7-9. What do we see there? Raw, anguished doubt. Asaph seems to question God on just about everything. No wonder he is distressed! In fact, his doubts were causing more distress than the original problem (whatever that had been).

I'm not saying we should never doubt. That would be asking the impossible. Doubts will come.

Nor am I saying that we shouldn't confess our doubts to God. In fact, if Asaph is any indication, then telling God is the best thing we can do. Asaph certainly didn't try to hide his doubts.

Confessing his doubts seemed to clear the way for Asaph to do something much better. Instead of focusing on his dingy little heap of doubts, Asaph raised his eyes to God! When Asaph started praising God for His greatness, his distress disappeared.

*"In my distress I called upon the L*ORD*, and cried to my God: and he did hear my voice out of his temple" (2 Samuel 22:7).*

VESSEL IN THE WATERFALL

DAILY BIBLE READING: 1 JOHN 4:7-11

"Herein is love, not that we loved God, but that he loved us, and sent his Son to be the propitiation for our sins" (1 John 4:10).

"Beloved, let us love one another." As Christians, we have no other option. We must love one another. But can we truly love one another in the way we should? It seems like a tall order.

How will we go about this business of loving? Will we be like the man who was given a large tank to fill with water? In grim determination, he grabbed his little pail and ran to the stream bank to fill it. Pail after pail after pail of water he carried to that tank. How slowly it filled up! The tank seemed to grow bigger by the minute, while his own puny pail seemed to shrink with every trip to the stream.

Another man was also given a tank to fill. One glance told him that he couldn't do it by carrying water in his own little vessel. So this man took the tank and placed it right beneath a waterfall, where the stream roared wide and full over the brink. Instantly the tank was full and overflowing!

The tank is like God's command to love one another. Our own efforts are puny, our love toward God and our fellow man feeble. But God's love toward us is like a mighty, rushing waterfall! If our lives are centered in the divine stream of love that sent His Son to die for us—why then, love will overflow and spill to those around us.

"If God so loved us, we ought also to love one another" (1 John 4:11).

A PSALM FOR THE HUNGRY

DAILY BIBLE READING: PSALM 34:8-10

"There is no want to them that fear him" (Psalm 34:9).

Why do we call this a psalm for the hungry? Is it because verse 8 speaks of tasting? Partly, yes; but there's more to it than that. In these verses we are shown a blessed state of complete satisfaction, of not wanting *anything*. David says in verse 9 and repeats in verse 10: "They that seek the LORD shall not want any good thing." He makes the picture all the more vivid by contrasting the satisfaction of believers with the restless, roaming hunger of a young lion.

But really, this is perplexing. Is David promising that a Christian will always get everything he could possibly want? No, of course not.

Let me tell you a little story that will help us understand what David means. Picture a small house where lives a poor, lonely widow. It is wartime, and one day some plundering soldiers crash down her door. Grabbing food from her pantry, they declare, "We'll leave you with nothing!"

"No matter," replies the widow. "I shall not want, as long as God is in Heaven."

Can we grasp now what David is saying? If we have God, we have all that we really need—even if we face poverty and hardship.

You see, God knows that our deepest needs are spiritual. He may even ask us to "go hungry" in the earthly sense to teach us that we need God more than anything else and to learn that spiritually, we have no want if we have God.

"The LORD is my shepherd; I shall not want" (Psalm 23:1).

HE'S THE EDITOR TOO

DAILY BIBLE READING: HEBREWS 12:1-3

"Jesus the author and finisher of our faith" (Hebrews 12:2).

If you've ever written for publication, you know how important an editor is. You are the author: the idea for the story came to you, and you put it down on paper. But after you send the story off to a publisher, an editor will scrutinize it from a different perspective. He will notice areas where improvements could be made and kindly point them out to you.

This passage in Hebrews 12 presents the startling thought that Jesus is not only the author, but also the editor of our faith. You see, the word given as *finisher* in the KJV can also be translated as *perfecter*. I can't think of a better description for an editor than to call him a perfecter.

In Ephesians 2:10, Paul suggests that God is composing a masterpiece as He leads us onward in faith. Can we grasp that picture? God is being an author and an editor. If you've ever written a poem, you know it can be quite an exercise in rewriting as you choose the proper words for rhyming and rhythm. Let's visualize our life of faith as a poem that God is composing. By His grace, faith is born in our hearts. That's why He's called the author. And because He diligently corrects and adjusts to form the masterpiece He desires, He is the editor too.

Who better qualifies to be our editor than Jesus? He has been here, has run the same race that we must run, and has endured for our sakes the shame of the cross.

"I have finished the work which thou gavest me to do" (John 17:4).

UNFULFILLED DREAMS

DAILY BIBLE READING: 2 TIMOTHY 4:6-8

"I have fought a good fight" (2 Timothy 4:7).

It's natural for young people to dream. We dream of things we hope to accomplish. We dream of happy times ahead. Perhaps we have golden dreams of what our own home and family will be like.

Life goes on. Trials come our way. Gradually we realize that some—perhaps even most—of our youthful dreams will remain unrealized. Life is more rugged than we thought.

Does that mean there is no happiness for us on earth? Will our highest dreams remain forever unfulfilled?

A resounding *no* to both questions! To explain why, let's look again at Paul's words here in 2 Timothy 4. Paul had nearly reached the end of his life. Upon looking back, what did he say? "I've had a pretty good life, lots of good times, an easy ride"?

Again, a resounding *no*. For Paul, life had been a fight, a race, a striving to keep the faith.

But I believe Paul was happy as he wrote these words because he could say he had kept the faith. In earthly life, there is no higher dream for us than to keep the faith, regardless of the rough waters we sail.

There was more to Paul's happiness. He knew that now at last, on eternity's shore, his dreams would be realized. They would be fulfilled beyond his wildest dreams once that crown of righteousness was placed upon his brow. So too for us. In Christ, we have a right to dream—because of eternity.

"Blessed is the man that endureth temptation: for when he is tried, he shall receive the crown of life, which the Lord hath promised to them that love him" (James 1:12).

VIGOROUS VERBS

DAILY BIBLE READING: 1 TIMOTHY 6:11-14

"Fight the good fight of faith, lay hold on eternal life" (1 Timothy 6:12).

Do some people picture Christianity as an armchair religion? Do they think we can simply rest in God's grace and forgiveness, secure and lazy because of what Jesus has done for us? Do we fancy that we can sit in a rocking chair and let God do all the work?

If so, we have a false view of faith. Consider the vigorous, active verbs Paul uses here to describe the Christian life. First there's *follow after.* To "follow after" something is to actively pursue it. Precious ingredients like godliness, righteousness, faith, love, patience, and meekness are not added to our lives without active participation.

In verse 12 the action gets more intense. *Fight! Lay hold!* No wonder the Christian is depicted as a soldier in full armor, with sword and spear at the ready. Swords and shields are not meant for use from the safety of an armchair. They are meant for active service on the battlefield.

Elsewhere, Paul likens the Christian to an athlete training for competition. It's good if we can view life as a training ground, a place for discipline and obedience. What a daily challenge we have, to bring carnality into submission and conquer the tendency to evil. Self must be sacrificed; our all must be focused on the command of the King.

"No man that warreth entangleth himself with the affairs of this life; that he may please him who hath chosen him to be a soldier" (2 Timothy 2:4).

AVOIDING THE ROOT OF ALL EVIL

"The love of money is the root of all evil" (1 Timothy 6:10).

Perhaps we as women are tempted to think that we do not love money. But do we love the things money can buy? I am afraid we sometimes do. Those little conveniences and enjoyments and frills that we cling to—at their roots, they are tied to the love of money.

How can we avoid this pitfall? Paul gives us some good suggestions in this chapter. For one thing, if we do have money we should "be rich in good works, ready to distribute" (verse 18). Is there a better use for money than to help others with it?

To avoid the love of money, let's cultivate a love for people instead. That thought is implied in verse 11, where Paul gives us a list of things we should pursue, or follow after; love is one of them.

Instead of loving money, we ought to be consumed with a love for God's work in general: righteousness, godliness, faith, patience, meekness. Focusing on those leaves little room to spare for money.

Then too, it helps a lot to remember that riches don't last. "We brought nothing into this world," Paul reminds us in verse 7, "and it is certain we can carry nothing out." Whereas in verse 17 he charges us to not "trust in uncertain riches, but in the living God."

Ultimately, we could say that contentment is the best safeguard against the love of money.

"And having food and raiment let us be therewith content" (1 Timothy 6:8).

SO MANY QUESTIONS

DAILY BIBLE READING: PSALM 89:46-49

"Lord, where are thy former lovingkindnesses?" (Psalm 89:49).

I wonder how many questions there are in the Psalms. David and the other psalmists weren't shy about bringing their questions out in the open. Here in this passage, the psalmist seems to plaintively ask God, "How long must this go on? Where is Your unfailing love, anyway?"

Psalm 77 is another psalm full of questions. And for each question, we can find an answer elsewhere in the Bible. First the psalmist asks, "Will the Lord cast off for ever?"(Psalm 77:7). We find the answer in Romans 11:1: "Hath God cast away his people? God forbid."

Next he asks, "Will he be favourable no more?" (Psalm 77:7). Lamentations 3:32 answers that question: "But though he cause grief, yet will he have compassion according to the multitude of his mercies."

"Is his mercy clean gone for ever?" wails the psalmist in 77:8. Another psalm gives a resounding reply: "For as the heaven is high above the earth, so great is his mercy toward them that fear him" (Psalm 103:11).

"Doth his promise fail for evermore?" he wonders, also in Psalm 77:8. Second Corinthians 1:20 replies: "All the promises of God in him [Jesus] are yea, and in him Amen."

"Hath God forgotten to be gracious?" is the next question in Psalm 77. Exodus 34:6 emphatically replies, "The Lord, The Lord God, merciful and gracious, longsuffering and abundant in goodness and truth."

Finally comes this heart-wrenching question: "Hath he in anger shut up his tender mercies?" And again, Lamentations 3 has the answer.

"It is of the Lord's mercies that we are not consumed. They are new every morning: great is thy faithfulness" (Lamentations 3:22, 23).

USEFUL OR USABLE?

DAILY BIBLE READING: 1 SAMUEL 13:5-14

"Thou hast done foolishly: thou hast not kept the commandment of the Lord thy God . . . now thy kingdom shall not continue" (1 Samuel 13:13, 14).

Saul's reign started gloriously. Picture the Prophet Samuel announcing to Israel, "See ye him whom the Lord hath chosen, that there is none like him among all the people?" And with one accord the people shouted, "God save the king."

Saul had plenty of talents. With his imposing height and handsome appearance, he was quite a kingly figure. He had courage, and he was a man of action.

But as you know, Saul failed. God rejected him. The last years of his reign were miserable. Why did such a promising reign turn out to be a dismal failure?

At the beginning of Saul's life, we could say that his talents made him a potentially useful man. But his weaknesses destroyed him. Acting impulsively, he disobeyed God. He took things into his own hands.

We all have weaknesses. Will we let them destroy us?

Let's not despair. God can use our weaknesses. It depends on what we do with them. If we refuse to recognize them and forge ahead in our own "strength" the way Saul did, we are doomed.

But if we are aware of our shortcomings, they give us a constant, keen reminder that we need a Master Craftsman in control of the abilities (or tools) He gave us. Our weaknesses can make us usable because they force us to hand over our strengths to God so that He can use them according to His will.

"Stubbornness is as iniquity and idolatry. Because thou hast rejected the word of the Lord, he hath also rejected thee from being king" (1 Samuel 15:23).

ENEMIES OF TRUTH

DAILY BIBLE READING: GALATIANS 4:15, 16

"Am I therefore become your enemy, because I tell you the truth?" (Galatians 4:16).

Can we fathom the pain Paul felt? He reminded the Galatians how warmly they had received him at first. But when he confronted them with their error, things were different. Paul seems to say, "Are we enemies now, just because I've been honest with you and told you where you should change?"

Paul knew the importance of being truthful. To the Ephesians he wrote, "Speak every man truth with his neighbour: for we are members one of another." Really, being less than honest with one another doesn't make sense—no more than if my hand tried to hide something from my foot. Since we're all members of the body of Christ, honest confrontation is what we need. That's also why Paul, when describing the Christian's armour in Ephesians 6, exhorted us to have our "loins girt about with truth" (verse 14).

How do we react when someone honestly confronts us about a mistake we have made? How do we feel when our ministers faithfully preach the truth—and step on our toes in the process? Are we filled with indignation? Do we become enemies?

That is folly. Our ministers need to be like the priest described in Malachi: "The law of truth was in his mouth" (2:6). When the truth is preached, let's praise God. Instead of becoming enemies, let's receive the admonition, take it to heart, and allow it to work a change in us.

"The man that ... will not hearken unto the priest that standeth to minister there before the LORD thy God ... even that man shall die" (Deuteronomy 17:12).

WITHOUT BLEMISH

DAILY BIBLE READING: LEVITICUS 22:17-22

"But whatsoever hath a blemish, that shall ye not offer: for it shall not be acceptable for you" (Leviticus 22:20).

Concerning the offerings, God's word to Moses was very clear: only the best would do. I'm afraid if I had been asked to bring an offering, I would have selected a lame animal. Or one with sores on its body. Or a runt. Why not choose something I wanted to get rid of, since it would only be burned up anyway?

But such reasoning was unacceptable to God. The animals brought for offerings had to be perfect. Why? Because they were meant to foreshadow God's eternal offering of Jesus Christ. God gave His best for us! His only Son—holy, sinless, without blemish. Nothing less would do to take away the sin of mankind.

Today, God does not require literal burnt offerings from us. But He certainly desires our sacrifices. In Isaiah 1 God explains that He doesn't want animal offerings anymore. "Stop bringing me such futile gifts when your hearts are not right!" He seems to say.

Then He goes on to describe the sacrifices He desires: stop doing evil and start doing good. The Hebrews writer says the same: "To do good and to communicate forget not: for with such sacrifices God is well pleased" (13:15).

Because we ourselves are not perfect, there is only one way we can offer acceptable sacrifices. We must receive the cleansing Isaiah describes: "Wash you, make you clean . . . though your sins be as scarlet, they shall be white as snow" (Isaiah 1:16, 18). Only through Jesus can we be made "white as snow" to offer an acceptable sacrifice.

"Offer up spiritual sacrifices acceptable to God by Jesus Christ" (1 Peter 2:5).

A PRIZE FOR PEACE

DAILY BIBLE READING: JEREMIAH 6:13-15

"Saying, Peace, peace; when there is no peace" (Jeremiah 6:14).

Alfred Nobel was a very rich man who died in the late 1800s. In his will, he made a unique provision for his vast wealth. Each year, prizes were to be awarded to people who made important contributions to mankind in areas such as medicine, literature, and world peace. Each year, the Nobel Peace Prize is awarded to someone who has promoted the cause of peace in the world.

Though I've known about this prize for a long time, I only recently learned how Alfred Nobel made his money. He invented dynamite, which is used to make explosives. Talk about irony. Money from a product used in warfare is dedicated to a prize given in the name of peace.

Was Nobel's conscience troubled by the fact that his invention could be used to kill? We don't know. Perhaps it was to assuage his conscience that he established an endowment to promote peace.

Somehow there is a hollow ring to all this. It makes us think of people who say, "I'm trying to do enough good to outweigh the bad things I've committed, in hopes I'll be allowed into Heaven."

It is all a part of the devil's delusions. We can never earn our way out of the pit of sin. Futile and pitiful is our insistence of "peace, peace" when there really is no peace apart from Jesus.

Jeremiah mentions "the time that I [the Lord] visit them." On the day the Lord returns, only one kind of righteousness will avail anything. It is the kind Paul describes in Philippians 1:11.

"Being filled with the fruits of righteousness, which are by Jesus Christ" (Philippians 1:11).

QUACK DOCTORS

DAILY BIBLE READING: JOB 13:1-5

"Ye are all physicians of no value" (Job 13:4).

Job was pretty hard on his so-called friends, wasn't he? After all, they really wanted to help him. Yet Job reacted to their "help" by calling them liars.

Much of what those friends said was correct. For instance, they maintained that God is just, and that He punishes sin. Those principles are true. But Job's friends felt sure they knew how these principles should be applied to Job. Because God is just, and because He punishes sin, the friends wrongly concluded that Job's trials were a just punishment for his sins.

Job's friends were like quack doctors. *Quack*, as you know, is the term for a person who considers himself an expert when he is not. Imagine the disastrous results if an uneducated man would start calling himself a heart specialist! None of us would want a quack doing open-heart surgery on us.

No wonder Job called his friends "physicians of no value." Well-meaning though they were, their diagnosis completely missed the mark in Job's situation. The principles they mentioned were based on truth—but the application was wrong.

I'm afraid we are sometimes like Job's friends. "Tut-tut!" we say, surveying another's circumstances. Even though we barely understand what's going on, we freely offer our judgments and opinions. "He should do this. Why don't you try to do better? It's really her own fault."

Let's not be quack doctors. God is the Great Physician; let's leave matters in His hands and ask Him for true love and compassion to offer our fellow man.

"Who art thou that judgest another man's servant?" (Romans 14:4).

YOU ARE JUST AS BAD

DAILY BIBLE READING: ROMANS 2:1-4

"Therefore thou art inexcusable . . . thou that judgest doest the same things" (Romans 2:1).

Let's try to picture a Christian church in ancient Rome. The congregation assembles eagerly, for they have heard that a special treat awaits them today: a letter from the Apostle Paul. With bated breath the people watch the minister unrolling a well-worn scroll.

Paul's letter starts in with a striking description of sin in its worst forms. Heads nod. Yes indeed, Paul's anger against such sin is justified. Perhaps some of the people even congratulate themselves for not taking part in evil of that sort.

Suddenly (in Chapter 2) the tone of the letter changes. Paul seems to turn and point a finger at those self-righteous folk. "You are just as bad as they are!" he seems to declare. Faces pale as the truth hits home.

The truth is that we have all sinned repeatedly. Some sins may seem more "socially acceptable" than others. You and I may think we are not as bad as people who drink and murder. But we have no excuse for condemning others. Often it is the sins we notice most clearly in others that have also taken root in our own hearts.

The point Paul wants to drive home is that we have all sinned and fallen short of God's glory. "There is none righteous, no, not one" (Romans 3:10). Our only hope is in Jesus. God in His righteousness, goodness, and patience is leading us to repentance and saving faith.

"Wherein thou judgest another, thou condemnest thyself" (Romans 2:1).

FIRE BAN

DAILY BIBLE READING: JAMES 3:5-7

"The tongue is a fire" (James 3:6).

Almost every summer there is a fire ban in our area. Due to prolonged weeks without rain, fires are a real threat. No campfires are allowed. Even something as small as a smoldering match tossed carelessly aside can cause untold damage. In some parts of the country we hear of whole townships engulfed in flames. And behind each raging conflagration there was once a spark—a tiny spark that grew.

Do you know what is just as bad as lighted matches tossed upon a tinder-dry forest floor? Words tossed carelessly from an untamed tongue. What evil can result from gossip and unkind words! "A world of iniquity . . . setteth on fire the course of nature." That's how James describes the disastrous results of an unruly tongue.

In our hearts we should always enforce a "fire ban." No lighted matches allowed! No idle or hateful words tolerated beyond the watchful gate of our lips. Because you see, an uncontrolled tongue has its source in Hell.

You and I could never bring a raging forest fire under control. Nor can we reverse the damage done by careless words. Relationships can be reduced to ashes, congregations destroyed, by the lighted matches tossed carelessly from our tongues.

"An ungodly man diggeth up evil: and in his lips there is as a burning fire. A froward man soweth strife: and a whisperer separateth chief friends" (Proverbs 16:27, 28).

LOOK OUT FOR OTHERS

DAILY BIBLE READING: PHILIPPIANS 2:4

"Look . . . on the things of others" (Philippians 2:4).

Today's reading is very short—just one verse—because the other verses might take our focus off the thought for today. The thought can be expressed this way: "Look out for others. Truly sympathize. Take genuine notice of others' feelings."

The word translated *look* comes from the Greek root word *skopos,* the same root from which we get our English words *telescope* and *microscope.* That gives you an inkling of just how intently we are to peer at the "things of others."

This is not to advocate minding other people's business. Not at all. The Bible speaks clearly against being meddlesome. *Skopos* encourages us to care about others' feelings. In fact, to care more for others than for ourselves!

That goes against our human nature. If we do what comes naturally, we care more about our own feelings than anyone else's.

How can we overcome this natural tendency of looking out for ourselves first? We must look to Jesus. His amazing example is described in the verses immediately following Philippians 2:4. So now I'm encouraging you to read more verses after all. Truly, Jesus looked out for others and not Himself. Being God, He could have clung to Heaven's privileges—but for our sakes He became a man and died a criminal's death on the cross.

His example of "looking out for others" leaves us with no excuse for being selfish.

"Don't be concerned for your own good but for the good of others" (1 Corinthians 10:24 NLT).

GOD'S ANGER

DAILY BIBLE READING: PSALM 30:2-11

"His anger endureth but a moment" (Psalm 30:5).

We humans are really not qualified to analyze the anger of God. Is God's anger at all to be compared with ours? Probably not. Like everything else about God, His anger is sure to be absolutely righteous.

God's anger is so much higher than ours that we hardly dare to take a peek at it. Still, here in Psalm 30 David gives us a glimpse.

Apparently David had a serious illness and almost died. That, to David, was an experience of God's "anger." But it didn't last long. Soon David was singing, "I cried unto thee, and thou hast healed me . . . thou hast brought up my soul from the grave" (verses 2, 3).

David recognized that he had learned from his experience. He realized that when all was going well, he became far too self-sufficient. When God "hid his face" by sending adversity, David felt shattered. The result? He earnestly sought the Lord again and ended up praising Him.

So David could say that God's anger "endureth but a moment." We should have the same attitude toward trials that God allows. When we receive a shot in the arm from a doctor, there is momentary pain, but it's quickly over. Yet the good effects of the shot linger on. God's anger can be painful, but so effective in turning us from sin. And never forget—in the morning there will be a shout of joy.

"He will not always chide: neither will he keep his anger for ever" (Psalm 103:9).

EPISTLE OF PRAISE

DAILY BIBLE READING: HEBREWS 1:1-3

"Upholding all things by the word of his power" (Hebrews 1:3).

If someone were to ask us which book of the Bible contains the most praises for God, we would probably say Psalms; it simply bulges with praise to God. If you need an example of bubbling praise, try Psalm 145. "I will speak of the glorious honour of thy majesty, and of thy wondrous works" (verse 5).

What about the New Testament? Is there a certain book that excels in praise? All the books are for God's glory, of course; but if we specifically seek words of praise for our Saviour, we could point to the Epistle to the Hebrews.

Notice how much praise for Jesus is crowded into the first three verses. Jesus is "the heir of all things"—everything ultimately belongs to Him. Jesus was a coworker in the Creation: "by whom also he made the worlds." Jesus radiates the very glory of God: "Who being the brightness of his glory . . ." In fact, Jesus expresses to us the character of God, "the express image of his person." And just try to grasp this: by His power, Jesus sustains the universe. "Upholding all things by the word of his power."

There is more praise—much more. Read through the Epistle to the Hebrews and find the writer extolling Jesus the Saviour again and again as he explains how much better He is than the old covenant.

Praise. Do we recognize how vital, how important, how life-changing it is? While we are praising God, we are looking away from the pettiness of self. And that is always good.

"But we see Jesus . . . crowned with glory and honour; that he by the grace of God should taste death for every man" (Hebrews 2:9).

FOUR TONGUES

DAILY BIBLE READING: PROVERBS 26:22-28

"A lying tongue hateth those that are afflicted by it" (Proverbs 26:28).

The Bible has much to say about the tongue, especially in James and Proverbs.

Often the Bible warns us against the evils of the tongue. That's certainly the case in today's reading. Not only the tongue, but also the mouth and the lips, are mentioned in connection with such evils as lying, deceit, flattery, and talebearing.

Of course, we must remember that the tongue in itself is not evil. It's what we do with it—our manner of speaking and what we say—that can be either good or evil.

In Proverbs we read about four different "tongues," or ways of speaking. Some people have a *careless* tongue: their manner of speech easily includes angry words, lies, or even curses. "He that goeth about as a talebearer revealeth secrets: therefore meddle not with him that flattereth with his lips" (Proverbs 20:19).

Then there's the *conspiring*, or scheming, tongue—always ready to spread gossip and slander. The first verse of today's reading vividly describes such a tongue: "The words of a talebearer are as wounds, and they go down into the innermost parts of the belly" (Proverbs 26:22).

Now for two good tongues. There's the *caring* tongue, full of truth and encouragement: "The tongue of the wise is health. The lip of truth shall be established for ever" (Proverbs 12:18, 19).

Finally we have the *controlled* tongue, that knows when to speak and when to be silent.

"The heart of the wise teacheth his mouth, and addeth learning to his lips" (Proverbs 16:23).

WHAT REALLY WAS THE PROBLEM?

DAILY BIBLE READING: EXODUS 17:1-7

"And the people thirsted there for water; and the people murmured" (Exodus 17:3).

The children of Israel certainly had a problem. At first glance we could think their main problem was lack of water. They were thirsty, with neither stream nor spring in sight.

But was thirst their biggest problem? Let's face it. Their biggest problem was their attitude. They murmured. They complained. They argued. They blamed Moses (and God).

What should they have been doing? They should have brought to God their concern about the lack of water. In other words, they should have prayed. They should have stood firm in the faith that "all things work together for good" (Romans 8:28).

Looking at the ungrateful Israelites, we think, *We would never do that. We wouldn't be so quick to complain against God.* But remember, the Israelites didn't even realize they were complaining against God. They were simply venting their feelings about an everyday inconvenience.

I wonder how often we complain about small everyday inconveniences. Maybe a water line is frozen. Or nobody has time to clear the driveway of snow. Or . . . There are hundreds of instances where we are tempted to complain.

Let's resist that temptation. Let's pray instead. Thus we will stay aware of the great truth God revealed to Moses: "Behold, I will stand before thee there." God is right here, every day, and He is much greater than our problems!

"And the water came out abundantly, and the congregation drank" (Numbers 20:11).

A FORM OF GODLINESS

DAILY BIBLE READING: 1 SAMUEL 4:1-10

"Let us fetch the ark of the covenant of the LORD out of Shiloh unto us, that, when it cometh among us, it may save us out of the hand of our enemies" (1 Samuel 4:3).

Reading this story reminds us of the words in 2 Timothy 3:5: "Having a form of godliness, but denying the power thereof." This is not to say that the ark of the covenant was merely a "form of godliness"; the Bible says that the Lord of hosts dwelled "between the cherubim" on the lid of the ark.

But what kind of relationship did Israel have with the Lord of hosts? Did they acknowledge His claim on their lives? Were they living in obedience to Him?

I am afraid not. The fact is, at this time Israel had fallen far from God. The previous chapter tells about God's promise of judgment on the high priest Eli's wicked sons. We must face it: Israel didn't have a proper faith in God. Yet when they were defeated by the Philistines, they came up with the idea that they should bring the ark to the battle. Why did they do that?

I'm afraid they saw the ark as little more than a "good-luck charm." True, they raised a triumphant shout when they saw the ark coming—but they weren't obeying God. So their idea didn't work. They were soundly defeated by the Philistines.

The survivors must have been puzzled. Hadn't they brought the ark? Didn't that mean God's presence was among them? Why didn't He give victory?

But because Israel wasn't obedient, that ark was merely a "form of godliness" to them. Through their disobedience they were "denying the power thereof."

We can be guilty of the same thing. We may try to comfort ourselves with a "form of godliness," but through inner disobedience to the spirit of God, we may be "denying the power thereof." Outward religious actions, such as churchgoing and rule-following, cannot give us victory over sin. Only an obedient relationship with God can do that.

"They profess that they know God; but in works they deny him, being abominable, and disobedient, and unto every good work reprobate" (Titus 1:16).

BROKEN IDOLS

DAILY BIBLE READING: 1 SAMUEL 5:1-4

"Only the stump of Dagon was left to him" (1 Samuel 5:4).

Yesterday we learned that the ark of the covenant did not serve as a "lucky charm" for Israel. Today we find the Philistines also hoping the ark will be a lucky charm for them. Having captured the sacred symbol from Israel, they placed it in the temple of Dagon, their major idol.

Lucky charm the ark was not—but a symbol of God's presence it certainly remained. No idol could stand in that presence. The first morning, the Philistines propped up their fallen Dagon and went back home. But when they returned the next morning, Dagon was in pieces. Only his stump remained.

Our hearts are temples. Do we still cherish idols there? Are we clinging to earthly things for happiness?

How we need God's presence in the temple of our hearts! No idols can stay standing there if we truly yield to God's power. Jesus alone can cleanse our hearts.

The battle will not be won in a day. Our carnal nature specializes in salvaging fallen idols and propping them up again. But if we truly seek deliverance, one day we will find our idols smashed to pieces, with nothing left but a stump to remind us of Christ's victory in our souls.

"We know that an idol is nothing in the world, and that there is none other God but one" (1 Corinthians 8:4).

ALL THINGS NEW

DAILY BIBLE READING: 1 SAMUEL 6:7, 8

"Now therefore make a new cart, and take two milch kine, on which there hath come no yoke" (1 Samuel 6:7).

The Philistines no longer wanted to have the ark of the Lord in their midst. In fact, they were very much afraid of it. So they asked their wise men what to do. The wise men told them to build a new cart to send the ark away; and the cows that pulled the cart must be new to the task—never before under a yoke.

Now let's flip to 2 Samuel 6, where we find King David bringing the ark home to his own city. Guess what? Verse 3 says, "And they set the ark of God upon a new cart."

Doesn't this remind us of something we read in the New Testament? Turning to Mark 11, we find Jesus riding upon an ass "whereon never man sat." And in Matthew 27:60 we find Christ's body being laid in a new tomb, never before used.

What might be the significance of all this newness? Let's think for a moment of a parable Jesus told: "New wine must be put into new bottles," He says in Mark 2:22. What does the "new wine" signify? It means the Holy Spirit, the life of God that seeks to indwell us. Jesus was saying that the Holy Spirit can only reside in a new life: a life regenerated, born again through repentance and faith in the atonement of Christ.

The presence of God will come to abide only when the old has been crucified. Why? Because Jesus is the "new and living way" spoken of in Hebrews 10:20. By Him, if we are made new, we may enter the holiest place.

"Therefore if any man be in Christ, he is a new creature: old things are passed away; behold, all things are become new" (2 Corinthians 5:17).

PUT ON THIS ARMOR

DAILY BIBLE READING: EPHESIANS 6:11-17

"Put on the whole armour of God" (Ephesians 6:11).

The armor of God is so complete. First and foremost, there is truth, likened to a belt that girds us about. Only God's truth can defeat the devil's lies.

The next item of our armor is righteousness—the righteousness of God that is ours through Jesus Christ. This is our body armor, the breastplate that protects our vulnerable heart. If we know that God approves of us and considers us righteous through His Son, no darts of the devil can pierce this armor.

The next piece of armor is for our feet: our shoes are the preparation of the Gospel of peace. With our feet shod thus, we are ready to proclaim peace everywhere.

We must not forget the shield. Faith is our shield. Through faith we believe ultimate victory is ours, even when the devil's arrows are flying thick and fast.

Of course our heads need the protection of a helmet. God's salvation is our helmet. The devil tries to make us doubt our salvation, but the helmet of salvation will protect our minds from doubt.

Only one weapon is included in our suit of armor: the sword of God's Word. With this sword we attack the temptations of the devil.

So there it is—the full armor of God. It's available and complete. But we have our part to do: we must put it on. In other words, we must avail ourselves of Christ's power through prayer.

"Let us therefore cast off the works of darkness, and let us put on the armour of light" (Romans 13:12).

ETERNITY IN THE HEART

DAILY BIBLE READING: ECCLESIASTES 3:10-15

"He hath set the world in their heart" (Ecclesiastes 3:11).

If you check the Hebrew dictionary, you will find that the original word for "world" can have the sense of *eternity*.

A young girl once admitted, "Ecclesiastes confuses me. Sometimes it even depresses me. Solomon seems so negative when he keeps insisting that 'all is vanity.'" I know exactly what she meant. If we read only part of Ecclesiastes, it is possible to get depressed.

It's important to keep in mind the main thought that Solomon wanted to bring out. As the wealthy ruler of a wealthy empire, he had everything the world could offer. Yet what does he tell us in his sermons? All is vanity! Nothing satisfies. Don't spend your life trying to find satisfaction in worldly things, because you will never be content. The more you have, the more you will want.

And why is that so? Today's key verse explains it. God has planted eternity in our hearts! That is why nothing on earth can satisfy. Deep within us, our spirits are linked to things eternal. Nothing but the eternal God can satisfy the spirit's thirst.

This helps to explain the restless yearning we sometimes feel. God has created us in such a way that we seek perfection. In other words, we seek the eternal God! Only in Him can we find fulfillment as we travel earth's lonely, rugged road.

"O God, thou art my God; early will I seek thee: my soul thirsteth for thee, my flesh longeth for thee in a dry and thirsty land, where no water is" (Psalm 63:1).

Day 233

THE PERFECT HEART

DAILY BIBLE READING: 2 CHRONICLES 16:7-10

"To shew himself strong in the behalf of them whose heart is perfect toward him" (2 Chronicles 16:9).

I certainly want God to show Himself strong toward me! But how can I have a perfect heart, one that is completely loyal to God?

Let's look at Asa's story to find out more about a heart that is perfect toward God. King Asa's reign started very well. For the first ten years, Asa served the Lord. In 2 Chronicles 14, Asa is faced with an army of a million Ethiopians. What did Asa do? He cried to God: "Help us, O LORD our God; for we rest on thee, and in thy name we go against this multitude" (verse 11). Isn't that a good picture of a perfect heart?

And God certainly showed Himself strong. His might quickly put that host to flight.

But now, two chapters later, the army of Israel attacked Judah. What did Asa do this time? Was his heart still perfect toward God?

No. Asa came up with a plan of his own—a human plan that left God completely out of the picture. Instead of asking God for help, Asa made an alliance with a heathen king. How sad!

One failure led to the next. When the Prophet Hanani rebuked Asa for not keeping a perfect heart, Asa flew into a rage and cast the prophet into prison. Worse still, Asa took out his anger by oppressing his own people.

Oh, let us pray that we can keep our hearts perfect toward God so that He can continue to show Himself strong toward us.

"My strength is made perfect in weakness" (2 Corinthians 12:9).

DRAW NOT NIGH

DAILY BIBLE READING: EXODUS 3:4-6

"Draw not nigh hither: put off thy shoes from off thy feet" (Exodus 3:5).

"Moses, Moses." That was God calling. And Moses responded right away: "Here am I."

Was Moses bewildered by the next words the Lord spoke? God had called to him; obviously He wanted his attention. He wanted to speak to Moses. Why, then, does God seem to hold out a warning hand, saying, "Draw not nigh?"

But you see, Moses needed to have the right attitude to come before God. He needed to recognize that he was a subject coming into the presence of his King. So off went his shoes, while his hands covered his face—showing how small and unworthy he felt.

God calls us too. Jesus said in John 12:32 that He will "draw all men" unto himself. James says, "Draw nigh to God, and he will draw nigh to you" (4:8). In Hebrews 10:22 we are invited to "draw near with a true heart."

Yet for us too, it's necessary that our hearts be properly prepared. In a sense we, too, are warned to "draw not nigh"—until we have taken off our shoes. In other words, we need to have our sins forgiven through the blood of Jesus. We need to come humbly and penitently before God.

Jesus is our Friend. He said so in John 15:15. But we do well to remember that He is also our King. Let us not be careless and casual in His presence, but rather let us come before Him in awe and reverence.

"And the captain of the LORD's hosts said unto Joshua, Loose thy shoe from off thy foot; for the place whereon thou standest is holy" (Joshua 5:15).

Day 235

FOUR DIFFICULTIES

DAILY BIBLE READING: EXODUS 3:10-14

"And Moses said unto God, Who am I . . . that I should bring forth the children of Israel out of Egypt?" (Exodus 3:11).

During his forty years as a shepherd, Moses had learned humility—but now he needed to learn faith. Let's stand at Moses' side as he gets four lessons in faith. Each lesson begins with a protest from Moses.

First he protested, "Who am I . . . that I should bring forth the children of Israel out of Egypt?" Back came the answer from God: "Certainly I will be with thee" (verse 12). Believe. Have faith. Stop worrying about your own inadequacy.

Then Moses had another difficulty, another protest. "When I tell the people God has sent me, they might ask, 'What is His name?'" And God answered, "I AM THAT I AM." Can we grasp the power and the mystery of those words? God is who He is. Have faith in Him!

But Moses was still not finished. At the beginning of Chapter 4, we find him asking, "What should I do if they don't believe me?" So God gave Moses a handful of miraculous signs that would demonstrate His power.

By this time, Moses should have learned that there was no difficulty too great for God. But Moses had one more protest. "I am not eloquent . . . I am slow of speech" (Exodus 4:10). God's reply was a powerful exhortation to faith: "Who hath made man's mouth? . . . have not I the LORD?" (4:11).

All four of Moses' protests were centered on himself. Moses had to learn to look beyond himself and trust in God. Don't we all need to learn this lesson?

"Not that we are sufficient of ourselves . . . but our sufficiency is of God" (2 Corinthians 3:5).

PEACEFUL SLEEP

DAILY BIBLE READING: PSALM 3:1-6

"I laid me down and slept; I awaked: for the LORD sustained me" (Psalm 3:5).

Sometimes when life gets difficult, it's hard to sleep peacefully. We lie awake while our minds rehearse our problems, over and over again.

Here is a psalm to put us to sleep! With David, we may say, "Thou, O LORD, art a shield for me . . . I cried unto the LORD with my voice, and he heard me . . . I will not be afraid of ten thousands."

And notice the heading in your Bible above this psalm. David wrote it during the time of Absalom's rebellion. That means he was running for his life, forced into hiding by his own son. Did David have something to keep him awake at night? I would think so.

Yet he slept peacefully, and this is why: David believed that God heard his prayers. He believed God was in control, no matter how chaotic the situation seemed.

So when we are tempted to lie awake at night, worrying about our circumstances, let's do as David did. Let's pour out our worries to God. And let's believe that He hears us. Let's believe He is in control.

"When thou liest down, thou shalt not be afraid: yea, thou shalt lie down, and thy sleep shall be sweet. Be not afraid of sudden fear, neither of the desolation of the wicked, when it cometh. For the LORD shall be thy confidence, and shall keep thy foot from being taken" (Proverbs 3:24-26).

A NEW STARTING POINT

DAILY BIBLE READING: MATTHEW 19:16-26

"What good thing shall I do, that I may have eternal life?" (Matthew 19:16).

Like the young man in this story, we all seek assurance of eternal life. We want to know what we must do to attain it.

But this young man was quite self-confident. When Jesus mentioned some commandments he needed to obey, the man shot back, "I've kept them all."

Jesus' next words took the young man by surprise. "Sell all you have and follow Me!"

That young man needed to realize that good deeds alone would never assure him of eternal life. In fact, he needed to lay down all his own "doings." He needed a whole new starting point!

What was this starting point? Forsaking his own righteousness and humbly following Jesus. Faith in Christ is what gives eternal life. Love for God comes before all the other commandments.

Again we realize how very like that young man we are. We, too, are tempted to depend on ourselves and our doings for salvation. But that is not the way to build up "treasure in heaven." It is through faith that we enter the kingdom and become a child of God—faith in the blood Christ shed for our atonement.

Faith, then, is the starting point. Having faith, we can go on in God's power and seek to obey His commandments. Eternal life is ours—as long as we keep the "faith which worketh by love."

"For in Jesus Christ neither circumcision availeth any thing, nor uncircumcision; but faith which worketh by love" (Galatians 5:6).

PREPARING TO ENTER

DAILY BIBLE READING: HEBREWS 10:19-22; LEVITICUS 16:1-25

"Enter into the holiest . . . by a new and living way" (Hebrews 10:19, 20).

Do you see why these two passages are connected? Leviticus tells us what God's people had to do under the old covenant when they wished to approach Him. What a complicated process it was!

For one thing, the holiest place, where the Lord's presence hovered above the mercy seat, could only be entered once a year.

For another thing, only the high priest could do it. And he could do it only after elaborate preparations. The finest details, such as bathing and dressing, were carefully prescribed.

How many animals needed to die so that their blood could make atonement for entering the holiest? Leviticus 16 tells it all. In those days, it was no easy thing to actually come before God.

But in Hebrews we find such an encouraging contrast. Because of the blood of Jesus, we are invited—no, entreated!—to enter boldly and freely into the holiest place and partake of God's mercy. We can do it daily, hourly, minutely. Our access to God is without limit and without difficulty.

However, Leviticus 16 still holds a message for us. We cannot enter carelessly or lightheartedly into the holiest place. Without prayer and consecration and a desire for holiness, we are still not welcome there. So, though Aaron's elaborate rituals are abolished, our hearts still need to be prepared.

"Let us draw near with a true heart" (Hebrews 10:22).

THE TWO GOATS

DAILY BIBLE READING: HEBREWS 10:11-18

"For by one offering he hath perfected for ever them that are sanctified" (Hebrews 10:14).

Now that you've read Leviticus 16, there are some more treasures we want to mine from that chapter. The two goats are so significant, the picture of Christ's sacrifice so vivid. They illustrate the two aspects of Christ's atonement for mankind.

The first goat is a picture of forgiveness. The goat had to be slaughtered and its blood sprinkled on the mercy seat as a sin offering. Jesus has done that once and for all! Because of His shed blood, God can forgive our sins; atonement is secured between the sinner and the righteous God. We can never be thankful enough for this forgiveness of our sins.

As for the second goat, upon its head were laid the sins of all the people. Then it was taken outside the city, to the wilderness, and left alone to die. In so doing it removed the people's guilt.

Does not that recall for us the cross? Jesus was taken outside the city to die, to bear our sins and provide a way for our guilt to be removed. Praise God, when we repent from our sins and trust in Jesus, we, too, are forgiven. The days of the two goats are long gone, but in Jesus their work is perfected and more effective than ever.

"So Christ was once offered to bear the sins of many" (Hebrews 9:28).

CHRIST, OUR SWEET INCENSE

DAILY BIBLE READING: LEVITICUS 16:12, 13

"And he shall put the incense upon the fire before the LORD...that he die not"
(Leviticus 16:13).

Here is another treasure from the "atonement chapter," another beautiful symbol of Jesus Christ. When Aaron went into the holiest place, he carried a censer, or bowl, full of hot coals taken from the Lord's altar. Just as he lifted the veil to enter, he threw handfuls of incense upon those coals. What a powerful aroma this must have created—and what a cloud of smoke!

That smoke stood between Aaron and the presence of God. In Exodus 33:20 God declared, "There shall no man see me, and live." God is a consuming fire. He is so holy that anything unholy coming near Him will be devoured. Without this cloud of incense between himself and God's presence, Aaron would have died.

Meanwhile, the scent of the burning incense was a sweet-smelling savor to God. It canceled out the foul odors that must have prevailed where so many animals were sacrificed and so much blood was spilled.

Today, Jesus is that sweet-smelling savor, canceling out the stench of flesh and sin that hangs about us. Because of His intercession, our prayers can rise into the presence of God.

Jesus is also that protecting cloud, standing between unholy sinners and a holy God. Jesus said in John 14:6, "No man cometh unto the Father, but by me." We, by ourselves, cannot see God and live. His holiness would consume us as with fire. But Jesus is our way of coming into God's presence—our sweet incense and mediating cloud.

"And the smoke of the incense, which came with the prayers of the saints, ascended up before God" (Revelation 8:4).

WHERE IS OUR FOCUS?

DAILY BIBLE READING: NUMBERS 11:7-9

"There is nothing at all, beside this manna, before our eyes" (Numbers 11:6).

Almost we feel like crying "Shame on you!" at the ungrateful Israelites. God was doing such great and wonderful things. With a high hand He had freed them from slavery, delivering them out of Pharaoh's power. Now He was shaping Israel into a nation, preparing the people for His amazing gift of a land flowing with milk and honey. Meanwhile, He sustained them with nutritious manna straight from Heaven.

But did the people stay focused on those extraordinary things God was doing for them? Did they praise God daily for deliverance and sustenance?

Obviously not. Numbers 11 is a sad chapter. It seems that among the Israelites were some foreigners who began to crave the kinds of food they'd known in Egypt. Soon these cravings and complainings rubbed off on the Israelites. They forgot God's mighty deeds and became stuck on one thing: this manna that turned their stomachs and made them gag because they were so tired of it.

"We want meat! We want fish and onions and melons and garlic like we had in Egypt!" Had they forgotten the harsh price they used to pay for those delicacies, the long weary days beneath the taskmasters' whips?

"What folly!" we exclaim. "They should have been ashamed."

Really, though, have we any right to point fingers at Israel? I'm afraid we're guilty of the same things. We, too, allow the world around us to influence us. We, too, start craving the world's luxuries. And what happens? Our focus is drawn away from what God gives us, and we can think only of our petty wants. Let us watch and pray that we can keep our focus in the right place.

"But I fear, lest by any means, as the serpent beguiled Eve through his subtilty, so your minds should be corrupted from the simplicity that is in Christ" (2 Corinthians 11:3).

TWO DIFFERENT RESPONSES

DAILY BIBLE READING: NUMBERS 11:10-17

"And Moses said unto the Lord, Wherefore hast thou afflicted thy servant? I am not able to bear all this people" (Numbers 11:11, 14).

Most of the time, we look up to Moses. His example of humility and dependence upon God is one we desire to follow. But here we see Moses in a weak moment. The people's complaining was just too much for him, like the last straw that broke the camel's back. And Moses complained in the bitterest terms to God.

Notice something interesting: The people complained, and Moses complained. Yet God's reaction to the people was entirely different from His reaction to Moses. Why?

It appears that the people did their whining to one another, standing in the doorways of their tents, griping about this sickening manna they were forced to eat. Such complaining accomplished nothing. It was negative, and God's reaction was negative too. He sent fire into the camp and took the lives of many people.

Whereas Moses took his burden straight to God. And God has a solution for every problem! Positive indeed was God's response: "There's no need for you to bear this alone. Delegate some others to help you."

You and I are only too expert at complaining to each other. But that is negative and useless. Let's bring our burdens to the Lord, who always knows what kind of help we need.

"Casting all your care upon him; for he careth for you" (1 Peter 5:7).

TABLE IN THE WILDERNESS

DAILY BIBLE READING: NUMBERS 11:18-23

"Shall all the fish of the sea be gathered together for them, to suffice them?" (Numbers 11:22).

This particular day doesn't seem to have been a very good day for Moses. I've sometimes wondered if he was depressed. What happens when we're under a cloud of depression? We tend to forget God's many good gifts to us. Our faith runs low. We start doubting God's power.

That's what Moses did here. When God told him He would provide enough meat to last Israel a month, Moses couldn't believe it. After all, he had about a million people in his charge. He exclaimed, "Even if we slaughtered all our livestock and caught all the fish in the sea, we wouldn't have enough!"

Moses, have you forgotten all the miracles God has performed in the past? Where is your faith?

The thing is, it's not hard to believe in God's power when we're experiencing it. Anyone can testify to God's power when they're on a mountaintop with Him. But in the humdrum grind of daily life, our faith can so easily run low. We get depressed and allow ourselves to lose sight of God's strength.

If it could happen to Moses, it can happen to any of us. It happened to Jesus' disciples too. When Jesus proposed to feed five thousand people, they asked in disbelief, "Shall we go and buy two hundred pennyworth of bread, and give them to eat?"

Let's never underestimate the strength of the eternal God. What He has promised He will deliver. Remember this: Unbelief asks, "Can God?" Faith replies, "God can!"

"Yea, they spake against God; they said, Can God furnish a table in the wilderness?" (Psalm 78:19).

GRAVES OF GLUTTONY

DAILY BIBLE READING: NUMBERS 11:31-35

"There they buried the people that lusted" (Numbers 11:34).

Kibrothhattaavah—a mouthful of a name. The meaning in Hebrew is "graves of gluttony." A place where greedy, gluttonous, lusting people were buried.

When the quail came blowing in from the sea, the Israelites caught them by the bushel. (Ten homers were fifty bushels—and that was the smallest amount gathered.) In their lust they gorged themselves on the meat.

This may seem like a morbid subject. But again, there is something here for us to learn. It begins with this question: is all desire wrong? In blazing anger, God struck down the people because they had complained and desired better food. Does that mean we should quench all our natural desires?

Not necessarily. Desires are part of the human makeup. If babies didn't desire food, they wouldn't grow. Desire becomes sin is when it turns into a greedy craving, and we start to feel that it is our right to fulfill that craving. Strong drink, rich food, sports, possessions, power, even knowledge—all these are things that can turn into cravings.

How can we know whether our desires have gone overboard into lust? A danger sign is when we get to the point where we can't think of anything but our obsession (just like the Israelites). May God guard and keep us from a grave of gluttony.

"The wrath of God came upon them, and slew the fattest of them, and smote down the chosen men of Israel" (Psalm 78:31).

SPIRITUAL MATURITY

DAILY BIBLE READING: GENESIS 44:30-34

"For how shall I go up to my father, and the lad be not with me?" (Genesis 44:34).

As we read Judah's eloquent plea for the safety of Benjamin, we get a striking picture of spiritual maturity. The picture is all the more vivid if we compare it with the way Judah acted years earlier when Joseph was "just his little brother."

Back then, Judah hated Joseph for relating dreams that made him feel inferior. Today, we see a Judah who recognizes his own weaknesses and is ready to acknowledge the guilt of his earlier treatment of Joseph: "God hath found out the iniquity of thy servants" (verse 16).

Back then, Judah stepped forward to sell his brother. Today, Judah steps forward to offer himself as a substitute for his brother.

Back then, Judah was concerned about personal gain: he thought selling Joseph would be more profitable than killing him. Today, Judah is willing to sacrifice his own life.

Back then, Judah hid his crime by telling lies. Today, Judah is completely honest, not trying to hide anything.

Back then, Judah didn't take any blame. Today, he takes all the blame on his own shoulders.

Back then, Judah didn't worry about other people's feelings. Today, he agonizes over the way his father would feel if Benjamin were lost to him.

How encouraging it is for us to see what the years did for Judah's spiritual maturity. It gives us hope that we, too, can grow spiritually as the years go by.

"Thy servants shall bring down the gray hairs of thy servant our father with sorrow to the grave" (Genesis 44:31).

WAS THE ATTITUDE RIGHT?

DAILY BIBLE READING: GENESIS 4:3-5

"But unto Cain and his offering he had not respect" (Genesis 4:5).

Why was Cain's offering not acceptable to God? The Bible does not tell us in so many words. Perhaps Cain did not bring the right kind of offering; perhaps, too, he brought it with a wrong attitude.

When we come before God, it's important to have the right attitude. Proverbs 21:27 says, "The sacrifice of the wicked is abomination: how much more, when he bringeth it with a wicked mind." In our own wording, we could say that a "wicked mind" means a wrong attitude.

Let's think about some wrong attitudes that could obstruct our relationship with God. It could be that Cain brought only what was leftover of his crop—the part he could easily spare. If so, it would have been a contrast to Abel's sacrifice: he brought the "firstlings" and the "fat thereof." Our offerings and prayers to God must not be mere second-best or leftover.

Or perhaps Cain came before God with a disobedient attitude. In Jeremiah 6:19 we read of people who "have not hearkened unto my words, nor to my law, but rejected it." And what did God say of the sacrifices these people brought to Him? "Your burnt offerings are not acceptable, nor your sacrifices sweet unto me" (Jeremiah 6:20).

The most important question may be this: did Cain come in faith? Was he penitent, seeking the grace of God? Or was his attitude one of careless arrogance, simply bringing an offering because it was the thing to do?

If that was Cain's attitude, we can again see the great contrast between his sacrifice and Abel's. According to Hebrews, Abel's sacrifice still speaks to us today—because Abel had the righteousness that comes through faith.

"By faith Abel offered unto God a more excellent sacrifice than Cain, by which he obtained witness that he was righteous, God testifying of his gifts: and by it he being dead yet speaketh" (Hebrews 11:4).

THEY HAD NO LEADERSHIP

DAILY BIBLE READING: JUDGES 17:1-6

"Every man did that which was right in his own eyes" (Judges 17:6).

What a mixed-up story this seems to be! We have an Ephraimite who stole eleven hundred pieces of silver from his mother. Then, fearing her curse, he confessed his thievery and returned the money. At this point we could get the impression that the woman feared God: she said, "Blessed be thou of the LORD" and spoke of dedicating the silver to the LORD.

But then what did mother and son do? They used some of the silver to make statues. The son, named Micah, built a "house of gods" for the statues, installed one of his sons as priest, and began to worship them.

Verse 6 explains why such strange things were going on. Israel had no leader, so people did whatever they wished. Doesn't that sound like the world around us? People no longer acknowledge God as King. They do just as they please. How quickly a society can descend from the worship of God to the idolatry of materialism!

We need leadership. We need to submit to the leaders of our church. Above all, we need to enthrone the Lord as King in our hearts. Left to ourselves, we, too, start doing whatever is right in our own eyes.

Reading further in the ensuing chapters of Judges, we find chilling stories of terrible sin and civil war. The picture is clear: people who do not submit to leadership descend into chaos.

"Be not deceived; God is not mocked: for whatsoever a man soweth, that shall he also reap" (Galatians 6:7).

HIS WAY IS IN THE SEA

DAILY BIBLE READING: PSALM 77:13-20

"Thy footsteps are not known" (Psalm 77:19).

Sometimes the Bible seems to contradict itself. Look at verse 13: "Thy way, O God, is in the sanctuary." Now look at verse 19: "Thy way is in the sea." The sea and the sanctuary are two widely different things. How can they both be used as an allegory for God's ways?

But there is no contradiction; instead, it is an expression of God's greatness. His goodness has so many aspects that many things can be used to symbolize it. God is everywhere. Better still, He is in all our circumstances. Is your pathway hard just now? Do you feel as though you are in the thick of a storm, with the voice of thunder and the sound of many waters?

Fear not. God is there. His way is in the sea.

During a difficult time, we may not understand how He can be working good for us. But we are not asked to understand. Remember? It says right here, "Thy footsteps are not known." We cannot fathom God's ways any more than the Israelites could have predicted how marvelously God would make a way for them through the Red Sea.

Nor can we fathom God's power. Consider verse 16. So great is God's power that the waters flee before His face, and even the depths are troubled at His approach.

Yes, God's way is in the sea—but never forget, it is also in the sanctuary. What a comfort for us! Anything God does or allows is always in accordance with His holiness and His love.

"Canst thou by searching find out God? canst thou find out the Almighty unto perfection?" (Job 11:7).

EVERYBODY ELSE DOES IT

DAILY BIBLE READING: 1 SAMUEL 8:11-22

"Now make us a king to judge us like all the nations" (1 Samuel 8:5).

Israel wanted a king because everyone else had one. Samuel saw the folly of the people's request. His heart was pained by the fact that they were rejecting his own leadership—and worse still, God's kingship. He went to the Lord for guidance. "Do as they ask," God replied, "but warn them about the consequences."

Samuel did. In detail he described all they could expect from a king with dictator-like powers. Their sons, their lands, and their resources would no longer be their own, but the king's. In a sense the people were asking to become slaves.

You know the outcome of the story. Nothing Samuel said distracted the people from their consuming desire: They still wanted a king. So they got one—and the rest is history.

The whole thing sounds somehow familiar, doesn't it? Human nature hasn't changed. When I want something, I *really* want it. And often, the only reason I can give for wanting it is the same reason Israel had: because everybody else is doing it. I want to be like the others. I don't want to be left behind. Give me my desire; never mind the consequences.

Oh, the tyranny of our carnal nature! If we insist on fulfilling such desires, we, too, are selling ourselves into slavery. Our own desires can control and enslave us to a frightening degree.

Is that how we want to live? Or shall we listen to the call of Jesus in John 8?

"Verily, verily, I say unto you, Whosoever committeth sin is the servant [slave] of sin. If the Son therefore shall make you free, ye shall be free indeed" (John 8:34, 36).

I HAVE A RIGHT

DAILY BIBLE READING: COLOSSIANS 3:5-10

"Mortify therefore your members which are upon the earth" (Colossians 3:5).

"Well, that's just how I am." Have you ever said that? I know I have. We use those words to try to justify ourselves for something less than kind we have said or done. We think our little weaknesses can be excused. We even go so far as to say, "I've a right to be who I am, haven't I?"

Hmm. We'd better be careful what we say about our rights. In God's eyes, how many rights do we have? Dare we really stand up before God and say, "I have a right to be this way"?

I don't know for sure about what "rights" God allows to us. But I do know about one right He offers. In fact, He urges us to take advantage of this right. We have the right to become children of God.

What a precious privilege! By belonging to God's family, we have a right to all the riches of His mercy and grace.

Before you run away with such a right, remember this: the way to become God's child is by believing in Jesus. Faith in Jesus means we partake of His accomplishments, because by faith we are one with Him. His two great accomplishments on earth are death and resurrection.

This means, therefore, that we are dead with Christ. We have put off the old man. If something is dead, does it still have rights? Do we have any right to anger or covetousness or self-indulgence, or even personal likes and dislikes? This passage in Colossians does not say that we have any such rights.

But we have a far greater right than the right to petty whims and fancies. We have the right to resurrection. To being risen with Christ. To a new life that consistently seeks holiness.

Yes, and if you read on in this chapter, you find that we have the right to a power that imparts love, humbleness, kindness, meekness, longsuffering. Are there any "rights" that you would rather have?

"But as many as received him, to them gave he power to become the sons of God, even to them that believe on his name" (John 1:12).

NO LONGER YOUR MASTER

DAILY BIBLE READING: ROMANS 6:12-14

"Sin shall not have dominion over you" (Romans 6:14).

Picture two opposing armies facing each other for war—one arrayed in red, one in blue. The blue army is the army of the Spirit, and grace is the master of all who enlist. The red army is the army of the law; sin is the master there.

At first you belong to the army of the law. What a weary existence! The law is very exacting, constantly condemning you because you cannot live up to its demands. Thus, because you cannot keep the law, you become a helpless slave of sin. Sin is your master, always peering over your shoulder, always holding you captive.

At last you throw down the useless weapons issued by the law. You cross over to the army of the Spirit. Now you are under a new law—the law of the Spirit of life in Christ Jesus. What a difference it makes to be under grace instead of under sin! Whereas the former law neither justified you nor offered power to obey, the law of the spirit of life proffers mercy for justification and grace to help with every weakness.

Sin is no longer your master. You have transferred your allegiance from sin to grace.

Notice, however—sin is still there. The red army still stands, and it will continue to make war on you. There may be times when it gets the best of you. But the fact remains, you are now wearing blue. The law that reigns over you is a law that justifies and gives grace to help. Sin shall not have dominion over you.

"If ye be led of the Spirit, ye are not under the law" (Galatians 5:18).

ETERNAL GOSPEL

DAILY BIBLE READING: REVELATION 14:5-7

"Having the everlasting gospel to preach unto them that dwell on the earth" *(Revelation 14:6).*

Do you sometimes have negative feelings when you hear a certain minister preaching? Do you sometimes find the sermons boring? Do you tend to have "favorites" among the ministers?

Such things are not necessary for a child of God. Instead of hearing the voice of a certain minister—boring or otherwise—learn to hear the voice of our beloved Saviour. The Bible is God's Word, the eternal Gospel. Regardless how it is delivered, regardless who delivers it, God's Word is precious because we love Him; we want to hear every word He speaks.

Consider what Paul says about his ministry in Ephesians 3:7-11. He marvels that God has given him this grace, this power to preach. He speaks glowingly of the Gospel, calling it "the unsearchable riches of Christ," the "manifold wisdom of God," "the eternal purpose," and "the fellowship of the mystery."

Yes, our ministers are revealing a mystery to us when they preach—the mystery of the everlasting Gospel. How can a gospel be everlasting? Paul says in Ephesians 3:9 that it has been hidden from the beginning of the world in Jesus Christ, by whom God created all things.

Our ministers can speak of this mystery for a lifetime, but they will never be finished. You and I can stay open and receptive to the preaching all our lives, yet we will never be finished discovering the eternal Gospel.

No, indeed, it is not necessary to be bored or negative when the Word of the eternal God is being preached. For we are those . . .

"To whom God would make known what is the riches of the glory of this mystery" *(Colossians 1:27).*

MY HEART IS FIXED

DAILY BIBLE READING: PSALM 112:1, 7, 8

"His heart is fixed, trusting in the LORD" (Psalm 112:7).

Isn't that what we all yearn for? A heart that is firmly established on the solid rock of Jesus Christ. A heart that can sing, "I shall not be moved." A heart undisturbed by any evil tidings, any trials, any adverse circumstances.

What does it take to have an established heart? The answer lies in the first verse of this psalm: "Blessed is the man that feareth the LORD." It has been said that he who fears God can live a fearless life. Nothing on earth can make him afraid.

How can fearing the Lord make us fearless? When we fear the Lord, we recognize Him as almighty, all-knowing, and utterly trustworthy. We become able to sing the song of Moses and the Lamb: "Great and marvelous are thy works, Lord God Almighty; just and true are thy ways, thou King of saints" (Revelation 15:3).

Thus believing, we stand on the solid Rock. We know without a doubt that our just and true God has only one purpose in the trials He allows: to draw us away from all things earthly, ever closer to Himself. Oh, indeed, our hearts tend to waver; earthly allurements often distract us—but if we fear God, our hearts can be fixed. And why should we ever fear evil tidings, if we know God's purpose is always for our eternal good?

"Whoso hearkeneth unto me shall dwell safely, and shall be quiet from fear of evil" (Proverbs 1:33).

SPIRITUAL BLINDNESS

DAILY BIBLE READING: NUMBERS 22:16-23

"And the ass saw the angel of the LORD standing in the way" (Numbers 22:23).

I shudder when I think how it would be if I could not see. Imagine a world that is always dark. Being blind would be hard.

But being spiritually blind is even worse than being physically blind. The Pharisees in their day were spiritually blind—blind to God's truth. Jesus called the Pharisees "blind leaders of the blind."

What causes spiritual blindness? In the story of Balak and Balaam we find a common cause for this serious form of blindness.

You know the story. Terrified of the Israelite army encamped against him, Balak king of the Moabites sent some of his princes to Balaam the sorcerer, asking him to come and curse Israel. At first Balaam refused, because God had forbidden him to do it.

Balak didn't give up easily. He sent more princes and promised great riches to Balaam if he would do this thing. That's when Balaam started to falter. Greed kicked in! Finally he set out with the princes.

God sent an angel to stop Balaam—but Balaam did not see that angel. Balaam's donkey had better vision than he!

Spiritual blindness prevented Balaam from seeing God's truth in the form of the angel. What caused Balaam's spiritual blindness? Greed. He couldn't forget the enticing riches promised by Balak.

Let's take this as a grave warning. The enticing riches of the world—if we give them a foothold in our lives—can cause us to become spiritually blind.

"In whom the god of this world hath blinded the minds of them which believe not, lest the light of the glorious gospel of Christ, who is the image of God, should shine unto them" (2 Corinthians 4:4).

MOMENT OF TRUTH

DAILY BIBLE READING: NUMBERS 22:22-29

"I would there were a sword in mine hand, for now I would kill thee" (Numbers 22:29).

Many of us know how to put up a good front. We can speak and act in ways that make us appear quite spiritual—or at least religious.

Balaam was such a man. He acknowledged the existence of God. He even proclaimed that he could not do anything God did not allow. But beneath that outer layer of Balaam's seeming spirituality lurked corruption. In reality he was a sorcerer and a man who coveted wealth more than the approval of God.

This incident with his donkey brought out the truth. Notice how angry Balaam became when the donkey thwarted his plan by refusing to move, even threatening to kill the beast. That anger revealed what was really inside Balaam.

How do we react when something blocks our path to what we want? Are we blinded by anger, like Balaam? Do we lash out at those around us, blaming them for our misfortune? Such moments tell the truth about us. Lashing out at others is a sure sign that something is very wrong inside us.

Maybe something has embarrassed us. Maybe our pride got hurt. Will we turn around and hurt others? Or will we recognize how sinful such revengeful anger is?

Balaam was so blinded by anger that he didn't even recognize the hand of God when the donkey miraculously spoke. Oh, let us pray that God may open our eyes to see the angel of the Lord standing with sword drawn against sin!

"And the angel of the Lord said unto him . . . behold, I went out to withstand thee, because thy way is perverse before me" (Numbers 22:32).

O MAN OF GOD

DAILY BIBLE READING: 2 KINGS 1:9-14

"Thou man of God, the king hath said, Come down" (2 Kings 1:9).

You almost have to read the whole chapter in order to get the drift of this story, but here's what happened: King Ahaziah fell out of a window and hurt himself. When the injury didn't heal, he sent messengers to a heathen god to enquire whether he would recover. But God sent Elijah to rebuke those messengers for going to Beelzebub rather than God Himself. The dumbfounded messengers hurried back to the king and told him about the man who had stopped them.

It didn't take Ahaziah long to guess who might do such a thing! In anger he sent a captain with fifty soldiers to arrest Elijah. They found him sitting on top of a hill. The captain commanded, "Thou man of God, come down."

You've read the rest of the story, how the first two captains with their fifties were destroyed, but the third one received mercy. Here's what we want to notice: those first two captains used religious words to address Elijah. They called him "man of God." But did they truly believe in God? Were they genuine? Apparently not. Religious words alone do not gain favor in the sight of God. Unless our hearts believe, religious words are in vain.

The third captain started in with the same words, "O man of God . . ." But his attitude was different. He came pleading for mercy, with a heart that truly feared God. Because he feared God, he came in respect and humility.

God is not impressed by high-sounding words. He sees into our hearts. Our attitude is far more important than our words. Remember the parable of the Pharisee and the publican.

"And the publican, standing afar off, would not lift up so much as his eyes unto heaven, but smote upon his breast, saying, God be merciful to me a sinner" (Luke 18:13).

A HAPPY HEART

DAILY BIBLE READING: PROVERBS 15:15-17

"He that is of a merry heart hath a continual feast" *(Proverbs 15:15).*

Yesterday we learned about the need to have right attitudes toward God. Today's verses show that we need to have right attitudes toward life in general.

At first glance we could think verse 15 is saying that if we suffer affliction, our days will be sad. But let's look at this verse from another angle. Solomon was actually talking about the need to maintain right attitudes: "If we are despondent, then every day seems to be full of trouble. A negative attitude of despondency casts a dark cloud over everything."

On the other hand, if there is cheer in our hearts, we can be happy regardless of what happens. No, we can't choose what happens to us. But we certainly can choose what attitude we take.

In verse 16 we see a person who has little in the way of earthly goods, but he has the fear of the Lord in his heart. His is an attitude that brings cheer, regardless of circumstances. Whereas a man can own all the world's treasure, and still be unhappy if there is turmoil in his heart. So too in verse 17—a cheerful attitude can turn a simple stew into a great feast!

How can we have this cheerful attitude? Paul tells us the secret: Think on the good things; dwell on the pure and the true and the lovely (Philippians 4:8).

It worked for Paul. He could be happy even in chains, in the deepest, darkest dungeon, because his heart was happy in the Lord.

"A merry heart doeth good like a medicine: but a broken spirit drieth the bones" *(Proverbs 17:22).*

CHRIST'S KINGDOM VERSUS THE WORLD

"Blessed are the poor in spirit" (Matthew 5:3).

"The kingdom of Heaven is at hand!" That's the announcement Jesus was making in Chapter 4. People were curious and intrigued. They flocked to hear their new "prophet," seeking answers to their question: how can I partake in this new kingdom?

So Jesus sat down on a mountainside and told them. The kingdom of Heaven was in direct opposition to worldly kingdoms, worldly values, worldly attitudes. Point by point Jesus pictured God's set of values, which always clash with the values of the world.

Those who enter Christ's kingdom are the poor in spirit—the people who recognize their need for God. The world, by contrast, takes pride in personal independence.

Kingdom people mourn because of their sin; worldly people claim they are all right.

Kingdom people are humble; the world values power and prestige.

Kingdom people have a yearning, a thirst, for God's righteousness; in the world, people are only concerned about their carnal desires.

Kingdom people are merciful; the world worships strength that destroys the weak.

Kingdom people are pure in heart; the heart of the world is corrupt to the core.

Kingdom people pursue peace; the world is at war and in chaos.

Kingdom people will be persecuted for pursuing these unworldly values—but they can rejoice and be exceeding glad, for a great reward awaits them in Heaven.

"The Lord shall deliver me from every evil work, and will preserve me unto his heavenly kingdom" (2 Timothy 4:18).

A DIFFERENT KIND OF RIGHTEOUSNESS

DAILY BIBLE READING: MATTHEW 5:17-20

"Except your righteousness shall exceed the righteousness of the scribes and Pharisees, ye shall in no case enter into the kingdom of heaven" (Matthew 5:20).

Jesus here is still speaking to a crowd that wonders how they can be a part of the kingdom of Heaven. "Don't misunderstand Me," He seems to say in verse 17. "I'm not going to abolish the law. The righteous law of God still stands." And that's still true today. The moral law of righteousness will never change.

How do you think people felt about what Jesus said in verse 20? "In fact," He said in effect, "if you wish to enter the kingdom of Heaven, your righteousness must be better than that of the Pharisees!" Jaws must have dropped in astonishment. Who could possibly keep the law better than the Pharisees? No one was more exacting and particular than they! The Pharisees could quote the law by heart; they were the last word in law-keeping.

But what Jesus really meant was that kingdom people need an altogether different kind of righteousness. Yes, the Pharisees were good at outwardly keeping the law. But what about their hearts? God knows our motives and attitudes. The only motive that counts in God's eyes is love and worship for Him.

This different kind of righteousness can issue only from God's work in our hearts. It does not depend on what we ourselves accomplish. Furthermore, this righteousness seeks only to reverence God. It is not mere "doing good" that aims to win the approval of other people.

Most important of all, kingdom righteousness goes deeper than law-keeping. It is based on the principles behind the law. Our greatest concern, then, is not what others see us doing. We are concerned about our attitudes. God sees the heart.

"For they being ignorant of God's righteousness, and going about to establish their own righteousness, have not submitted themselves unto the righteousness of God" (Romans 10:3).

HUMILITY BEFORE HONOR

DAILY BIBLE READING: 2 CHRONICLES 6:18-21

"Behold, heaven and the heaven of heavens cannot contain thee; how much less this house that I have built!" (2 Chronicles 6:18).

Picture the newly finished temple in all its gold-plated splendor. A vast tier of steps leads up to the holy place; at the top stands King Solomon, no doubt clad in a magnificent robe. For the congregation of Israel standing below, it must have been an imposing spectacle. But listen to the sermon Solomon delivers from that awe-inspiring summit. Are these the words of a conceited, self-satisfied man? No, not at all. To me, this address is a beautiful example of true humility.

Solomon's humility told him that his glorious temple was as nothing to the God who created the universe. Solomon asks, "Will God actually deign to dwell here, when in reality the heaven of heavens cannot contain Him?" In his meekness Solomon could scarcely conceive the thought.

Humble though the young King Solomon was, God bestowed enormous honor upon him. But that would not have happened had there not first been humility. The fear of the Lord precedes wisdom; humility precedes honor.

Solomon's humility was rewarded. By sending the Shekinah cloud, God did come to dwell in the temple prepared by the young king. Today we are the temple of the living God; but He will not dwell in us unless we are adorned with the spirit of humility.

One day we, too, shall receive honor beyond anything we can imagine—providing we lived a life of humility and faith here on earth.

"Whosoever shall exalt himself shall be abased [humbled]; and he that shall humble himself shall be exalted" (Matthew 23:12).

WHERE CAN GOD REST?

DAILY BIBLE READING: ISAIAH 66:1, 2

"Where is the place of my rest?" (Isaiah 66:1).

Yesterday we read how God graced the humble King Solomon's temple with His presence. Today, we find a plea from God: He is still in need of a dwelling place on earth. He still seeks on earth a place of rest.

The Jerusalem temple was destroyed hundreds of years ago. What can we offer God today? How can we prepare a dwelling for One whose throne is Heaven and whose footstool is the earth?

Verse 2 of this chapter gives the answer. It really is possible for us poor mortals to provide a dwelling place for the Most High. His chosen place is a contrite heart that is poor in spirit and that fears God. Though we cannot erect an ornate temple, this we can do: humbly we can bow before God, confess our sins, and receive His Holy Spirit in our penitent hearts. Thus we provide for Him both a throne and a footstool, right in our hearts.

The key is the same as it was in Solomon's day: humility opens the way for God to dwell with us. We all know the sad story of Solomon's later life, how pride overtook him, and he wandered away from the Lord. How earnestly we must watch and pray to guard against the pride that might destroy the lowly temple of our contrite hearts!

If we remain faithful, we can look forward to an eternal city where no temple is needed. John wrote of the New Jerusalem: "I saw no temple therein: for the Lord God Almighty and the Lamb are the temple of it" (Revelation 21:22).

"Behold, the tabernacle of God is with men, and he will dwell with them, and they shall be his people" (Revelation 21:3).

HE OFFERED FREEDOM

DAILY BIBLE READING: GENESIS 3:1-6

"The woman saw ... that it was ... a tree to be desired to make one wise" (Genesis 3:6).

We could say that the serpent was pretending to offer freedom. "God's pretty strict, making rules like that," Satan seems to say. "Why should God curb your freedom? Why must you be kept from the knowledge of good and evil? Come on! You were created with freedom of choice. Now be brave and exercise that freedom. Surely you want more knowledge—the knowledge of good and evil. It's yours for the taking!"

If you have ever felt restricted by rules, you may understand how Eve felt as she listened to Satan's wily offer. Freedom from rules and restrictions looked very appealing. After all, Satan was correct. She was free to choose. Free to disobey God.

Adam and Eve got what they wanted. Their choice certainly led to knowledge of good and evil—especially evil. But did they get freedom? True freedom? Had disobedience liberated them?

No, oh no. Disobedience did to Adam and Eve what it has done ever since. It brought them into bondage—the bondage of sin.

True freedom comes not from escaping rules and restrictions, but from true obedience. The obedience of love, the obedience of faith: that is what brings us to the only One who said, "If the Son therefore shall make you free, ye shall be free indeed" (John 8:36).

"Ye shall know the truth, and the truth shall make you free" (John 8:32).

HEALING TOUCH

DAILY BIBLE READING: DANIEL 10:7-11

"Understand the words that I speak unto thee, and stand upright" (Daniel 10:11).

By the time of Daniel's vision, he was more than eighty years old. God must have laid a very heavy burden upon Daniel's spirit, because we read earlier in this chapter that he fasted for three whole weeks.

At the end of those three weeks came this vision. If you want a description of the heavenly messenger Daniel saw, read verse 5 and 6. But our focus today is not on the vision, marvelous though it was; we want to look at how the vision affected Daniel.

It left him totally *without strength.* In fact, from verse 9 we gather that Daniel fainted and fell flat on his face.

Daniel was very *frightened.* Quite likely he was troubled, and his peace was disturbed. In verse 15 we find that Daniel was left speechless.

What a picture of *helplessness* Daniel was after that vision. Fearful, speechless, faint, without strength—flat on the ground.

But one touch from the Master's hand took care of all Daniel's ills. In the form of a messenger, God came and lifted Daniel up. He touched Daniel's lips so that he could speak. He brought reassurance for Daniel's fear and peace for his troubled heart.

Doesn't this remind us of Jesus when He lived on earth? All it took was a touch from His hand to heal whatever ailed the people. Nothing that befalls us is beyond the restoring power of Jesus!

"And the whole multitude sought to touch him: for there went virtue out of him, and healed them all" (Luke 6:19).

A MODEL FOR OUR PRAYERS

DAILY BIBLE READING: DANIEL 10:12, 13

"Thy words were heard" (Daniel 10:12).

Although the words *pray* and *prayer* are not actually used here, this chapter gives us a beautiful illustration of how the believer should pray. We can see five points.

First, Daniel prayed in *fear.* The fear of God is a necessary ingredient of our prayers.

Second, Daniel prayed with *fervor.* He had mourned for three whole weeks. Was that not an earnest petitioning? When the will of God is clear to us, how earnestly we may pray for its fulfillment!

Third, we see deep *humility.* Daniel chastened himself before God (verse 12).

Fourth, we see *boldness,* or confidence. Fear, fervency, and humility should always be combined with confidence: this God to whom we pray is our God (verse 12). As a child toward his parents, we can have complete confidence in Him.

Fifth, we see *expectancy* in Daniel's prayer. He expected a response—and it came.

Daniel's prayer was fully answered. A messenger from God assured him that his words were heard. In fact, Daniel's prayer had been heard even during those three long weeks of mourning when he may have felt that God was not listening at all. Daniel was told, "from the first day thou didst set thine heart to understand"—right from the beginning of his prayer—God's ears had been tuned.

"Let him ask in faith, nothing wavering" (James 1:6).

HOW GREAT IS GOD'S LOVE?

DAILY BIBLE READING: DANIEL 10:16-19

"O man greatly beloved, fear not" (Daniel 10:19).

"Fear not." The angel's message to Daniel is still God's message to us today, when we tremble before the unknown, or beneath a fiery trial. Fear not.

And why was Daniel not to fear? What takes away our fear? Why, the fact of God's love. We are greatly beloved. Why should we fear?

Do we realize how much God loves us? Probably not. Our finite minds are hardly elastic enough to grasp the length and the breadth and the height and the depth of God's love.

How much does God love us? He loved us so much that He gave His only begotten Son. He loved us so much that He went to the cross and shed His blood in terrible pain—for us. God loves us so much that He delivers us from the bondage of sin. He loves us so much that His tender pleas lead us to repentance. He loves us so much that He will not let us go.

How much does God love us? There are a few words in John 13:1 that give us a remarkable glimpse of God's love. Jesus, knowing He would soon leave this earth, "having loved his own which were in the world, he loved them unto the end."

Yes, even though He knew all His disciples' weaknesses, Jesus loved them to the end. Does that merely mean He loved than to the end of His earthly life? I do not think so. I think it means He loved than to the uttermost, to the full, into eternity.

How do we know? Because in John 15:9 Jesus told His disciples, "Continue ye in my love." His love has no end. It is eternal. So why should we fear?

"Behold, what manner of love the Father hath bestowed upon us" (1 John 3:1).

THE PIERCING WORD

DAILY BIBLE READING: LUKE 12:13-21

"For the word of God is quick, and powerful . . . piercing even to the dividing asunder of soul and spirit" (Hebrews 4:12).

You have probably heard this parable of the rich fool from Luke 12 since early childhood. Even as a schoolgirl, you could see the folly of trying to satisfy one's soul by building big barns.

Yes, this is a familiar parable; but I would like to ask, are we just as familiar with the occasion that prompted Jesus to tell this story? The occasion is significant because it demonstrates to us how God answers prayer. We're sometimes tempted to think He doesn't answer, but that's not true at all. We just fail to catch on to what His answers are. Read verses 13 and 14 in Luke 12 again. Here we see a man who wanted Jesus to help him with a personal problem. The man's brother was being selfish, refusing to share his father's estate with him.

At first glance we could think Jesus didn't even address the man's problem. In fact, He seems to change the subject. But no. Jesus was wielding the piercing "sword of the Word," cutting through the outer layers of the man's problem to its heart. What the man really needed was some teaching about covetousness! And so Jesus told him this parable of the rich fool.

Often I'm like that man with his estate problem. I get all tangled up in a thorny little problem. I bring it to God in prayer. I wait. I start thinking God isn't helping me at all. But if I remain open to His still, small voice, I will find that His piercing sword is at work, probing into my heart, uncovering the wrong motives that cause my problem.

That's God's way. He wants us to bring our problems to Him—but then He directs us to the big picture of obedience to His heavenly principles; in other words, of becoming "rich toward God." Let's thank Him for His piercing Word!

"Hath not God chosen the poor of this world rich in faith, and heirs of the kingdom which he hath promised to them that love him?" (James 2:5).

PLEASING OTHERS

DAILY BIBLE READING: 1 CORINTHIANS 10:31-33

"Even as I please all men in all things" (1 Corinthians 10:33).

This statement is really quite startling. Paul's main goal in life was to please others!

You know as well as I do that this goes against human nature. We tend to please ourselves first and foremost. We tend to be insensitive to those around us.

However, we need to strive in the power of the Holy Spirit against that me-first nature. Paul didn't just say that he tries to please others—he also exhorted every one of us to do the same. In verse 24 of this chapter, he says, "Let no man seek his own, but every man another's wealth [well-being]." And in Romans 15:2, 3, "Let every one of us please his neighbour for his good to edification. For even Christ pleased not himself."

How can we "please all men?" Should we be very sensitive and mostly do nothing for fear of displeasing someone? Or should we be easy-going and go along with everything in hopes of gaining everyone's approval?

Hardly. It is not men's approval, but God's, that we seek. To please others is not to seek their favor. Rather, our goal should be as Paul wrote in the verse above— "for his good to edification." This is clearly not something we can accomplish by ourselves. It will take the love of God and the power of the Holy Spirit.

"I am made all things to all men, that I might by all means save some" (1 Corinthians 9:22).

WHAT IS WORLDLINESS?

DAILY BIBLE READING: 1 JOHN 2:15-17

"Love not the world, neither the things that are in the world" (1 John 2:15).

We could say that the key message of these verses is "Don't be worldly!"

What should we do to keep from being worldly? Should we try to avoid worldly people, worldly places, and worldly activities?

That should help, of course. But did Jesus avoid all worldly people? Not really. He mingled with crowds of very worldly people. Yet we know He was never tainted with worldliness.

Outwardly avoiding worldly things, then, is not the only answer. According to what John wrote here, worldliness is most of all a matter of the heart. John portrays three worldly attitudes: cravings for physical pleasure, cravings for the things and the power of the world around us, and taking pride in what we have and can do.

Those are the temptations we face. And did you know that Jesus faced similar temptations during His wilderness test? The devil tempted Him with physical cravings, with cravings for power, and with pride—in other words, with worldliness.

Jesus passed the test. He said no to all the cravings and attitudes of the world. May Christ's power rule our hearts so that we can have a spirit of self-control, of generosity, and of humble service instead of "the lust of the flesh, and the lust of the eyes, and the pride of life."

"And they that use this world, as not abusing it: for the fashion of this world passeth away" (1 Corinthians 7:31).

WHEN WE ARE STRONG, WE ARE WEAK

DAILY BIBLE READING: MATTHEW 4:1-11

"If thou be the Son of God" (Matthew 4:3).

The devil knows there are two main circumstances when we are liable to succumb to temptation: when we are weak, and when we are strong.

That may sound like a contradiction. But let's look at the way the devil tempted Jesus, and we'll be able to understand.

On the one hand, we could say that the devil tempted Jesus when He was weak. Out in the desert, alone, hungry after days without food, probably tired—it's an understatement to say that Jesus, as a man, felt weak. You and I also know what it's like to be assailed by temptation when we're sleepless or sick or weary. The devil knows a weak moment when he sees one!

On the other hand, we could also say that the devil was attacking Jesus in the area of His strengths. "Are you the Son of God?" he challenged. "Then use your power. You could turn these stones to bread. You could make a big impression on the world by jumping from this pinnacle." And so on.

Jesus knew how wrong that would be, how detrimental to His mission of saving the world through sacrificial love. Jesus was able to spurn such insidious appeals to His strengths.

God gave strengths to you and me. But if we use those strengths wrongly—if we trust in our own abilities rather than God's strength—that's the devil's way of making us fall.

How can we avoid this? By always remembering that our strengths are gifts from God—and we need to dedicate them back to Him.

"When I am weak, then am I strong" (2 Corinthians 12:10).

REMEMBRANCE LEADS TO REALITY

DAILY BIBLE READING: 1 CORINTHIANS 11:23-26

"This do in remembrance of me" (1 Corinthians 11:24).

Reading these words raises a question: What does the Lord's Supper really mean to me?

The Lord's Supper is very deep and has many aspects. Today, let us look at the aspect the apostle shows forth in these few words: remembrance. Jesus Himself tells us to remember Him as we take the cup; it reminds us of Christ's blood shed on the cross. The broken bread reminds us of His body broken for our salvation. Sweet remembrance! We can never praise Him enough; we can never remember His sacrifice too often.

But does not this remembrance lead us on to something even deeper? Does it not bring home to us the reality of Christ's life and death, thus affecting our own lives at the deepest level?

This reality that we take to ourselves along with the cup and the bread...how shall we describe it? Perhaps Paul's words in Philippians 3:10 say it best: "That I may know him, and the power of his resurrection, and the fellowship of his sufferings, being made conformable unto his death."

The reality is that the life and death of Jesus must become our very own. Not only must we die with Him, but we must also live with Him. The old man must be truly crucified, and the new man truly alive! That's what Paul says in Galatians 2:20: "I am crucified with Christ: nevertheless I live; yet not I, but Christ liveth in me."

Remembrance of Christ's suffering is good and needful. But let us not stop there. Let the remembrance lead us on to real participation every day in the life and the death of Jesus.

"If we be dead with Christ, we believe that we shall also live with him" (Romans 6:8).

HOW CAN WE BE WORTHY?

DAILY BIBLE READING: 1 CORINTHIANS 11:27-29

"Wherefore whosoever shall eat this bread, and drink this cup of the Lord, unworthily, shall be guilty of the body and blood of the Lord" (1 Corinthians 11:27).

Many a person has been alarmed by this verse. What a terrible thing, to be guilty of the body and blood of Jesus!

Yet how can we be worthy? We look at ourselves, and we see failures; we see weakness; we see sin. We definitely do not see people who are worthy of this precious service that proclaims our oneness with Jesus.

If we view it from that angle, then the fact is that all of us are unworthy—always. But here is the answer to this seeming impossibility: in recognizing our unworthiness, we become worthy. Acknowledging our sin is what turns us in repentance to Jesus. All He desires of us is that we believe His gospel—His great, loving, sacrificial act of redemption on the cross—and apply it to ourselves. But how could we apply it to ourselves if we did not recognize our unworthiness?

That is one aspect of what renders us worthy. Another aspect is found in verse 29: "not discerning the Lord's body." What is the body of Christ? It is the church. The body of Christ is one. It has many members, yes; but they are one. So if I do not discern, or recognize, that oneness, if I think I can harbor in my heart a taint of dissension or disobedience, I am not discerning the true oneness of the Lord's body. I am not part of that oneness. All such taints must go if I want to be worthy to partake of the emblems of oneness.

"Examine yourselves, whether ye be in the faith; prove your own selves" (2 Corinthians 13:5).

NOT WITH ALL HIS HEART

DAILY BIBLE READING: 2 KINGS 10:29-31

"But Jehu took no heed to walk in the law of the LORD God of Israel with all his heart"
(2 Kings 10:31).

At first glance we might think that Jehu was a king after God's own heart. He certainly didn't lack zeal. When God told Jehu to accomplish something, he was up and at it with all the force of his aggressive nature.

For an example of Jehu's fiery zeal, we can read the previous chapter (2 Kings 9). His reign over Israel began when Elisha sent a young prophet to anoint him king. Along with the anointing, Jehu received orders: he was to completely exterminate the family of wicked King Ahab and get rid of Baal-worship in Israel.

Off went Jehu with his army to fulfill God's command. Apparently Jehu was known for his swift chariot-driving. One who saw him coming on this God-appointed errand commented, "The driving is like the driving of Jehu son of Nimshi; for he driveth furiously" (2 Kings 9:20).

Lots of zeal. Lots of action. Outwardly performing God's commands. Rebuking and punishing sin in other people's lives. Was that enough? Was Jehu truly a man after God's heart?

No. He lacked the most important quality. Heartfelt obedience was missing. Jehu was not careful to get rid of sin in his own life. He was not committed by faith to the Lord.

This is very sobering. It is possible for us to be doing God's work, being zealous for Him—and fall far short of what God desires. Unless our hearts are surrendered to Him in full obedience, we cannot be a true child of God.

"Thou shalt love the Lord thy God with all thy heart" (Matthew 22:37).

WHAT IS A BABY CHRISTIAN?

DAILY BIBLE READING: 1 CORINTHIANS 3:1-3

"I...could not speak unto you as unto spiritual, but as unto...babes in Christ" (1 Corinthians 3:1).

There is no such thing as a Christian baby. Babies are unable to have a saving faith in Jesus Christ. But according to Paul here in 1 Corinthians 3, it is possible for Christians to be babies! Obviously, he means a Christian who is spiritually immature—still a "babe" in the faith.

What are the characteristics of a baby? One thing is clear: a baby is totally controlled by its own desires. When a baby is hungry, it wants something to eat—*now!* Nothing else matters. When a baby wants a certain toy, it will insist upon having it. Two babies will quarrel when both want the same toy.

Did Paul see characteristics like that among these "baby" Corinthian Christians? Were they still controlled by their carnal desires instead of surrendering to God's will? Were they quarrelsome and divisive? Things like that are definite signs of spiritual immaturity.

Let's examine ourselves. We may have repented of our sins and been forgiven through Christ's blood—yet we still have to struggle against carnality. We may find that we still have self on the throne; daily we must remove self and choose to let the Lord reign. How stunted our growth will be if we try to serve both self and the Lord!

Do we want to stay "babes in Christ"? Or do we seek to grow up in Him?

"That we henceforth be no more children...but speaking the truth in love, may grow up into him in all things, which is the head, even Christ" (Ephesians 4:14, 15).

JUSTIFIED BY WORKS

DAILY BIBLE READING: JAMES 2:21-26

"Ye see then how that by works a man is justified" (James 2:24).

What? Are the apostles contradicting one another? Doesn't Paul state in Romans 3:28, "Therefore we conclude that a man is justified by faith without the deeds of the law"? Yet here James declares that we are justified by works.

No, it's not a contradiction. Let's take a closer look. Think about the meaning of the word *justify.* To be justified is to be pronounced righteous before God. That's a very special thing, and something we definitely don't deserve! With all our sins and failings, how could we possibly be considered righteous by our perfect God?

Yet it does happen. Because of Jesus, we truly can be justified—on one condition. We must have faith. We must believe that it is so. Paul's statement, therefore, is correct: we are justified by faith. What we do can never justify us. Only through believing and accepting God's grace are we justified.

But James is correct too. How so? Because true faith results in active obedience. True faith transforms our lives. Think about Abraham or Rahab—two people the Bible holds up as pioneers of faith. Their faith transformed their lives. From being a wealthy city dweller, Abraham faithfully followed God into the poverty and danger of wilderness life. From being a harlot, Rahab became one of God's people and eventually a link in the chain of ancestors that brought God's Son into the world.

It is true that faith justifies and brings salvation, yes; but it takes works to show that our faith is true. The love of God reflects from the heart of justified man in the form of faithful, loving service.

"For in Jesus Christ neither circumcision availeth anything, nor uncircumcision; but faith which worketh by love" (Galatians 5:6).

TWO GENEALOGIES

DAILY BIBLE READING: JAMES 1:15-18

"The Father of lights . . . of his own will begat he us" (James 1:17, 18).

This passage has so many facets that it could be compared to a diamond. Each facet is unique, each sparkles when touched by the light, and each offers nourishment for our spirits.

But we will focus on only one facet today. Has it occurred to you that this passage portrays genealogies? You know what a genealogy is: a list or chart of grandparents, parents, children, and grandchildren.

The first genealogy here in James 1 could be called the genealogy of sin. It is a very ugly portrait. Lust is the grandparent. Sin is the offspring of lust. And what is the offspring of sin—the grandchild of lust? Death. Sin gives birth to death. What a dark picture! It makes us shudder, because usually we think of birthdays as something joyful.

Let us turn quickly to the second genealogy, found in verses 17 and 18. First let's notice: there is no grandparent here. There is only a Father—the Father of lights. No darkness here either. And through His own blessed will He gives birth to—who? Why, to us! To the born-again believers, the firstfruits of the new creation, of faith.

Why are there no grandchildren? Because each new believer is begotten directly through the will of the Father of lights, the Father of our Lord Jesus Christ.

Glorious birth! Marvelous begetting! And if we truly are the Father's first fruits, may our life be as sweet as the sweetest grapes of paradise.

"Which were born, not of blood, nor of the will of the flesh, nor of the will of man, but of God" (John 1:13).

ONLY A HINT OF ETERNITY

DAILY BIBLE READING: REVELATION 21:10-12

"And he ... shewed me that great city, the holy Jerusalem" (Revelation 21:10).

In Revelation 21 and 22, we find the Bible's most comprehensive description of the eternal city. The soaring words picture for us a place filled with the glory of God, a city with a wall great and high, perched on a great and high mountain. But is this description complete? Are there enough words in any earthly language to describe eternity?

I think not. What we have here in Revelation are merely hints. Wonderful hints, to be sure: a city of pure gold transparent as glass; a place so bright with God's presence that no sunlight is required; a street watered with the crystal waters of the river of life. But still, only hints.

We don't need more. Why not? Because the Bible is filled with something far more important to us today. The Bible's main message is to explain how that eternal city can become ours. Our focus must mainly be on the advice and instructions God gives us in His Word.

You see, He wants to share His eternal city with us. He gives us those brief, tantalizing hints so we are drawn to seek Him. He pours four thousand years' worth of divine utterance and history into the Bible, so we can know the way to His city.

The gates stand open! God's Word—if we heed it—will take us through to the glory beyond.

"Who shall ascend unto the hill of the LORD? or who shall stand in his holy place? He that hath clean hands, and a pure heart" (Psalm 24:3, 4).

EVEN SO, COME, LORD JESUS

DAILY BIBLE READING: REVELATION 22:18-21

"Come . . . Surely I come . . . Even so, come" (Revelation 22:17, 20).

We look around at the evil, the immorality, the desperate problems of this world—and we all chime in with the desperate plea; "Lord Jesus, come!" We are those of whom Paul writes in Romans 8, who wait in "earnest expectation"— who "groan in pain"—looking forward to deliverance from the bondage of this present world.

The answer comes from the Lord Himself, warm and assuring: "Surely I come quickly."

Quickly? Doubt gnaws at our hearts. If Jesus told John two thousand years ago that He will come quickly, why are we still here today? We are tempted to be like the scoffers of 2 Peter 3, who scornfully claim, "all things continue as they were."

But that is not the response God desires of us. We must remember that we serve an eternal God, to whom time as we know it has no meaning. A thousand years in His sight are like a day—or a day like a thousand years. If He has said He will come quickly, then so it will be: "In a moment, in the twinkling of an eye" (1 Corinthians 15:52).

What then should be our response? It is there in the Bible's second-to-last verse. Let us echo it from the bottom of our hearts: "Amen. Even so, come, Lord Jesus." Amen and amen! So let it be. Only because of His grace can our response rise in a mighty chorus to the gates of Heaven: "Even so, come, Lord Jesus."

"Behold, I come quickly: hold that fast which thou hast, that no man take thy crown" (Revelation 3:11).

A FEW OF CHRIST'S "I AM'S"

DAILY BIBLE READING: REVELATION 22:16, 17

"I am the root . . . the offspring . . . the bright and morning star" (Revelation 22:16).

If we want to learn to know Jesus better, pay attention to what He calls Himself. In the Gospel of John, Jesus says "I am" in seven different ways, giving Himself titles such as *Good Shepherd, Bread of Life,* and *Resurrection.* Here in Revelation 22, we also find Jesus revealing some titles for Himself.

Jesus says He is both the Root and the Offspring of David. How can one person be both an ancestor and a descendant of another? Only Jesus can do it, because He is God the Creator—therefore the Source of David's being. But as we know, Jesus chose to become a man. As such He is David's Offspring—"Born of David's line," as the old hymn says. Let us praise this wonderful Creator who entered His creation in order to redeem!

The next title Jesus gives Himself has a double intent. Jesus is the "Morning Star" of salvation, breaking as a dawning light into the darkness of sin. He is also the Sun of the eternal day. As we read in Revelation 21, "the Lamb is the light thereof." Jesus, the Sun of the heavenly city, far exceeds the brightness of our present sun.

"I am Alpha and Omega." Jesus the Lord is the beginning and the end. Past, present, and future are all wrapped up in Him. May He be your all and mine from beginning to end.

Verse 17 implies the statement Jesus made directly in John 7:37: He is the water of life. And Jesus is the Coming One. He is real, and someday we shall see Him, gloriously arrayed in all His majestic titles!

"I am the first and the last: I am he that liveth, and was dead; and, behold, I am alive for evermore" (Revelation 1:17, 18).

THE RIGHT TO THE TREE OF LIFE

DAILY BIBLE READING: REVELATION 22:13-15

"That they may have right to the tree of life" (Revelation 22:14).

A right to the tree of life—such a great privilege! What gives us this right? According to these verses, the right to the tree of life is given to those who do the commandments of God.

We need to be careful how we understand these words. If we strive to be righteous in our own strength, does that mean we can say, "Now I have a right to the tree of life"? Or, to put the question another way, is our salvation by works? Is it because of my works that I can have the right to the tree of life?

No, no. Nothing that I can do will give me this great and blessed privilege. Nothing, that is, except to repent from my sin and hearken to the commandment of God: "Believe on the Lord Jesus Christ, and thou shalt be saved" (Acts 16:31).

The ancient Bible manuscripts don't all have the same wording for this passage. Some translations use an alternate wording: instead of, "Blessed are they that do his commandments," they say something like, "Blessed are they that have washed their robes."

Is this a contradiction? Does one translation speak of salvation by works and the other salvation by grace? Not at all. Both speak of the same thing—the grace of God. It is the grace of God that produces faith and obedience in us; so ultimately, it is the grace of God that gives us the "right to the tree of life."

"The fruit of the righteous is a tree of life" (Proverbs 11:30).

THE TIME IS AT HAND

DAILY BIBLE READING: REVELATION 22:10-12

"Seal not the sayings . . . for the time is at hand" (Revelation 22:10).

These verses remind me of Daniel 12, where we see Michael the archangel standing before all the world's people, in his hand a book. What a book that is! All those whose names are written therein will arise at the last day to eternal life.

In Daniel's time, that great book of testing was not opened. "Shut up the words, and seal the book, even to the time of the end" (Daniel 12:4). Daniel's glimpse of the Judgment Day told of something yet to come. For the time being, for the intervening centuries, the great book was to remain sealed.

But in Revelation we see a dramatic difference. The angel cries to John, "Don't seal the book! The time has now arrived! Judgment Day is here."

Such an immediate, present view of the last day sends a shudder through our souls. And well it may, for there is a definite ring of finality to the words. Once that day is here, nothing can be changed. The unjust must remain unjust. Repentance will no longer be an option.

Here's a comforting thought though: the opposite is also true. Those who wear robes washed clean in the blood of the Lamb shall surely be found righteous. By the grace of God let us be holy, let us be righteous, so that we may be ready on the final day.

"But the end of all things is at hand: be ye therefore sober, and watch unto prayer" (1 Peter 4:7).

HOW TO BE A STAR

DAILY BIBLE READING: DANIEL 12:2, 3

"And they that be wise shall shine as . . . the stars for ever and ever" (Daniel 12:3).

In today's world, many people aspire to be "stars": movie stars, rock stars, or famous and rich in some other field. They think that will be fulfilling.

But such "stardom" is only temporary—and false to the core. By contrast, these two exquisite verses tell us how to achieve true stardom, one that lasts forever.

What an amazing thing, that mere humans can one day shine as stars! Jesus Himself gave us this promise of the resurrection: "Then shall the righteous shine forth as the sun in the kingdom of their Father" (Matthew 13:43). Paul wrote at least three times of the marvelous change that takes place in the resurrection. In 1 Corinthians 15:43, he wrote this of our body: "It is sown in dishonour; it is raised in glory." Then in Philippians 3:21 he told us that Christ "shall change our vile body, that it may be fashioned like unto his glorious body." And in Colossians 3:4 he declared, "When Christ, who is our life, shall appear, then shall ye also appear with him in glory."

But, going back to Daniel 12, we notice it is only the wise and the righteous who will become stars. How can weak humans have the wisdom and righteousness to make our lives radiant through eternity?

There is only one way. We are like the moon; of ourselves we have no shining, no radiance. Our faces must be turned toward God, that great Light. "But we all, with open face beholding as in a glass the glory of the Lord, are changed into the same image from glory to glory, even as by the Spirit of the Lord" (2 Corinthians 3:18). The New International Version uses these words: "And we, who with unveiled faces all reflect the Lord's glory, are being transformed into his likeness with ever-increasing glory, which comes from the Lord, who is the Spirit."

"They looked unto him, and were lightened" (Psalm 34:5).

A ROBE AND A SEED

DAILY BIBLE READING: MATTHEW 22:11-14

"Friend, how camest thou in hither not having a wedding garment?" (Matthew 22:12).

You know how this parable of Christ's begins. A certain king prepared a wedding banquet, but the guests he originally invited refused to come. So the king sent his servants out into the byways to invite everybody and anybody: a picture of God's invitation to all—"whosoever will"—to partake of the salvation He offers.

The poor and needy flocked to the king's banquet. But unless they received the wedding garments provided by their host, the guests could not stay.

What does this wedding garment signify? We can find the answer to that question in Isaiah 61:10. "My soul shall be joyful in my God; for he hath clothed me with the garments of salvation, he hath covered me with the robe of righteousness." The righteousness of Christ is the garment which allows us to stay for the banquet. When we repent of our sins and put our trust in the One who died as a ransom for sin, we may partake of God's bounteous provision at the wedding feast.

What proves that we have received this robe of righteousness? The next verse has the answer: "As the garden causeth the things that are sown in it to spring forth; so the Lord GOD will cause righteousness and praise to spring forth" (Isaiah 61:11). The righteousness God gives us through faith in Christ is not only like a robe, but also like a seed. It will grow and "spring forth" in our lives in the form of praise and good works that glorify God.

"For he hath made him to be sin for us, who knew no sin; that we might be made the righteousness of God in him" (2 Corinthians 5:21).

SHEPHERD OF THE STARS

DAILY BIBLE READING: ISAIAH 40:26, 27

"Why sayest thou, O Jacob, and speakest, O Israel, My way is hid from the LORD, and my judgment is passed over from my God?" (Isaiah 40:27).

We may sometimes feel rather like Jacob, or Israel, in these verses. Jacob seems to be asking God, "Why don't you see my troubles? Why do you ignore me?" We may get the feeling that God doesn't concern Himself with our little trials and cares. Though we don't say it in so many words, secretly we wonder whether He even wants to help us.

It's time to read verse 26 and do as Isaiah bids us: "Look up into the heavens at night. Think about the One who created all those stars—millions of them. And God knows each individual star. He has a name for each one."

Isaiah is very poetic, comparing the stars with a vast flock of sheep. God is their Shepherd. He "bringeth out their hosts by number." So great is the Shepherd's power that not one sheep will be lacking—not one star will fall.

Now let's see ourselves as part of that vast flock in the tender care of the Shepherd. If He knows every star by name, does He not also know each of us? Does He not care about every detail of our lives? If He guides the stars in their heavenly orbits, does He not desire to guide and lead us?

Oh, we of little faith. We pain the loving heart of God if we start thinking He doesn't care. Of course He cares! He is like a shepherd, carrying each lamb close to His bosom.

"He shall gather the lambs with his arm, and carry them in his bosom, and shall gently lead those that are with young" (Isaiah 40:11).

A GENERIC NAME

DAILY BIBLE READING: LUKE 23:18, 19

"Release unto us Barabbas" (Luke 23:18).

Who was Barabbas? He was a criminal. Reading the four Gospel accounts, we see that Barabbas was guilty of the worst crimes: treason, murder, robbery.

But who *was* he? Does his name give us any idea what family he came from? Many Bible names indicate parentage. For instance, *Simon Bar-Jonah* was Simon son of Jonah. So what does the name *Barabbas* mean? Divide it into two parts, *Bar-Abbas,* and it simply means "son of father."

If ever there was a generic name, Barabbas must be one. *Generic* is a word that means "describing an entire group or class." In other words, Barabbas means you. It means me. It means all mankind. We're all sons or daughters of our fathers.

And in another very real sense also, you and I are Barabbas. We are sinners, guilty, deserving of a death sentence. But, like Barabbas, we have been released. Set free. Why? Because Jesus, the innocent One, suffered for us, going to the cross to die.

Did Barabbas perhaps go to Golgotha that terrible afternoon? Did he witness the suffering of Jesus? Did he say in his heart, "That should have been me"?

We don't know if Barabbas did that. But you and I should definitely do it. We should view the cross daily and realize it is ourselves who deserved death. And we should be eternally grateful to the One who made us truly "sons of the Father" through faith.

"That they may be blameless and harmless, the sons of God" (Philippians 2:15).

Day 285

BORN OF ENVY

DAILY BIBLE READING: COLOSSIANS 3:8

"Put off... malice" (Colossians 3:8).

Today we want to focus on a single word in the reading: *malice*. What is malice? How is it different from anger, wrath, or hatred?

The dictionary says that malice is wanting to see others suffer. For examples of malice in the Bible, we could turn to John 12:10, where we find the Jews wanting to kill Lazarus. Or to Acts 7:54-60, where the Jews wanted to kill Stephen. We could go all the way back to the Book of Esther, where Haman wanted to destroy the whole Jewish race.

In each of these instances, if we tried to put a finger on the underlying cause of malice, we might settle upon the word *envy*. Is it not true that malice is often born of envy? Does not human nature, when it is envious of another's fortune, wish to see that person suffer?

This brings us to the Bible's most dramatic instance of malice, in Matthew 27. I cannot picture a group of people more filled with malice than those outraged Jews who demanded the death of Christ.

What gave birth to their malice? Even Pilate recognized the root cause: "He knew that for envy they had delivered him" (Matthew 27:18). These people had heard the hosannas when the triumphant King entered Jerusalem. They were filled to the brim with envy, and the resulting malice wanted only to destroy Jesus.

Malice, then, is a terrible thing. Oh, let us guard our hearts! At the slightest sign of envy, let us be rid of it—lest it lead to malice.

"Wherefore laying aside all malice" (1 Peter 2:1).

CAREFULLY WITH TEARS

DAILY BIBLE READING: HEBREWS 12:16, 17

"He found no place of repentance, though he sought it carefully with tears" (Hebrews 12:17).

Have these verses ever puzzled you? Have you wondered whether it's actually possible to come to the place where repentance is not an option?

Before we answer that question, let's ask another. Was Esau really seeking true repentance? I don't think so. True repentance means a desire to forsake sin. Esau had no desire to forsake his sin. Also, he wanted to kill Jacob: more proof that he wasn't truly repenting.

So what were Esau's tears for? They definitely were not tears of true repentance. Instead, they were merely tears of regret that he had lost the birthright and that he could not change his father's mind. Basically, the "repentance" Esau sought was a repentance on his father's side, a change of mind that would let Esau have the birthright after all.

What a grave message is here for us! We need true repentance, the repentance that desires to forsake sin, that is willing to take up the cross and follow Jesus.

True repentance opens the door to God's mercy. If we do not repent now, we will one day be as Esau, crying in vain with bitter tears of regret, wishing our Father would change His mind. We will be like the scoffers who pounded on the door of the ark while floodwaters rose around them. Then the time for repentance will be past.

"And ye returned and wept before the LORD; but the LORD would not hearken to your voice, nor give ear into you" (Deuteronomy 1:45).

A GREAT NAME

DAILY BIBLE READING: GENESIS 11:4; 12:2

"I will bless thee, and make thy name great" (Genesis 12:2).

Both of these chapters speak about having a great name. Genesis 11 shows us the human way of trying to "make a name" for oneself. Human nature says, "I want to be important." The people on the plain of Shinar wanted to be important, so they built themselves a tower.

We all know what happened to those people. God put an abrupt end to their rebellious plans, annihilating the name they sought to make for themselves. "For whosoever exalteth himself shall be abased," says Jesus in Luke 14:11.

In Genesis 12 we see a completely different attitude. Abraham definitely wasn't out to make himself a great name. In fact, he was willing to completely forsake his name by leaving home and family and starting out with faith in God as his only guide.

But God wanted to give Abraham a great name. Why? Simply because Abraham was willing to forsake all greatness and humbly obey God. Jesus also said in Luke 14:11, "He that humbleth himself shall be exalted."

What a contrast! In Genesis 11 we see the old nature, striving for human greatness. In Genesis 12 we see the old nature crucified, humbly receiving the "great name" given to all repentant, believing, obedient hearts: sons of God and heirs of Christ.

"That we should be called the sons of God" (1 John 3:1).

IN SPITE OF THE BARRIERS

DAILY BIBLE READING: MATTHEW 8:5-7

"There came unto him a centurion" (Matthew 8:5).

When I think of all the barriers that could have kept this centurion from coming to Jesus, I am amazed that he actually did. After all, a centurion was a Roman soldier—quite a prestigious man. To think that he came in humble supplication to a wandering Jewish teacher! *Pride* could have prevented him from approaching Jesus.

Doubt could also have been a barrier. The centurion could have asked himself, "Will it be worth the trouble? Is that rabbi's healing power really all that people seem to think it is?"

Another barrier might have been *lack of time.* Centurions were busy people. He could have decided it would take far too much time to travel all the way to Capernaum and find the rabbi.

Self-sufficiency might have hindered him. The centurion could have thought, "I'll try my own doctors first; or we might check out some home remedies to see if we can heal this servant on our own."

But the centurion did not allow any of those barriers to keep him from Jesus. He came, and he came in faith. The rewards were great.

The devil is very good at setting up barriers between us and Jesus. He wants our pride, or our busyness, or our doubts, or our self-sufficiency, to hinder our relationship with God. Let's be like the centurion: come to Jesus, and come in faith.

"As thou hast believed, so be it done unto thee" (Matthew 8:13).

SPEAK THE WORD ONLY

DAILY BIBLE READING: MATTHEW 8:5-10

"Speak the word only, and my servant shall be healed" (Matthew 8:8).

Over telephone wires or across radio waves, a word spoken by humans can flash around the world in seconds. Our spoken words can accomplish amazing things in this age of technology.

But there is a Word far more amazing, far more powerful, than the human word. This is the eternal Word, of which John says, "In the beginning was the Word, and the Word was with God, and the Word was God" (John 1:1). John goes on to declare that all things were created by this Word.

We cannot fathom it. God had only to speak His powerful word—and the universe came into being.

Even more amazing, this powerful eternal Word came to earth in the form of a man and dwelt among humans as Jesus Christ. During that earthly sojourn, the Word was active and powerful, preaching and healing.

The centurion in our reading recognized the power of Christ's word, for he was himself a man who only needed to speak a word to have his command carried out. "There's no need for you to come," the centurion protested when Jesus offered to walk the distance to his home. "Just speak the word!"

This little happening shows the key that can release the power of the eternal Word in our own lives. The key is faith. Because the centurion believed, the Word flashed out its healing power.

"He sent his word, and healed them, and delivered them from their destructions" (Psalm 107:20).

THE DEVILS BELIEVE

DAILY BIBLE READING: MATTHEW 8:28-34

"What have we to do with thee, Jesus, thou Son of God?" (Matthew 8:29).

Matthew 8 is a chapter that radiates God's power. In it we see our Creator God walking among humans, cleansing a leper, healing a servant, driving out a fever, stilling the sea—and finally, conquering the devil's power.

It seems that everyone watching Jesus perform these miracles would surely realize that He is divine. Yet here is a sobering question: who in this chapter best recognized Jesus as Creator and God? Was it humans—or was it the devils?

The people around Jesus seemed so shortsighted. Yes, they witnessed His healing acts; yet when a crisis arose—such as a storm at sea—little real faith was evident. "O ye of little faith," Jesus mourned in verse 26. In verse 10 He implies that He has not seen much faith among His own people.

Back to that sobering question—who recognized Jesus for who He was? It was the devils who clearly saw Him as the Son of God. They were a striking testimony to the words in James 2:19: "The devils also believe, and tremble."

As for the people who watched Jesus destroy those devils, did they display any faith at all? No! They asked Jesus to leave.

How sad. We think, "Surely I wouldn't have done that. If our Creator were here today, I wouldn't send Him away."

But wait. Our Creator *is* here. Daily He probes our hearts, seeking to rid us of vices and sin. Do we resist Him? Do we wish He would leave us alone? Are we reluctant to let Him uncover those dark places still lurking in us? Perhaps we are no better than the Gergesenes, who "besought him that he would depart out of their coasts" (Matthew 8:34).

Instead, let's be like the disciples at Emmaus, who "constrained him, saying, Abide with us" (Luke 24:29).

"Abide in me, and I in you" (John 15:4).

THE SMALL POINTS TO THE GREAT

DAILY BIBLE READING: 2 CORINTHIANS 9:12-15

"Thanks be unto God for his unspeakable gift" (2 Corinthians 9:15).

We might wonder why Paul spends so much time talking about the Macedonian believers' gift to the Jerusalem believers. Why is Paul so preoccupied with finances? Is money really so important to him?

I don't think the money itself was important to Paul. By concentrating on the Macedonians' financial gifts, he is bringing out some very important aspects about God and our relationship to Him.

For one thing, Paul shows us how essential thanksgiving is in the Christian life. In verses 11 and 12 he's saying, "Your giving results in abundant thanksgiving." Few things enrich our lives more than a well of thanksgiving springing up in our hearts. For, as Paul points out in verse 13, it is in thanksgiving that we glorify God. What's more, Paul is saying that by our cheerful, bountiful giving we reflect the heart of God. Was there ever a giver who could match the eternal Giver—the One who gives us all things, including life itself? Read verse 8 and notice the words *all* and *every.* All! Everything! Abounding! Sufficient! Paul seems hardly able to find words to describe God's giving.

Considering God's unbounded giving, we realize there can be no such thing as a stingy Christian. We are one with Christ; therefore, we must become like Him. Stinginess is not one of Christ's attributes.

In the final verse we catch a glimpse of Paul's ultimate reason for extolling the Macedonians' generosity. Their giving points us to the greatest gift of all: Jesus Christ, given to the world as the Saviour of mankind.

"Every good gift and every perfect gift is from above, and cometh down from the Father of lights" (James 1:17).

THE BOOK OF SALVATION

DAILY BIBLE READING: ISAIAH 61:10, 11

"He hath clothed me with the garments of salvation" (Isaiah 61:10).

If I were to ask you which book of the Bible could be called the *book of salvation*, you could probably name any one. Certainly any of the four Gospels could be called a *book of salvation*, because they tell the salvation story. Today, however, we shall call Isaiah the *book of salvation*. Why? The Hebrew name *Isaiah* means "salvation."

If you've ever tried to read the Book of Isaiah, you may have found it difficult. Many parts are hard to understand.

Sometimes it's good to take a greatly simplified view. Isaiah has 66 chapters. The Bible has 66 books. There are 39 books in the Old Testament, and 27 in the new. Amazingly enough, the first 39 chapters of Isaiah pronounce judgment on sinful humanity, whereas the next 27 are filled with the hope of salvation. So we could say that Isaiah corresponds with the whole Bible, which certainly makes it a book of salvation.

Here are some of the beautiful references to salvation we find in Isaiah: "But Israel shall be saved in the LORD with an everlasting salvation" (Isaiah 45:17).

"Therefore his arm brought salvation unto him" (Isaiah 59:16). Picture the arm of God reaching out, through Jesus Christ, to save the world from sin. In the very next verse (59:17) we read of the "helmet of salvation." God's arm provides the whole armor of salvation for us.

Isaiah 62:1 gives us a vivid picture of the light of salvation: "I will not rest, until . . . the salvation thereof [go forth] as a lamp that burneth."

"Thus saith the LORD, In an acceptable time have I heard thee, and in a day of salvation have I helped thee" (Isaiah 49:8).

BRIDE AND GROOM

DAILY BIBLE READING: REVELATION 19:7-9

"Blessed are they which are called unto the marriage supper of the Lamb" (Revelation 19:9).

These verses provide a lovely picture of the heavenly wedding feast. Though we are not told in so many words who the Bridegroom or bride are, we know from other Bible passages that Jesus is the Bridegroom and the church His bride.

The heavenly Bridegroom loved the church so much that He died for her. "Even as Christ also loved the church, and gave himself for it" (Ephesians 5:25).

The bride causes the Bridegroom to rejoice. "As the bridegroom rejoiceth over the bride, so shall thy God rejoice over thee" (Isaiah 62:5).

The Bridegroom's great love covers all the defects (sin) of the bride. "Thou art all fair, my love; there is no spot in thee" (Song of Solomon 4:7).

And one day the Bridegroom will come to claim His bride. "Behold, the Bridegroom cometh; go ye out to meet him" (Matthew 25:6).

What do we read about the bride? From today's reading we know that she has been purified and is dressed in spotless white robes. Isaiah 61:10 implies that the bride is adorned with jewels—the jewels of righteousness. All this was made possible through the redeeming love of the Bridegroom.

Still, the bride feels her unworthiness. "Look not upon me, for because I am black" she says in Song of Solomon 1:6. Unworthy or not, the bride dearly loves the Bridegroom. "My beloved is mine, and I am his" (Song of Solomon 2:16).

And who issues the invitations to that glad marriage supper? Why, the bride. It is up to the church—through the power of the Spirit—to make sure that all know they may come.

"And the Spirit and the bride say, Come" (Revelation 22:17).

HOW DO WE RESPOND TO REPROOF?

DAILY BIBLE READING: MARK 6:17-20

"For Herod himself had sent forth and laid hold upon John, and bound him in prison" *(Mark 6:17).*

Here is a riddle for you: How is Herod Antipas like the Jewish religious leaders?

Here is the answer: To both Herod and the Jewish leaders, God sent a man who reproved them for their sin. Both Herod and the Jews responded in the same way. Instead of getting rid of the sin, they got rid of the man who showed it to them!

Consider Herod. God sent John the Baptist to tell Herod that he had sinned by marrying his brother's wife. Herod put John in prison, hoping to shut up the voice of reproof. Eventually he even had John killed. But did Herod ever really get rid of his sin? No; his life remained troubled and uneasy.

As for the Jewish religious leaders, we know whom God sent to reprove them: His own Son. How many times did Jesus boldly point out their sin and hypocrisy? We also know how the Jewish leaders tried to get rid of Christ's reproof. They had Him crucified.

You and I are also like Herod and the Jewish leaders, in that we have sin in our lives. We need reproof. God is faithful; He has ways to reprove and point out our sin. How do we respond? Do we eradicate the sin—or do we merely try to get rid of the reproof?

King David, who once received a very sharp reproof from the prophet Nathan, is our example. He recognized and repented of his sin.

"And David said unto Nathan, I have sinned against the Lord" (2 Samuel 12:13).

HOW TO RECEIVE THE INHERITANCE

DAILY BIBLE READING: MARK 10:17-22

"What shall I do that I may inherit eternal life?" (Mark 10:17).

The rich young ruler's question reveals one right concept and one wrong concept. His concept of eternal life was right. Eternal life is an inheritance, an undeserved gift that we receive by becoming the children of God.

But the young man's concept of how to receive that inheritance was wrong. "What shall I do?" he asked. We gather that he was thinking, *I've kept the Law—I must be a good candidate for eternal life.*

Jesus looked lovingly upon this young man. We can imagine Him wondering how to show this man how far off the mark he was. How could he be made to see that receiving the inheritance was not primarily a matter of doing the Law? That it was rather a matter of letting go and having faith?

So Jesus probed the young man's weakest spot. He asked him to give up his wealth so that he could honor the first commandment—loving God with all our heart, soul, and mind. Jesus invited the young ruler to take up his cross and follow Him.

This young man had come into Jesus' presence asking what he could do. He came strong and self-confident. But now, faced with a demand on his cherished wealth, he could not let go. He walked away sorrowful and greatly humbled. He had thought he could do anything for the sake of inheriting eternal life. Yet Jesus had confronted him with the one thing he could not—or would not—do.

So the young ruler turned and went away. In so doing, he walked away from eternal life. Let us be willing to give ourselves up completely to Jesus! In so doing, we tear down the barriers that would keep us from our inheritance in Heaven.

"Blessed be the God and Father of our Lord Jesus Christ, which according to his abundant mercy hath begotten us again unto a lively hope by the resurrection of Jesus Christ from the dead, to an inheritance incorruptible . . . reserved in heaven for you" (1 Peter 1:3, 4).

AN IRONIC SIGN

DAILY BIBLE READING: LUKE 23:35-38

"A superscription also was written over him...THIS IS THE KING OF THE JEWS" *(Luke 23:38).*

My dictionary explains *irony* as the use of words to convey the opposite of their literal meaning. So we could say that the sign placed on Christ's cross was meant to be ironic. Surveying this broken, bleeding Man as He hung on the cross, the onlookers could have said, "Ha! King of the Jews? If ever He was a king, He is stripped of His kingdom now."

Today, when we see signs along the road, we do not expect them to be ironic. A sign posting a speed limit of sixty miles per hour does not mean that you should drive twice that speed. Signs mean exactly what they say.

The Romans who put that sign on the cross may have meant it ironically. But the irony was totally different from what they thought—the sign actually conveyed the greatest truth in the universe! That sign above Christ's head was literally, majestically true. Christ is King! And not only King of the Jews, but of all creation.

Neither the Romans nor the Jews grasped what kind of kingdom Christ's is. It is completely different from the world's kingdoms. In fact, Christ's has been called the "upside-down kingdom," because that is how it appears to the world. Through His ignoble death on the cross, Jesus conquered all His enemies and mounted the throne as supreme ruler of the universe.

Thus we might say that Jesus on the cross was the quintessential irony. Life through death. Victory through defeat. And we all want a part in this life that begins by dying!

"That through death he might destroy him that had the power of death" (Hebrews 2:14).

GUARDIAN CHERUBIM

DAILY BIBLE READING: EXODUS 26:31-34

"And thou shalt make a veil . . . with cherubims shall it be made" (Exodus 26:31).

Did you know that there were cherubim embroidered on the veil that hung between the holy place and the holy of holies in the temple? Those cherubim remind us of the cherubim we read about in Genesis 3:24: "So he drove out the man; and he placed at the east of the garden of Eden Cherubims, and a flaming sword which turned every way, to keep [guard] the way of the tree of life."

In these two instances, the cherubim, some of God's mighty angels, served as guardians. They guarded the gate of Eden so that no sinful person could access the tree of life. The embroidered cherubim on the heavy dividing veil remind us that sinful man is separated from God. Unredeemed man cannot enter the holy of holies because it is guarded by God's cherubim.

What a sad and hopeless case it would be if the story ended there! We could not possibly get past those mighty angels into the presence of God. Because of our sin we would be barred forever from the holiness of Heaven.

But praise God, through Jesus we have hope. On the day Jesus gave His life—on the day His flesh was torn and bleeding—the heavy dividing veil with its guardian angels was torn in two. The way was opened! We can go back to Eden—back to the heart of God, back to the One who gave His Son because He loved us enough to remove the grim guards that stand between Him and sinful humanity.

Today we can fly to the mercy seat. And there too we will find God's cherubim. Now they are not wielding a flaming sword—their wings are outstretched to welcome the penitent sinner.

"And over it the cherubims of glory shadowing the mercyseat" (Hebrews 9:5).

SIN MISUSES THE LAW

DAILY BIBLE READING: ROMANS 7:10-12

"Sin ... by the commandment ... slew me" (Romans 7:11).

It's sad, but it's true. Sin takes God's commandments and uses, or misuses, them to kill us—spiritually, that is. It happened in the Garden of Eden, and it has been happening ever since. Satan persuaded Eve to forget all the lovely things God had provided, focusing instead on that one commandment. Wielding the commandment like an instrument of torture, Satan persuaded Eve to rebel.

We, too, become rebels if we have a narrow view of God's commandments. They appear restrictive to us, and even unfair. We rebel at the way God's commandments seem to hinder our freedom. And as soon as we rebel, we are spiritually dead. Do you see what happens? Sin, by misusing the commandments, kills us.

But, oh, there is a much better way to view God's commandments. We must allow our focus to be much, much wider so that we can see God's love and goodness. (If only Eve hadn't forgotten all the other beautiful trees in Eden to start harping on the one forbidden tree!)

Viewed in the perspective of God's great love, His commandments are not instruments of death at all. Instead, as we read in verse 12, the law is holy and just and good! We recognize that God's law has one purpose: to keep us from harm. If God says, "Don't do this," it's because doing it would damage us spiritually. If God says, "Do that," it's because the doing will lead to a greater realization of God and His love.

"I delight in the law of God after the inward man" (Romans 7:22).

OUR PRAYERS DELIGHT HIM

DAILY BIBLE READING: PROVERBS 15:8, 9

"The prayer of the upright is his delight" (Proverbs 15:8).

Isn't this amazing? God actually delights in the prayer of an upright person! We may picture God leaning forward, inclining His ear, stretching forth His hand—in every possible way, God welcomes those prayers.

But that is where a large question looms up in our minds. Who can stand upright before God? I am not upright. I am a sinner. How could God possibly take delight in my prayers?

Here is the first key to resolving this troubling question: in our own strength we cannot stand upright before God. The only way we can approach Him is on our knees, in the dust, repenting of our sins.

Then a wonderful thing happens. That very repentance puts us in touch with the Saviour. We are one with Christ. He is in us, and we are in Him. His righteousness becomes ours! In Christ, then, we become upright. That is how our prayer can be a delight to God—if we pray in the name of His Son.

That's why Hebrews tells us, "Let us draw near with a true heart in full assurance of faith, having our hearts sprinkled from an evil conscience" (Hebrews 10:22). Faith makes the connection; we must dare to believe that Christ's blood cleanses us and makes us upright before God. So let us yield ourselves to God in prayer, and He can use us for His purpose.

"For the Father seeketh such to worship him" (John 4:23).

REND YOUR HEARTS

DAILY BIBLE READING: JOEL 2:12, 13

"Rend your heart, and not your garments" (Joel 2:13).

Here Joel shows us two vivid pictures of repentance: one picture is of pretended, outward repentance; the other of true, heartfelt repentance.

This rending of garments is an Old Testament practice. People used to do it as an outward show of remorse or repentance. To us it seems slightly silly: getting so emotional that we actually grab our clothing and tear it. If that was as far as the person's remorse went—an outward tearing of clothes—it had little value before God. "Man looketh on the outward appearance, but the Lord looketh on the heart" (1 Samuel 16:7).

True repentance is so much more! When we are truly sorry for our sin, truly sorry for offending God, truly sorry for having wronged ourselves and others—then something happens that has far more power than ripping our clothing.

Joel's way of describing this event is simple yet direct. True repentance is a tearing of the heart. The psalmist calls it a "broken and a contrite heart" (Psalm 51:17), likening it to a sacrifice. Now that's a dramatic picture! The heart must be torn from the carnal bosom and cast in faith upon the altar of offering. There the keen, two-edged sword of God's Word must do its work, rending the heart wide open to receive the love and mercy of God.

Anyone can rend his clothes. But to rend the heart—that can take place only through the power of the Holy Spirit, by the love and grace of God.

"The Lord is nigh unto them that are of a broken heart" (Psalm 34:18).

NOT BECAUSE WE ARE SPECIAL

DAILY BIBLE READING: DEUTERONOMY 7:6-9

"The Lord did not set his love upon you...because ye were more in number" (Deuteronomy 7:7).

"I didn't save you because you were special," God says. And from a human viewpoint the tiny nation of Israel was hardly worthy of notice. Israel was probably one of the world's smallest nations at the time. So why did God go to all that trouble to save them?

It's true that Israel had the status of being "God's chosen people," since they were descended from Abraham. Yet where on earth could a more perverse people be found? Despite God's choosing and care, Israel seemed bound to stray, bound to disobey, bound to do everything they should not.

So why did God redeem from the bondage of Egypt this perverse, disobedient, decidedly un-special multitude?

And here is the answer: God didn't save them because they were special. They were special because God saved them! God had His reasons for saving Israel. But these reasons came from within His own great heart, not from any merit on the people's part. God's reasons were based on a love that we can never fathom and a mercy greater than the furthest stretch of our imagination.

All this is true of you and me. As believers, we are God's chosen and special people. But did He choose us and save us and redeem us because we're special? Because we deserve it? Because our good works merit it? Did He save us because we are worth more than others around us?

Definitely not. He redeems us because He loves us.

"For by grace are ye saved ... not of works, lest any man should boast" (Ephesians 2:8, 9).

THE RIGHT HAND

DAILY BIBLE READING: ISAIAH 41:10-13

"I will uphold thee with the right hand of my righteousness" (Isaiah 41:10).

Notice the repeated emphasis on the "right hand." In verse 10, God's right hand upholds us. In verse 13 He holds us by our right hand. I don't think this is intended to exalt the right hand over the left. The "right hand" is just a symbol of excellence, of superiority. So in saying that God holds us with His right hand, Isaiah is emphasizing how great and wonderful is God's care for us.

Is there anywhere we would rather be than held fast in the right hand of God's righteousness? His righteousness is unwavering and totally faithful, unlike the righteousness of man, which can (and does) flicker and fade and disappoint. God's righteousness is eternal!

Because of God's righteousness, we need not fear. Did you notice? The first verse of today's reading began with "Fear thou not." The last verse ends with "Fear not: I will help thee." God helps us just as a father helps his child who clings to his hand.

Humanly speaking, it's not logical for a father and his child to walk along, right hand in right hand. Wouldn't that be awkward?

But there's nothing awkward about God's right hand holding my right hand. I believe this only emphasizes the mysterious greatness of God's power. His care for us exceeds human logic.

So, even though the circumstances and the evidences may seem to the contrary, let's go on in the faith that God is with us. He will help us, and our right hand is firmly in the grasp of His right hand!

"They shall never perish, neither shall any man pluck them out of my hand" (John 10:28).

ONE IN HIM

DAILY BIBLE READING: JOHN 17:21-23

"That they also may be one in us" (John 17:21).

Perhaps the biggest mistake we can make concerning the oneness of the body of Christ is this: we think oneness is something we must manufacture. But that is not true. Oneness is a spiritual reality. A fact. It already exists.

If we, through believing in His saving grace, are one with Christ—then we are one with all other believers. Jesus illustrated this with a very simple fact. A branch is part of a tree, one with a tree. A branch need not be in a frenzy, trying to become one with the tree. It *is* one with the tree.

How does this oneness show up in the believers' daily lives?

If we are one, we pray for each other.

If we are one, we work humbly together.

If we are one, we do not gossip about each other.

If we are one, our lives exalt Christ, because our oneness is in Him.

If we are one, we refuse to argue about divisive things.

In short, if we are one, even as the Son and the Father are one, we love each other.

So now we know where our work lies. We do not need to create a oneness, because that exists already. But we certainly must work to keep and maintain it!

"Holy Father, keep through thine own name those whom thou hast given me, that they may be one, as we are" (John 17:11).

CHANGED BY HIS DEATH

DAILY BIBLE READING: LUKE 23:37-43

"To day shalt thou be with me in paradise" (Luke 23:43).

We know of at least four men whose lives were changed on the day Jesus died. There may have been many more, but these are the four the Bible tells us about.

First we have the thief. Like you and me, he was a sinner. But there on the cross, witnessing the patient suffering of the Innocent One, the thief repented, freely confessing that he deserved his punishment. And what came of this blessed change? The sinner was promised paradise.

Then there was the Roman soldier who saw Jesus die. We see him being changed from a hardened soldier to a convicted believer. "And when the centurion, which stood over against him, saw that he so cried out, and gave up the ghost, he said, Truly this man was the Son of God" (Mark 15:39). Can we imagine the power that rang in Christ's dying voice, piercing to the heart a man who had likely killed dozens of people without a qualm?

Finally we have the two men who buried the body of Jesus—Joseph of Arimathea and Nicodemus. They, too, were changed by the death of their Lord. It is true that they were believers before this day. But before Jesus died, they were only secret believers. They dared not speak their faith aloud.

Now, they could no longer hide their faith. Christ's death changed them into people who were ready not only to believe but also to proclaim their faith in action.

Nothing changes people more than recognizing the death of Christ and allowing it to touch their own lives. Christ's death must become our own death—death to the carnal man. That is true change!

"We preach Christ crucified... but unto them which are called... Christ the power of God" (1 Corinthians 1:23, 24).

BURNING THE BUSHEL

DAILY BIBLE READING: MATTHEW 5:14-16

"Neither do men light a candle, and put it under a bushel, but on a candlestick"
(Matthew 5:15).

Suppose you were to do that. Suppose you lit a candle and put a bushel basket over it. What would happen?

Why, quite likely the basket would be set on fire! In minutes it would be reduced to a ring of ashes around the candle, while the candle's flame burns on.

You and I are candles God wants to light. The Proverbs writer tells us so: "The spirit of man is the candle of the LORD" (Proverbs 20:27). When we come to Jesus in repentance and faith, a light sparks on in our spirit. But all too often, we obscure that light with the "bushel" of our own carnality.

The Gospel tells us about two men who had "bushel" trouble. Joseph of Arimathea and Nicodemus had both been kindled by the fire of faith as they observed Jesus during His life. However, these two devout Jews were afraid to let their faith be known. They covered their faith with a bushel basket.

But what happened to Joseph and Nicodemus when they witnessed Christ's terrible suffering and death? The flames on their candles burned high with love! Love consumed the flimsy bushel that had previously hidden their faith. Then faith broke forth into action as they lovingly cared for the body of their Lord.

Let's pray that our puny flames too may be fueled by love till every bushel basket is consumed.

"The path of the just is as the shining light, that shineth more and more unto the perfect day" (Proverbs 4:18).

TRANSFORMING THE VINDICTIVE

DAILY BIBLE READING: LUKE 9:52-56

"Wilt thou that we command fire to come down from heaven, and consume them?" (Luke 9:54).

Do you know what the word *vindictive* means? Here are some synonyms offered by my thesaurus: *vengeful, unforgiving, spiteful.* Not very pretty, is it?

In this story, James and John were inflamed by a spirit of revenge against the Samaritans, who had refused to receive Jesus. They asked Jesus, "Shall we destroy that village by fire?"

But Jesus rebuked them: "Ye know not what manner of spirit ye are of." In other words, "You don't realize how revengeful—how unforgiving—how vindictive you are."

I think Jesus could say the same of you and me. I'm afraid we often don't realize what a dark, vengeful spirit we hide in our bosoms. It's part of the Adamic nature. When we are wronged, we seek revenge.

Is there hope for us? Can our natural tendency toward spite and vengefulness be transformed?

Let's take hope by observing what happened to the disciple John. Turn to the epistles he wrote later in his life. "Beloved, let us love one another: for love is of God; and every one that loveth is born of God, and knoweth God" (1 John 4:7). Is there any lingering sign of vindictiveness or lack of forgiveness here? No! John's whole life has become permeated with love.

Let us open our hearts to God's Spirit of love, that He may sweep away all carnal vengefulness and make us disciples of love, like John.

"Beloved, if God so loved us, we ought also to love one another" (1 John 4:11).

NO BARRIERS!

DAILY BIBLE READING: PHILEMON 1:15-18

"Not now as a servant, but . . . a brother beloved" (Philemon 1:16).

There are no barriers! That is the supreme message of Paul's letter to Philemon.

And it's true. In Christ there are no barriers. Sadly, though, human relationships are full of them. In Paul's day there were all kinds of class barriers: noblemen, workers, slaves; Jews, Greeks, barbarians; priests, kings, subjects.

This little letter of Paul's transcends even the barrier of slavery. Onesimus had been a slave in Colosse, belonging to a man named Philemon. For some reason—perhaps due to shabby treatment—Onesimus ran away. Worse still, before leaving, he stole from his master.

By the providence of God, Onesimus made his way to Rome. There he came to know the imprisoned apostle—and Jesus entered the slave's life. Paul and Onesimus became brothers in the Lord.

Paul would have liked to keep Onesimus with him. But he chose a nobler path. "You need to go back and make things right with your owner," Paul urged the slave. "Philemon loves the Lord. I will give you a letter for him, reminding him that as brethren in faith, there can be no barriers between the two of you. As for the money you stole, I'll pay what it takes to right that."

Such a beautiful picture of barriers being torn down! What about us? Are we hanging onto any walls that really shouldn't be there? We don't own slaves, but what about walls of ill will? Grudges? Unforgiving attitudes? Misunderstandings? Let us pray that all the barriers can be demolished. Through Jesus it is possible.

"For he is our peace, who hath made both one, and hath broken down the middle wall of partition between us" (Ephesians 2:14).

TO THIS YOU ARE CALLED

DAILY BIBLE READING: 1 PETER 3:8, 9

"Knowing that ye are thereunto called, that ye should inherit a blessing" (1 Peter 3:9).

Peter in these verses gives us a list of six qualities that believers are called to have: We're to be united in spirit; to be sympathetic; to love one another as brethren and sisters; to be compassionate; to be courteous—or humble, as many translators render it; and we must never return evil for evil.

That's quite a list! As the saying goes, it's a tall order. Can weak, failing humans actually have all those qualities?

Think about the man who wrote these verses. What was Peter like before Jesus entered his life? From what the Bible tells us, we can gather that Peter by nature was rash. He was arrogant. He liked having things his way. He tended to be domineering and even belligerent.

That's quite a list too—a list that has very little connection with the qualities that Christians are called to have.

If Peter the brash and rude could become a man who enjoins us to peace and love and compassion, surely there is hope for us too.

But we cannot attain our calling to compassion and love in our own strength. It took the power of the Holy Spirit to make the divine calling a reality in Peter's life, and the same is true for us. As we fulfill our calling to bless our fellow man with love, we will receive in return the very blessing of God.

"Then shall the King say unto them on his right hand, Come, ye blessed of my Father" (Matthew 25:34).

CONSUMING FIRE

DAILY BIBLE READING: HEBREWS 12:28, 29

"Our God is a consuming fire" (Hebrews 12:29).

Leviticus 10:1-3 records a happening that shows God's "consuming fire" in action. Nadab and Abihu were Aaron's sons. As priests, they were allowed to enter the holiest place of the tabernacle. But they did not carefully follow the detailed instructions God had given. They entered the holy place carrying "strange fire." I don't know exactly what that strange fire was, but obviously, Nadab and Abihu, in their carelessness, had sinned.

Sin cannot enter the presence of God. So what happened? Fire from God flashed out and instantly consumed those two men. Sin could not exist in the holy place. It had to be consumed by the holiness and justice of God.

This happening could cause us to despair. What hope is there for us? We have sinned. Only God can cleanse us and give us power over sin. But if we cannot come before a holy God without being consumed, how can we be saved?

We need not despair. God provided a way for us to draw nigh to Him without being consumed. He taught the Israelites to bring a lamb without spot or blemish. This lamb was to be slaughtered before the Lord and the blood sprinkled as a purifying agent upon the sinners.

Today, Jesus is our Lamb without spot or blemish. Through the shedding of the Lamb's blood, and through the faith of the repentant sinner, sin is taken away. Through Jesus we can approach this God who is a consuming fire! Yes, we come in reverence and godly fear—but we may come. The way is open. Jesus' blood has quenched the flames of consuming fire.

"Having therefore, brethren, boldness to enter into the holiest by the blood of Jesus, let us draw near with a true heart in full assurance of faith, having our hearts sprinkled from an evil conscience" (Hebrews 10:19, 22).

 Day 310

ONLY THE BEST

DAILY BIBLE READING: MALACHI 1:6-8

"If ye offer the lame and sick, is it not evil?" (Malachi 1:8).

Malachi pictures a dialogue between God and His priests. "If I'm your Father, where is the respect I deserve?" God asks. "Why are you being contemptuous of My name?"

Back comes the priests' reply, in the form of an astonished question: "When have we ever acted contemptuously toward You?"

God then explains that it is wrong and disrespectful to offer sacrifices that are sick or lame or blind. He suggests, "Just try offering imperfect animals to an earthly ruler. Would he be pleased with such contemptible gifts?"

The priests must have known that God requires only the best. Only a perfect, unblemished animal can serve as an offering for sin. Over and over we read that fact in Leviticus and Deuteronomy. If we want our sins forgiven, only a perfect offering will do.

This realization makes our hearts swell with praise, for we know that today we have the perfect offering. Today we come to the altar of the Lord in the name of Jesus, who offered His own life as the perfect, sinless sacrifice for sin.

But if we look again at Malachi's dialogue, we see that God was concerned about the attitude of those priests. Their contempt and disrespect brought dishonor to the Lord's altar. What does this mean for you and me?

It means that our heart's attitude is very important. To receive the benefits of Christ's perfect offering, we must be humble and repentant, willing to offer our whole lives to God. Not that our lives in themselves would be acceptable, for we are blemished by sin. But justified and cleansed through the blood of Christ, my life and yours can be a pleasing sacrifice to the Lord.

"That ye present your bodies a living sacrifice, holy, acceptable unto God" (Romans 12:1).

LOVE ONE ANOTHER

DAILY BIBLE READING: JOHN 13:21-30

"One of you shall betray me" (John 13:21).

Try to imagine how you might react in a situation like this. Jesus had just finished eating supper with His dearest friends on earth. In His heart was a knowledge that made Him "troubled in spirit." He knew that Judas would betray Him. He also knew that Peter would deny Him. This was the kind of treatment He would receive from men who had stuck by Him for three grueling years as He traveled up and down the land of Israel.

Yes, in that hour, Jesus was fully aware of just how prone to failure humans are.

You and I also sometimes arrive at realizations like that. Maybe a dear friend disappoints us by something she does or says. Or perhaps we start noticing many weaknesses and failures in the people around us.

How do we react in such situations? By nature, we start feeling hurt. We feel we can't take the pain of being disappointed or betrayed. We want to throw up our hands and get away from these trying people who are making life miserable for us.

But Jesus didn't react that way. He showed us how to respond according to the Holy Spirit within. Read a little further in the chapter to find what Jesus tells us to do in the face of hurt, betrayal, failure, and denial. His words in verse 34 are some of the most powerful ever spoken; they shine with a blinding light out from the darkest of situations: "Love one another; as I have loved you" (John 13:34).

Jesus loved His disciples in spite of the terrible things they did. So too must we.

"But I say unto you, Love your enemies . . . pray for them which despitefully use you" *(Matthew 5:44).*

GLORIFIED IN LOWLINESS

DAILY BIBLE READING: JOHN 13:31, 32

"Now is the Son of man glorified" (John 13:31).

The traitor had left the room. Jesus knew where Judas would go. He knew that Judas would make his way to the high priest's palace to betray the whereabouts of Jesus. The wheels had been set in motion. Jesus was entering the final inexorable hours before the Crucifixion. Ahead lay capture, brutal trials before hostile courts, scorn and contempt from His fellow countrymen, and cruel suffering and death on the cross.

But what did Jesus say? He said, "Now is the Son of man glorified."

Glorified? When faced with such terror and darkness?

Yes, glorified—for Jesus knew this was why He had come into the world. As He said in John 17:1, "Father, the hour is come." All His earthly life He had been looking ahead to this hour. Still we are puzzled. How could Jesus be glorified in His darkest hour?

This is just another example to remind us that God's values are not like ours. As Albert Barnes said, "The lowest condition of earth is frequently connected with the highest honor of heaven."

Christ's cross was His throne. His thorns were His crown. From that darkest hour of His death burst forth the brightest light the earth has ever known!

It was because Jesus utterly humbled Himself that God glorified Him. Let this be our example. Let us be humbled under the mighty hand of God, that He may exalt us in due time.

"Let this mind be in you, which was also in Christ Jesus . . . who . . . humbled himself, and became obedient unto death, even the death of the cross. Wherefore God also hath highly exalted him" (Philippians 2:5-9).

BE AN EXAMPLE

DAILY BIBLE READING: 1 CORINTHIANS 4:15-17

"Be ye followers of me" (1 Corinthians 4:16).

Every good teacher knows the importance of using examples. Showing a student how to do something always works better than merely telling.

We all need good examples to look up to. But the sobering truth is that the New Testament urges each of us to also be a good example for others.

How can I in my weakness set an example worthy enough for others to follow?

For answers, let's look at what the New Testament says about following examples. First, the words of Jesus in Matthew 11:29: "Take my yoke upon you, and learn of me; for I am meek and lowly in heart." Jesus is saying, "Follow My example!" How can we do that? By obeying Him—taking His yoke upon us.

That's the primary answer to our question of how we can be examples. There is only one way, and that is by following Christ's example. The example we want to show the world is Christ Himself. If Christ dwells in us through faith and obedience, people will see Him and be drawn to Him.

That's why Paul wasn't afraid to say, "Be ye followers of me." It sounds a little presumptuous until we realize we are to follow Christ as we see Him in Paul's life.

Being an example wasn't something Paul boasted about. In 1 Timothy 1:15 he calls himself the chief of sinners, and then in verse 16 he goes on to explain how he thus becomes an example to all believers. In effect he is saying, "If God could save a sinner like me, there is hope for all."

"Brethren, be followers together of me, and mark them which walk so as ye have us for an ensample" (Philippians 3:17).

A TWO-PRONGED PSALM

DAILY BIBLE READING: PSALM 34:1-7

"The angel of the LORD encampeth round about them that fear him, and delivereth them" *(Psalm 34:7).*

Do you see the two prongs? On the one hand, this psalm describes many blessings that God gives to His children. On the other hand, it also gives many instructions on how we must live if those blessings are to be ours.

Let's look first at some of the blessings set forth. In verses 4 and 6, we see that God can free us from our fears: God "delivered me from all my fears" and "saved him out of all his troubles." Verse 7 makes us aware of how perfectly God guards and defends us.

In verse 8 we find God showing us His goodness. What a blessing! Verse 9 tells us that God supplies all our needs. Verse 15 has the blessed assurance that God will hear us when we cry to Him. And in verse 22 we find the greatest, most comprehensive blessing of all: God redeems us! (Through His Son Jesus Christ.)

Now. What is our part? Under what conditions will all these blessings be ours? First and foremost, we must trust God. Verses 4 and 10 make that clear. We must cry out to Him, as in verses 6 and 17. Yet we must also fear Him, as verse 9 makes plain.

Our hearts must be broken and contrite (verse 18). Our desire must be to serve God (verse 22). Verse 14 commands us to turn from evil and do good. It also calls us to seek peace. And verse 13 makes clear that all this must be in utter honesty.

What great blessings—yet what challenging conditions! May God give us grace that we can realize it all.

"None of them that trust in him shall be desolate" (Psalm 34:22).

A REVOLUTION BREWING

DAILY BIBLE READING: JOHN 6:14, 15

"When Jesus therefore perceived that they would...make him a king, he departed"
(John 6:15).

If you have studied history, you will have read about revolutions. Often a revolution centers around a certain man. He is held up as a figurehead and leader who will make life easier and better for a nation. For instance, during the Communist Revolution in Russia, Lenin claimed he would change everything for the better. So also when Communism came to China; Mao Zedong was practically idolized as a revolutionary leader. History has shown that these revolutions did not succeed in making life better.

In reading John 6, we gather that some people were expecting Jesus to bring about a revolution. The miracles He performed led them to believe that Jesus could throw off the yoke of Rome. They really thought a revolution was brewing! But Jesus wanted no part in that kind of revolution. He slipped away from those who wished to make Him king.

The people didn't give up easily though. They found Jesus on the other side of the lake and peppered Him with questions. As a result, we have Christ's teaching on the Saviour as the Bread of life.

But the revolutionaries could not grasp these spiritual depths. First they murmured against Jesus (41) and argued among themselves (52). They complained that Christ's words were hard to understand (60). Finally, in verse 66, we find large numbers of former disciples deserting Jesus.

When evening came, only a few people remained with Jesus. "Will ye also go away?" Jesus asked them.

Peter responded in the way you and I must also respond if we want a true spiritual revolution in our life: "Lord, to whom shall we go? thou hast the words of eternal life."

Jesus is indeed a revolutionary leader—but the revolution must happen in our hearts.

"And we believe and are sure that thou art that Christ, the Son of the living God"
(John 6:69).

GOD TOOK CARE OF THE DETAILS

DAILY BIBLE READING: GENESIS 7:13-16

"And they that went in, went in male and female of all flesh, as God had commanded him" (Genesis 7:16).

If Noah had been like me, he might have caused himself a lot of worries when this commandment of God's came to him. He could have asked frantically, "How am I going to collect such an array of animals? Some of the species are ferocious. How can I make them listen to me? Some of them live far away. How am I going to bring them to the ark? And however can I persuade them to live together in peace in the confines of the ark?"

But we are not told that Noah had any worries; he simply obeyed. "And Noah did according unto all that the LORD commanded him" (Genesis 7:5).

That is faith. Only by faith could this astonishing feat have taken place—faith in the power of God, who alone could have accomplished it.

There is nothing too difficult for God. He was the One who miraculously brought the animals to Adam so he could name them. Gathering them again into the ark was not any harder. After all, God created them!

Noah had things in the proper perspective. He built the ark and let God take care of the other details. Aren't we, too, often the opposite? We fuss and worry about details we can't control when we should be doing something about areas over which we do have control, such as our attitudes and relationships. Let's learn to leave the hard parts for God and concentrate instead on our small part in daily life.

"His lord said unto him, Well done, thou good and faithful servant: thou hast been faithful over a few things, I will make thee ruler over many things: enter thou into the joy of thy lord" (Matthew 25:21).

THE PATIENCE OF NOAH

DAILY BIBLE READING: GENESIS 8:7-14

"And he stayed yet other seven days" (Genesis 8:10).

People sometimes talk about "the patience of Job." Today, let's think about the patience of Noah.

The Flood happened in the year that Noah turned six hundred. On the seventeenth day of the second month God opened all the faucets from above and below. For forty days the rain continued; the water grew ever higher. At the end of forty days, when the rain stopped, even the highest mountains were submerged.

The world stayed like that for 150 days—five months. But God didn't forget Noah. He sent a wind that began to dry up the waters.

After the seventh month, the ark came to rest on the mountains of Ararat. Did Noah's heart speed up with anticipation? Was he sick and tired of being confined to that boat?

If so, he still needed a lot of patience. It wasn't until two-and-one-half months later that more mountaintops became visible. Noah was human. Perhaps at this point he began to think what he might do to discover what the situation was like. Still, he waited another forty days before he put his idea into action: he sent out a raven and a dove. Nothing much happened. The dove came back.

Noah waited seven days before sending out the dove again. It returned with an olive leaf! But Noah waited another seven days before releasing the dove again.

By this time the world had entered another year. Noah was six hundred one. On that day, the earth was almost dry! Yet still Noah had to wait. Not until two more months had gone by—a full year after entering the ark—did God call Noah out.

Can we thus look to God for patience during times when we must wait?

"But if we hope for that we see not, then do we with patience wait for it" (Romans 8:25).

BUT THE FEARFUL

DAILY BIBLE READING: REVELATION 21:6-8

"He that overcometh shall inherit all things ... but the fearful ... shall have their part in the lake which burneth with fire" (Revelation 21:7, 8).

These verses picture the two destinations in stark contrast. On the one hand we see the overcomers, those who thirsted after righteousness, drawing near at last to that eternal Fountain from whence all life flows. We see those who by faith became God's children. Coming home to their Father, they find it is His will they should "inherit all things." Stupendous inheritance! Can our imaginations even touch the fringes of what it means to inherit all things in eternity?

Now let's look at the other side. Oh, we would far rather not. Our eyes would prefer to turn away from the vision of that lake of fire where unbelievers will receive the second death.

But read again the list that describes those who will be consigned to the lake of fire: unbelievers, murderers, whoremongers, abominable, liars, idolaters. We may think, "I'm not on that list."

But did you notice the first category on the list? "The fearful." The cowards. Those who are afraid to stand up for the right. Those who shrink from bearing the cross. Those who fall away in the heat of persecution. Those who, like Peter, look around and tremble at the winds and waves of the world.

May we not be such of whom Jesus said, "O ye of little faith." For, as Matthew Henry so graphically states, "Those who cannot burn at the stake for Christ must burn in hell for sin."

"For God hath not given us the spirit of fear; but of power, and of love, and of a sound mind" (2 Timothy 1:7).

Day 319

WITHOUT A CAUSE

DAILY BIBLE READING: JOHN 15:23-25

"They hated me without a cause" (John 15:25).

Don't you think Jesus' voice was filled with sadness as He spoke to His disciples about the world's hatred for Him?

That hatred was so unjustified. "They hated me without a cause," Jesus said, quoting words from the Psalms. The fact is, in Jesus there was every cause that men should love Him. He went about doing good, teaching, and healing. Yet instead of loving Jesus, the world hated Him—without a cause.

The Greek word translated "without a cause" is *dorean,* meaning "unearned, unjustified, without a cause." There was no cause for hatred of Jesus. In no way did He earn the hatred heaped on Him by mankind.

Here's an interesting fact. That same Greek word *dorean* also appears in Revelation 21:6 where it is translated *freely:* "I will give unto him that is athirst of the fountain of the water of life freely."

Unearned! Without a cause! That's how we receive salvation. That's how God gives His love to mankind. Freely. *Dorean.*

Think of it. Is there any cause in sinful mankind that God should love us? No, there is no more cause that God should love man than there is cause that man should hate God.

Men hated Jesus freely, without a cause. God loves man freely, without a cause. We could never earn His love. It is *dorean*—a beautiful gift, unearned and undeserved.

"But not as the offence, so also is the free gift" (Romans 5:15).

THE PARABLE OF THE COLT

DAILY BIBLE READING: MARK 11:2-5

"They...found the colt tied by the door without in a place where two ways met" *(Mark 11:4).*

I realize this story is not a parable. It is an actual happening. Jesus did tell the disciples to go get this colt, and they did find it just as He had said they would. But it is very easy to see a vivid allegory in this little incident.

That colt is like my flesh. By nature I am wild, untamed, untrained; no one has mastered or controlled me. Yet I am tied up. I am in bondage. I have a master, called sin, or Satan. He keeps me from being free.

Notice, however, that I am tethered "where two ways" meet. I have a choice. Which way shall I choose?

But first I need someone to help me out of my bondage. Parents, church, ministry—all who teach me God's Word are reaching out to loose the knot that tethers me to sin.

How can this wild, untamed flesh be controlled? Only through Jesus. He has the power to free me, and to control me.

Satan will protest. He may ask indignantly, "What do you think you're doing? That's my colt!"

Jesus fears neither Satan nor the untamed nature. Praise God that His disciples (our parents and church leaders) take me gently down the way that leads to Jesus.

What freedom, to know that Jesus is in control! What freedom, to have the flesh tamed—yes, crucified—through the love of Christ.

"If the Son therefore shall make you free, ye shall be free indeed" *(John 8:36).*

COME IN . . . GO FORTH

DAILY BIBLE READING: GENESIS 7:1; 8:15, 16

"Come thou and all thy house into the ark" (Genesis 7:1).

Two words in particular I want you to notice in these verses: *come* and *go*. Do you see why they are significant? God did not tell Noah, "Go into the ark," as though God were outside directing him in. He said, "Come into the ark." God was inside! Through His Spirit, God was there in the ark with Noah throughout those 371 days he was confined.

Nor did God say, "Come out of the ark," as though God were outside bidding Noah to come out. He said, "Go forth," again showing that He was inside with Noah.

Today the church of Christ is the ark. Jesus through His Spirit dwells in the midst of the church. He is still saying *come*. "Come unto me, all ye that labour and are heavy laden, and I will give you rest" (Matthew 11:28). He also promises, "Him that cometh to me I will in no wise cast out" (John 6:37).

Noah's ark provided safety from the Flood. Today the church is also an ark of safety. There in the ark with God, we are protected from the deluge of evil that floods the world.

Jesus prayed in John 17:11, "Holy Father, keep through thine own name those whom thou hast given me." What a comforting thought! We are "kept in his name" in the ark of safety.

One blessed day, we, too, will hear the words "Go forth"—forth into the endless day of eternity, where no ark of safety will ever be needed. Then through the ages we can offer the sacrifices of praise, as Noah did when he left the ark.

"All that the Father giveth me shall come to me" (John 6:37).

THE BOOKS WILL BE OPENED

DAILY BIBLE READING: REVELATION 20:11, 12

"The dead were judged out of those things which were written in the books"
(Revelation 20:12).

These words from Revelation 20 make us tremble for two reasons. On the one hand, we tremble with joy: our names are written in the book of life!

Remember that time, recorded in Luke 10:17-20, when the seventy-two disciples reported to Jesus the great works they had been able to do? Jesus told them, "Don't rejoice because the spirits are subject to you; rejoice because your names are written in Heaven." It's not our works that cause our names to be written in the book of life, but the fact that we believe in Jesus. Oh, how we may rejoice in this merciful heavenly bookkeeping!

On the other hand, we tremble with awe and fear. Every day we live with the sure knowledge that *the books will be opened*. In this account we get the impression that there are other books besides the book of life. What is recorded in those other books? We are told that "the dead were judged . . . according to their works." Our works are being recorded, day by day.

Our works either deny our Lord or confess Him. Jesus said, "Whosoever shall confess me before men, him shall the Son of man also confess before the angels of God [when the books are opened]. But he that denieth me before men shall be denied before the angels of God [when the books are opened]" (Luke 12:8, 9).

"He that overcometh . . . I will not blot out his name out of the book of life, but I will confess his name before my Father, and before his angels" (Revelation 3:5).

WHEN WE SEE HIS HOLINESS

DAILY BIBLE READING: EZEKIEL 1:26-28

"And when I saw it, I fell upon my face" (Ezekiel 1:28).

Did you know that the ancient Hebrews forbade their young people to read some parts of the Book of Ezekiel before they were thirty years old? They felt Ezekiel's prophecies were so marvelous and complicated that an immature mind would only be confused by them.

We don't believe there are certain Scriptures a young person must not read. But knowing how the Hebrews felt about Ezekiel helps to explain why we can't grasp all of the Bible's mysteries. Few chapters are more mysterious and wonderful than Ezekiel 1. In it the prophet describes a vision of God Himself.

We will not try to analyze that vision. It is too great for us. We will merely focus on what Ezekiel did when confronted with the holiness of God: he fell on his face. That's really the only possible response of humans confronted with God's glory. The Bible says that "every knee shall bow"—and one day that will be true. On the day of judgment, no man can stand upright before Almighty God.

But there are two ways of falling on our faces. One is the way of the sinner—in dread and terror because he has not obeyed God. The other is the way of the believer—in awe and reverence and thankfulness for God's mercy. Because even here, in Ezekiel's description of God's flaming throne, we see the symbol of mercy and grace: the rainbow in the cloud.

When you and I appear before the throne, how will we fall before God? As terrified, unrepentant sinners who realize they are doomed? Or repentant, saved sinners eternally grateful for God's mercy?

"For it is written, As I live, saith the Lord, every knee shall bow to me, and every tongue shall confess to God" (Romans 14:11).

BECAUSE OF THE RESURRECTION

DAILY BIBLE READING: JOHN 7:3-5

"For neither did his brethren believe in him" (John 7:5).

The brothers of Jesus—sons of Joseph and Mary—must have recognized that He was someone special. They acknowledged that He was doing miracles, and for that reason they urged Him to go to Jerusalem. Apparently they lusted for greatness, for recognition from the public.

But these earthly brothers of Jesus didn't really believe in Him. Not in a life-changing way. They may have believed that He possessed the power to do wonderful things, but it wasn't a belief that touched their hearts.

Something changed though. We know it, because Acts 1 lists those who gathered in the upper room, prayerfully awaiting the advent of the Holy Spirit. Among them were the brothers of Jesus.

What brought about that change? What transformed them from fame-seeking, superficial "believers" to true, wholehearted believers seeking the Holy Spirit's power?

Christ's resurrection must have made the difference. From 1 Corinthians 15:7 we learn that Jesus in His resurrected body made a point of especially appearing to His brother James. Now His brethren could no longer deny that Jesus was truly the Son of God in His resurrection power.

Because of the resurrection, they understood and believed that Christ's words and promises were true. Because of the resurrection, they became genuine followers of Jesus.

Are we a little like the brothers of Jesus? Does our faith tend to be superficial? Do we acknowledge His miracles without acknowledging His power in our lives?

Let the power of the resurrection change all that! Because of the resurrection, we know that Jesus defeated death. We have a living hope that we, too, will be raised. In short, because of the resurrection we are born again!

"Blessed be the God and Father of our Lord Jesus Christ, which according to his abundant mercy hath begotten us again unto a lively hope by the resurrection of Jesus Christ from the dead" (1 Peter 1:3).

NOT I

DAILY BIBLE READING: 1 CORINTHIANS 15:8-10

"Yet not I, but the grace of God which was with me" (1 Corinthians 15:10).

If you're like me, when you think of a Pharisee, the word *self-righteous* quickly enters your mind. That description certainly fits the Pharisee described by Jesus in a parable in Luke 18. This Pharisee enjoyed using the pronoun *I*. When he prayed, he had much to tell God about all the good "I" had done. In His parable, Jesus pointedly mentions that this Pharisee stood while praying.

Another Pharisee in the Bible also mentions a few things he had done. In fact, he claims to have labored more abundantly than all the other apostles.

Yet there is such a difference between these two Pharisees. The second one—whose name was Paul—spoke in utter humility. It's easy to picture him bowed low before God. He mentioned his accomplishments only to point out that it wasn't really himself who did it, but the power and grace of God working through him.

Not I, but Christ. That is Paul's song. He used the same words in 1 Corinthians 7:10 and in Galatians 2:20.

We can learn so much from Paul's deep humility. If we are truly humble, we do not spend time trying to persuade ourselves that we are worthless. True humility simply says, "Not I, but Christ." True humility recognizes what God can do in and through us. True humility acknowledges our real worth in God's sight—all through the grace of God.

King David was one who could have boasted about many great accomplishments. Yet on his dying day, what really counted for him was what God had done through him.

"Now these be the last words of David. David the son of Jesse said, and the man who was raised up on high . . . said, The Spirit of the Lord spake by me, and his word was in my tongue" (2 Samuel 23:1, 2).

RELIGION OR RELIGIOUSNESS?

DAILY BIBLE READING: JOHN 19:31

"The Jews therefore . . . besought Pilate . . . that they might be taken away" (John 19:31).

Satan has a counterfeit for everything. He himself is a counterfeit (Jesus called him a liar). Satan claims to be lord of the earth, but his is a counterfeit lordship. Satan even offers a counterfeit "love" that might satisfy for a while, but in the end proves fleeting and false.

In this verse from John 19 we see an example of counterfeit religion. Perhaps we could call it "religiousness." True religion means faithfulness and devotion. But the "religiousness" we see in this verse makes us shudder.

The Jewish leaders were anxious to get those bodies off those crosses. Why? There were two reasons, and both came from the Jewish religious Law. For one thing, it was against the Law to leave a dead body exposed overnight. Furthermore, it was against the Law to do any work after sundown on Friday. It would have been terrible—simply terrible!—to have those bodies hanging there over the Sabbath; and what made it even worse, this Sabbath was special because it concurred with the annual Feast of the Passover. Dead bodies were not to spoil the ritualistic importance of that great and holy day.

Now do you see why this scene makes us shudder? The Jewish leaders were so very concerned about the details of the Law—*yet they had crucified God's Son.* To use Jesus' own words, they were "straining at a gnat" while "swallowing a camel."

Could it be that you and I sometimes get caught in a similar trap of "religiousness" while sadly neglecting true religion? Might we sometimes be fretting about rules (which do fill a necessary spot) while at the same time neglecting the love and mercy of God? May God save us from all that is counterfeit.

"Woe unto you, scribes and Pharisees, hypocrites! for ye pay tithe of mint and anise and cummin, and have emitted the weightier matters of the law, judgment, mercy, and faith" (Matthew 23:23).

THEIR BURDENS MADE THEM BETTER

DAILY BIBLE READING: EXODUS 1:8-12

"But the more they afflicted them, the more they multiplied and grew" (Exodus 1:12).

Revelation 2 and 3 contain many wonderful promises for "him that over-cometh": the tree of life, the crown of life, the hidden manna, a new name, the morning star, white raiment, a place on the throne—all are promised to those who overcome.

Think for a moment about that word *overcome*. The only way we can overcome is by facing trials, troubles, and burdens. We can't be overcomers unless we have something to overcome!

That's why we can rejoice when we are troubled and have heavy burdens to bear. Our burdens don't have to defeat us. Instead, they can make overcomers of us. They can make us better.

Perhaps by this time you understand why we read those verses in Exodus 1. Those Israelites were real overcomers. They were faced with horrible oppression. Pharaoh's plan was to exterminate them by means of impossible burdens.

But it didn't work that way. It seems the Israelites just worked harder and increased their output. The more they were afflicted, the more they increased.

Years ago when the Anabaptists in Europe were being sorely persecuted, the same thing was true. The government hoped to exterminate them through persecution—but the opposite took place. As Tertullian said, the "blood of the martyrs is seed." The more believers gave their lives for their faith, the more others were drawn to also be overcomers.

Let's pray that we, too, can be overcomers in the afflictions of everyday life.

"Him that overcometh will I make a pillar in the temple of my God, and he shall go no more out" (Revelation 3:12).

FOLLOWING AFAR

DAILY BIBLE READING: MATTHEW 27:55, 56

"And many women were there beholding afar off" (Matthew 27:55).

You and I can identify with these women who were "beholding afar off" at the cross. How they must have yearned to help their beloved rabbi! Yet they felt helpless. We all know how it feels when there's nothing we can do.

I wonder, had the women known about the sham trials held the evening before at the homes of Annas and Caiaphas? Were they "beholding afar off" there as well? Did they wish they could storm those makeshift courts and bring incontrovertible evidence of Jesus' innocence? Yet they could do nothing.

Did these women attend the trial at Pilate's court? Maybe they even cried out in protest against the crowd's roar of "Crucify Him!" But their voices were not heard. There was nothing they could do.

Still, they kept following. They trudged up Golgotha's steeps after Jesus, and I'm sure they would gladly have borne the cross for Him. But being women, they had not the strength for that. If it could have done any good, I suppose those women would have argued with the Roman soldiers who drove the nails. But they couldn't do that either.

Was there really nothing the women could do? Yes, there were some things—and they did them. They watched. They followed. They made sure they knew where the body was laid. Luke tells us that they went home and prepared spices to anoint Jesus' body.

These women were only human. They worried about who would roll away that stone. But they did what they could—and their reward was great. They were the first witnesses to the resurrection of Jesus.

You and I are also called to do what we can. It may not seem like much. We might be tempted to fret about the big, important things we cannot do. But let's be faithful in what we can do; we, too, will be rewarded.

"Now when Jesus was risen early the first day of the week, he appeared first to Mary Magdalene" (Mark 16:9).

SCHEMING

DAILY BIBLE READING: JOHN 11:47-53

"Then from that day forth they took counsel together" (John 11:53).

The Jewish high council was in a ferment. Something had to be done! That Galilean rabbi had raised Lazarus from the dead—and as a result more and more people were following Him. They needed to come up with a plan—this Man was disrupting the whole nation! Maybe the priests and the Pharisees were even wringing their hands, wondering how Jesus could be stopped.

Caiaphas the high priest didn't waste time wringing his hands. His mind was already made up. Jesus had to die, no question about it. The only question was—how would they do it?

From that moment the high council (or Sanhedrin) began planning. Oh, how they schemed! We will never know what elaborate plots they hatched.

When Judas played right into their hands with his offer of betrayal, the Jews must have been surprised and pleased. Things were falling into place!

What these schemers did not realize was how insignificant their planning was. They did not recognize that far above their malicious little schemes existed a master plan that encompassed the whole world and all of history.

Caiaphas probably never knew how prophetic his angry outburst had been: "that one man should die for the people." Unconsciously he had put into words the greatest plan of the universe—the plan of salvation.

We all like to plan. We look ahead and make decisions about things we will do. There's nothing wrong with that, but let's not forget how insignificant our plans are compared to the plans of the One who rules the universe.

"Ye know not what shall be on the morrow. For that ye ought to say. If the Lord will, we shall live, and do this, or that" (James 4:14, 15).

GREAT FAITH OR GREAT GOD

DAILY BIBLE READING: NUMBERS 14:6-9

"The Lord is with us: fear them not" (Numbers 14:9).

Looking at people who persevere courageously in the face of danger, we may be tempted to think, "If only my faith were as great as that."

Caleb was one such person. We admire him for his faith. He dared to take a stand, even though thousands were afraid! While most of Israel quailed in the face of Canaan's giants, Joshua and Caleb declared they could be conquered.

Let's take a second look at Caleb, though. Did he have great faith, or was it that he believed in a great God?

Caleb was only human. I'm thinking those giants of Anak made him tremble in his sandals too. But he didn't forget what God had promised. His faith was grounded in the fact that God was going to give this land to Israel.

Caleb's faith endured. For thirty-eight years he had wandered in the wilderness, watching his contemporaries die off one by one. For seven years after that, he fought with Joshua, taking the land.

Finally, in Joshua 14, we find Caleb asking for his portion of Canaan. "Give me the hill country, where those giants dwell. With God for my help, I'll drive them out!" There we see it again: Caleb's faith was in the great God of the universe.

When we tremble at the fiery onslaughts of the giant Satan, let's not waste time wishing for greater faith. Let's fix our faith wholeheartedly on our great God. He has promised, "Thou shalt tread upon the lion and the adder: the young lion and the dragon shalt thou trample under feet" (Psalm 91:13).

To be saved, we may not need a great faith—but we do need an enduring faith in a great God.

"He that endureth to the end shall be saved" (Matthew 10:22).

I AM AND I WILL

DAILY BIBLE READING: EXODUS 6:6-9

"I am the Lord, and I will bring you out" (Exodus 6:6).

Count how many times God says, "I will" in this passage. Seven times! "I will redeem you—I will take you to me—I will be to you a God—I will bring you in—I will give it to you for an heritage." Such a complete promise!

And notice how God sealed His promise with three strong statements of "I am the Lord." No greater guarantee could have been given for the fulfillment of His promise. I am the Lord. I will do it.

Then we come to verse 9. What a sad verse. Apparently, the people didn't believe Moses when he relayed this great promise to them. They were simply too discouraged.

Why were they so discouraged? The first time Moses had told the people what great things God had in store for them (Exodus 4:29-31), they had believed and bowed their heads in worship. But since then, hard things had befallen Israel. Pharaoh had decided to oppress them as never before. Now they were ordered to make more bricks, with fewer materials being supplied.

So, from a human viewpoint, Israel's discouragement in Exodus 6 is understandable. The minute they allowed their hopes to rise, dark clouds had rolled in and the situation became worse than ever.

Perhaps you have experienced something similar. You want to believe God's promises—but time goes on and your difficult situation doesn't change. Or if it does, it only seems to grow worse.

Take heart! When God says, "I will," He certainly will. Remember His words: "I am the Lord."

"I have also heard the groaning of the children of Israel, whom the Egyptians keep in bondage; and I have remembered my covenant" (Exodus 6:5).

TWO SIDES OF REALITY

DAILY BIBLE READING: ROMANS 5:1-5

"We have peace with God through our Lord Jesus Christ" (Romans 5:1).

By reading only the first two verses of Romans 5, we could think the Christian life ought to be trouble-free. Through faith, we have peace, we have access, we have grace, we stand, we rejoice, we have hope. Praise God! It is such a privilege to be His child.

Yet our day-to-day life contains problems, irritations, failures, and pressures. Does that mean we haven't attained to the life God wants for us?

What it means is that there are two sides to the reality of the Christian life. On the one hand, if we have repented of our sins and come to Jesus for forgiveness, we are complete in Him. His atonement is sufficient and sure. At the same time, we still need to grow. The reality of God's grace is something we must learn to live out every day. That's why we need to read beyond the first two verses of Romans 5. The next verses show us how to grow.

Let's look at a few more aspects of the two-sided reality of the Christian life. On the one hand, we rejoice and rest in the presence of Christ. But at the same time, we know that sin is also still present, waiting to tempt and lead us astray.

In Christ we are given a high status. Peter tells us we are priests before God; John, in Revelation, says we are kings and priests. Yet the other side of the reality is that we are slaves, bound in love to serve the Lord who saves us.

In Christ we have peace because He has made us right with God. However, that peace doesn't exempt us from the reality of daily problems.

So we needn't be discouraged if we face problems and pressures and failures. Let's view them as lessons that teach us to rely on the Holy Spirit more and more. In eternity there will no longer be two sides to the story; all will be one glorious reality!

"We are troubled on every side, yet not distressed; we are perplexed, but not in despair" (2 Corinthians 4:8).

TRUE COMMITMENT

DAILY BIBLE READING: JOHN 12:23-27

"If any man serve me, let him follow me" (John 12:26).

We all have some idea what the term *commitment* means. We know what it's like to make a commitment: we have committed our lives to follow Christ; perhaps we have committed ourselves to teach at a certain school or to honor and submit to a certain man. Today let's try to get a glimpse of the commitment Jesus made when He came to earth. And as we glimpse that, may we receive a new understanding of what it means to commit our lives to Him.

Jesus was committed to saving mankind from sin. That's what He refers to in verse 23—His glorification as the Saviour. But His glorification came at a tremendous cost. The only way Jesus could carry out that commitment was by dying on the cross. That's why He spoke of the grain of wheat. It can bear fruit only if it lies in the grave of the earth.

Verses 25 and 26 switch the focus from Christ's commitment to ours. Do we want to serve Him? That means we must follow Him. Follow where? Into death. To the cross. We may not be asked to literally lose our lives for His sake as a martyr. We will not literally hang on a cross.

But if we want to be Christ's, we must die. Our own nature, our own ideas and aspirations—they must die. We must hate our earthly life if we want to keep our spiritual life into eternity.

Does this stark reality of commitment trouble you? Don't be surprised. Even Jesus was troubled at the thought of His impending death (verse 27). But He was committed. "For this cause came I unto this hour." And the rewards—for Him, and for us if we truly commit—are "out of this world."

"That I may know him, and the power of his resurrection, and the fellowship of his sufferings, being made conformable unto his death" (Philippians 3:10).

THE STRENGTH IS IN THE CALL

DAILY BIBLE READING: MATTHEW 8:19-22

"Follow me" (Matthew 8:22).

While on the subject of commitment, we must certainly take a look at these four verses. They cast a revealing light on human efforts at commitment, and it doesn't look very impressive.

The first man, a scribe, seems like someone whose emotions have been stirred. This scribe had probably heard Christ's teaching and seen His healing. Impulsively he exclaimed, "I'll follow You wherever You go!" He was offering his commitment to Christ, perhaps expecting Jesus to be pleased that someone as noteworthy as a scribe wanted to be His disciple. We could even say that this was a self-centered commitment.

Jesus knows how shaky such an impulsive, emotion-based commitment can be. So He asks us to take a hard look at what it really means to follow Him. We may need to give up much that we hold dear on earth. Commitment to Jesus is not something that can be made lightly or on the spur of a moment.

What did Christ's forthright reply do to the scribe's commitment? We are not told. But we can use this as a searchlight upon our own commitment. Does my commitment go deeper than my emotions?

The second man also felt drawn to Jesus, but he wanted to procrastinate. To this man, the responsibility to care for his father until he died looked more important than discipleship.

Jesus' answer seems almost harsh, but in reality it is not. He is not contradicting the commandment to honor father and mother. But in no uncertain terms He is saying, "Follow *Me!* This must be your priority. This is your call, above any earthly calling."

By this time, we see that commitment to Jesus is an awesome thing. We may shrink back, unsure that we are up to its demand. This is our reassurance; if Jesus calls, "Follow Me," our strength comes from Him through that call—not from our own uncertain, wavering commitment.

"These are they which follow the Lamb whitersoever he goeth. These were redeemed from among men, being the firstfruits unto God and to the Lamb" (Revelation 14:4).

PREFERRING JESUS

DAILY BIBLE READING: MATTHEW 10:37, 38

"He that loveth father or mother more than me is not worthy of me" (Matthew 10:37).

It seems we are still on the subject of commitment. Today, however, we will give the thought a different slant by focusing on the word *preference*. It's a word we tend to use quite lightly. We have preferences in the foods we eat, the jobs we hold, the clothes we wear. Confronted with a choice, we might prefer pizza over a hot dog.

Where Jesus is concerned, preference takes on a far weightier meaning. He says that to be His followers, we must prefer Him over everything else.

For one thing, we must prefer Jesus over our nearest and dearest relatives. Any claims they have on us must give way to the greater claim that Jesus has upon us. This is not to say we are not to love our families—but we must love Jesus more.

Then too, we must prefer Jesus over earthly safety and ease. By nature we might prefer pleasure, leisure, comfort, financial security, absence of pain. But following Jesus means taking up the cross. It means our goals are no longer earthly but heavenly; thus earthly preferences may need to be sacrificed. Jesus was willing to bear the cross for our sakes; are we willing to prefer a cross over an easy life?

That brings us to the weightiest preference of all: preferring Jesus over life itself. Let's remember that Jesus is speaking of "life" in two ways here. When He asks us to be willing to lose our lives, He means the earthly life with its comforts. We dare not deny Christ for the sake of saving that earthly life! No, we would rather lose our earthly lives than deny Christ.

And the life that we thus find is eternal life. We must be willing to sacrifice the lower life because we prefer the higher life—abundant life in Jesus Christ.

"He that loveth his life shall lose it; and he that hateth his life in this world shall keep it unto life eternal" (John 12:25).

THE WATER AND THE WINE

"And there were set there six waterpots of stone, after the manner of the purifying of the Jews" (John 2:6).

This first miracle of Christ's can be taken as a picture of His whole mission on earth. To see the picture, we begin by looking at those waterpots. They were huge, holding perhaps twenty gallons each. Why did people need so much water at a wedding feast? Probably not for drinking; I'm told people in those days didn't drink much water, because it wasn't very pure. Since wine (or fermented grape juice) provides its own purifier because of the alcohol it contains, wine was safer to drink than water.

No, these waterpots were needed for washing—ceremonial washing. A great deal of washing took place at a feast like this. God's law required basic handwashing; Jewish law added many more occasions for handwashing and feetwashing. So we could think of these waterpots as a symbol of the Law.

Notice how quietly Jesus performed this miracle. He could have called together all the important people and announced that He was about to do a great thing. But He simply spoke to the servants. Did not the Son of God come to earth in a stable, attended by the lowliest of parents?

Jesus could have asked for special vessels, but He used the waterpots. He used water—among the commonest of earthly substances. Thus He showed Himself the Lord of creation. He causes rain to fall from heaven to water the grapevine so that wine can be produced; that same power could simply take the water and turn it into wine.

And now He tells the wondering servants to "draw forth" from the waterpots and let the governor taste it. The water had turned to wine! Even so, Christ came to fulfill the Law—to turn it into grace. No longer are we under the Law's demands; we can receive cleansing through the blood of Jesus. But like those servants, we must come and draw. The wine of grace is no help to us unless we drink deeply and allow its saving, purifying work to happen in our souls.

"If any man thirst, let him come unto me, and drink" (John 7:37).

FROM COMPLAINTS TO PRAISE

DAILY BIBLE READING: PSALM 3:1-4

"But thou, O LORD, art a shield for me" (Psalm 3:3).

Today we want to notice two things about David's psalms. One: many of them start on a troubled, complaining note, yet end with high praises to God. Two: many of them are connected to a specific happening in David's life.

Psalm 3 is a good example of this. The heading tells us that David wrote this psalm when he fled from his son Absalom. Can we hear the anguish in his words? "Many there be which say of my soul, There is no help for him in God." David didn't try to hide from God how he felt.

Yet by the third verse, David starts praising God. And by the end we see that he had learned something through it all: Salvation belongs to the Lord.

Psalm 56 is another such psalm, written during the days when David was a fugitive from Saul, and the Philistines were after him. "O God, people are hounding me on every side!" he seems to lament. But again, by verse 4 he is praising God for His promises. What had David learned? "What time I am afraid, I will trust in thee" (verse 3).

Try Psalm 142. There, David was hiding in a cave. He complained that his enemies were setting traps for him. But soon he came to this realization: God is my refuge.

Psalm 52 starts out as a sharp complaint against evil men. David wrote it upon hearing that Doeg had murdered eighty-five priests and their families. By verse 9, however, David said, "I will praise thee for ever." What had he learned? To trust in God, not in riches, for strength.

In each of these psalms, though David started by pouring out complaints, he was soon arrested by the realization that he was speaking to the God of Heaven. That realization was enough to change his laments into praise.

Like David, we are free to tell God how we feel—providing we allow Him to transform our heaviness into praise and teach us valuable lessons from each experience.

"Cast thy burden upon the LORD, and he shall sustain thee" (Psalm 55:22).

THE PROMISES—AND THE CONDITIONS

DAILY BIBLE READING: GENESIS 12:1-4

"I will bless thee, and make thy name great" (Genesis 12:2).

Oh, the remarkable promises God gave to Abraham! Four times in these verses, God says, "I will"; twice, He says, "shall."

"I will make of thee a great nation." Quite a promise for a man who had not even one child.

"I will bless thee." Can we receive anything greater than God's blessing?

"I will make thy name great." This reminds us of the promise in Revelation 3:12— "I will write upon him the name of my God. . . I will write upon him my new name."

"Thou shalt be a blessing." God promised that Abraham would bring many blessings to others.

"I will bless those that bless thee and curse him that curseth thee." God was on Abraham's side.

And finally, the culmination of all blessings: "In thee shall all the families of the earth be blessed"—because Jesus the Saviour would be born of Abraham's descendants.

Notice, however, that all these blessings came with a condition. They would come to Abraham only if he obeyed God's call. For a man so happily settled among his kindred in a goodly land, it was a challenging call: "Get thee out of thy country!" Abraham had to separate himself from the idolatrous influences around him.

Abraham's experience has a familiar ring to us. We, too, are offered great and precious promises in Jesus. God promises to bless us in Him beyond any blessings we have known.

And for us too there is a condition: We must step away from the carnal self and from sin. We must abandon the idols of iniquity in our hearts. We must realize that this world is not our home, and we look for a better land—the land of promise. God help us to meet the conditions so that He can truly bless us.

"And being fully persuaded that, what he had promised, he was able also to perform" (Romans 4:21).

ALL THE PROMISES

DAILY BIBLE READING: 2 CORINTHIANS 1:18-20

"All the promises of God in him are yea, and in him Amen" (2 Corinthians 1:20).

Yesterday we looked at the wonderful promises God gave to Abraham and similar great and precious promises He gives to us. Today we want to think about the fact that Jesus Christ is the fulfillment of all God's promises.

All of them! I have not counted the promises God makes in His Word, but someone has said there are ten thousand. But numbers are beside the point. God's promises are eternal and endless.

And Jesus is the great "Yea." He is a resounding "Yes!" to all that God would give us. There is no wavering in Jesus. As long as we rest in Him, we have assurance. "Jesus Christ the same yesterday, and to day, and for ever" (Hebrews 13:8). "Thou art the same, and thy years shall not fail" (Hebrews 1:12).

God is true. God is faithful. His Word is unchangeable. "For I am the LORD, I change not" (Malachi 3:6). Let's not forget though: God's unchangeableness does not refer only to His promises of blessing. His promises of judgment upon sin are also unchangeable.

For example, after Saul's disobedience, Samuel confronted him with an awful verdict: "Thou hast rejected the word of the LORD, and the LORD hath rejected thee" (1 Samuel 15:26).

Saul was devastated. As Samuel turned to go, Saul grabbed his garment, hoping perhaps to change Samuel's mind. Sternly came the rebuke. "The Strength of Israel will not lie nor repent; for he is not a man, that he should repent" (1 Samuel 15:29).

May we ever cling to the resounding "Yea" of God's promises in Jesus. If we do, we need not face the terrible "Nay" of God's judgment.

"These things saith the Amen, the faithful and true witness" (Revelation 3:14).

HE SHALL CONFESS

DAILY BIBLE READING: LEVITICUS 5:5-9

"When he shall be guilty in one of these things, that he shall confess that he hath sinned in that thing" (Leviticus 5:5).

God gave Israel a way to receive forgiveness of sins. To us it seems a very elaborate system, almost mind-boggling in the details that went with the sin offerings. But I want to focus today on one thing: the need to confess. Without confession, the whole elaborate system was useless. No matter how many beasts were offered on the altar, forgiveness could not come unless the sinner confessed. God's Word reminds us again and again of this need. "When a man or a woman shall commit any sin . . . then they shall confess their sin which they have done" (Numbers 5:6, 7).

In the days of Ezra, Israel realized that they had sinned and fallen far from God. So "Ezra the priest stood up, and said unto them, Ye have transgressed. Now therefore make confession unto the LORD God of your fathers, and do his pleasure. Then all the congregation answered and said with a loud voice, As thou hast said, so must we do" (Ezra 10:10-12).

The Psalmist David says, "I said, I will confess my transgressions unto the LORD; and thou forgavest the iniquity of my sin" (Psalm 32:5).

And in Proverbs we read, "He that covereth his sins shall not prosper: but whoso confesseth and forsaketh them shall have mercy" (28:13).

Why is confession so important? It shows that we realize we have sinned. It shows that we realize how holy God is and that no sin can stand before Him. Confession humbles us before God. Above all, confession brings us to the willingness we need—the willingness to forsake our sins.

As we know, animal sacrifices are a thing of the past. God sent His Son Jesus to be the ultimate sacrifice for sin. Oh, how precious and effective is the blood of the Lamb in cleansing us from sin!

Yet still today, this fact holds true: there can be no cleansing, no forgiveness, unless we confess.

"If we confess our sins, he is faithful and just to forgive us our sins, and to cleanse us from all unrighteousness" (1 John 1:9).

THE LORD LAUGHS

DAILY BIBLE READING: PSALM 2:1-4

"He that sitteth in the heavens shall laugh" (Psalm 2:4).

Such striking words. We do not often read of God's laughter. A few other places in the psalms also mention it; each time the setting is the same: God laughing at the futile raging of the heathen.

To say that God laughs is to use human language; it's a figure of speech. For an example of what the psalmist means by this laughter, picture this: a small child declares to his father, "I can run faster than you. I'll beat you to the barn!" You laugh, not so much in scorn, but because the idea is ridiculous.

Something similar is happening here. The heathen are in a tumult, imagining something that can never be; they dream of breaking away from God's control. It is a scene of violence, of angry scheming against God and of futility.

From God's viewpoint it is laughable. Regardless of what these puny nations think they can do, the universe is the Lord's. Christ is crowned King of the earth. That's what we see if we read on to the end of this psalm.

This messianic psalm speaks prophetically of Jesus. Few other psalms are more often quoted in the New Testament. Time and again the apostles quoted words from the second psalm in reference to Jesus.

For one example, go to Acts 4. There, the Jewish high council had taken Peter and John into custody. Upon releasing them, the Jews "commanded them not to speak at all nor teach in the name of Jesus." Peter and John hurried to the other believers, and together they prayed for boldness in the face of persecution. Part of their prayer quotes the first two verses of Psalm 2. What a testimony of power they were given from the Lord. The house was shaken, and they were filled with the Holy Ghost.

Those apostles faced seemingly impossible odds. But they remembered that God laughs at the scheming of men. It's a reminder for us too: God is in control!

"Blessed are all they that put their trust in him" (Psalm 2:12).

CONFUSION—SATAN'S TOOL

DAILY BIBLE READING: 2 KINGS 18:1-6

"He did that which was right in the sight of the LORD . . . He trusted in the LORD God of Israel" (2 Kings 18:3, 5).

We know that one of Satan's main tools is to cause us to sin through disobedience. But let's not forget that he has other tools with which to make us fall. One of those tools is confusion. If Satan cannot get us to commit outright sin, he may try to confuse us. He knows that will make us just as ineffective for God as sin would.

In reading these verses from 2 Kings 18, we are convinced that King Hezekiah did right to break down all the idol altars. But Satan, through the Assyrian king, tried to persuade Judah that Hezekiah had insulted God when he tore down those altars. Talk about confusion!

We read about this in Isaiah 36:7. If we read that entire chapter, we can see that Assyria wanted to break down Judah's trust in God. "Do you claim to trust in God?" the Assyrians taunted. "But isn't that the God whom Hezekiah insulted? God is angry at you, and He will not deliver you when we come to conquer Jerusalem."

Quite likely, some of the people who heard these taunts felt confused. But they obeyed Hezekiah's commandment to stay quiet (Isaiah 36:21). As for Hezekiah, he was not confused. Troubled, yes; but not confused. He did the right thing. He took his troubles to the Lord (see Isaiah 37:1). And Isaiah the prophet gave Hezekiah a mighty promise: God would smite the Assyrian armies. Thousands of soldiers would die, and the rest would return home; Judah would be saved by the hand of the Lord.

The way the Assyrian king spoke to Judah is the way Satan sometimes speaks to us. He tries to make us doubt whether we've done the right thing. He tries to confuse us.

Let's be like Hezekiah. Let's pay no attention to Satan's confusing thoughts, but instead bring our troubles before the Lord. He will save and deliver.

"Now therefore, O LORD our God, save us from his hand, that all the kingdoms of the earth may know that thou art the LORD, even thou only" (Isaiah 37:20).

HOW THE TEMPLE SITE WAS CHOSEN

DAILY BIBLE READING: 1 CHRONICLES 21:25-28

"And David built there an altar unto the LORD, *and offered burnt offerings and peace offerings"* (1 Chronicles 21:26).

God can bring good out of our mistakes and failures. The verses you just read are taken from a larger story that tells how God caused something wonderful to result from a mistake committed by King David.

The story begins when Satan tempted David to take a census of Israel, and David fell for the temptation. Some of his men strongly advised him not to do it. They realized it would cause David to take pride in his army. But David ordered the census to be taken anyway.

He soon realized his mistake. He saw that God was highly displeased with him, and he begged for forgiveness. The punishment for David's sin was a plague that killed seventy thousand people of Israel.

First Chronicles 21:16 is a dramatic verse: the angel of death standing above Jerusalem with a drawn sword, ready to strike many dead with the plague. But at that moment God decided to stop the plague.

Now we come to the part where God brings good out of this sad situation. Where had the angel of the Lord been standing? Right on the threshing floor of Ornan—a large flat rock situated above Jerusalem. God told David to build an altar there. So David bought the threshing floor from Ornan, built an altar, and offered sacrifices of gratitude to God for halting the plague's deadly advance.

Now an inspiration came to David: this threshing floor would be the site for the temple his son Solomon would build. What a glorious purpose for something that started out as a mistake!

"Then Solomon began to build the house of the LORD . . . *in the place that David had prepared in the threshingfloor of Ornan the Jebusite"* (2 Chronicles 3:1).

CONFLICT WITH SELF

DAILY BIBLE READING: ROMANS 7:21-25

"Bringing me into captivity to the law of sin which is in my members" (Romans 7:23).

We've come to Jesus and received justification through His blood. Now we long for sanctification. We want our life to become righteous, as befitting a child of God. We "delight in the law of God after the inward man."

But there is a problem. Our self is still with us. Our sinful flesh makes things very difficult. Whenever we try to do the right thing in our own strength, our flesh interferes and causes failure.

That's what Paul is describing here in Romans 7, which has rightly been called "the chapter of *I.*" That great big "I" is very much alive in Romans 7. It seeks to save itself; it seeks to make itself righteous. That big "I" is just like a three-year-old who, when someone offers to help him, insists, "I can do it myself."

Yet Paul finds out that's impossible. The conflict within him is so great, it brings him to despair. "O wretched man that I am! Who will deliver me from the slavery of self—this flesh that draws me down and keeps me from living the way I should? Who can save me from the condemnation I deserve because I keep failing God's holy law?"

Oh, we can identify with Paul. This inner battle is as real to us as it was to him. Gratefully we listen as Paul tells us what to do when we feel overwhelmed with sin.

We must remember how our spiritual life began. We came to Jesus, and He set us free from sin through His forgiveness. We may claim that freedom daily! Let's remember it's not "I" that can do this—but Jesus through the power of the Holy Spirit. And then, leaving behind the desperation of "I" in Romans 7, let's go on to read Romans 8—the chapter of the Holy Spirit.

"There is therefore now no condemnation to them which are in Christ Jesus, who walk not after the flesh, but after the Spirit" (Romans 8:1).

HE TRIED TO CLEAR HIS CONSCIENCE

DAILY BIBLE READING: MATTHEW 27:19-24

"And the governor said, Why, what evil hath he done?" (Matthew 27:23).

When I read the story of Pilate, one fact stands out: he didn't listen to his conscience. It's not that his conscience didn't speak. We can think of at least three ways his conscience became convicted of Jesus' innocence.

For one, Pilate's wife had dreamed about Jesus; she sent the governor a note begging him not to have anything to do with this innocent man. That must have made an impression on Pilate's conscience, but apparently he ignored it.

Then too, Christ's calm bearing must have had a mighty impact on Pilate's conscience. He knew this man was innocent. He said as much: "I, having examined him before you, have found no fault in this man" (Luke 23:14).

Finally, Pilate knew Roman law. He knew that, according to the law, no innocent man may be condemned. Don't you think that fact clawed at Pilate's conscience?

He did make several feeble attempts to clear his conscience. He sent Jesus to Herod, hoping the Galilean king would take the whole mess off his hands. That didn't work; Jesus was sent back to Pilate. He even appealed to the crowd's conscience, offering them Barabbas—but that didn't work either.

Finally, Pilate had someone bring him a basin of water. Publicly, solemnly, literally, he washed his hands of the matter. "His blood be upon you," he told the crowd.

Was Pilate's conscience free? No. He probably lived the rest of his life with an enormous burden.

Is your conscience free? Have you made vain attempts to free it from sin, yet the burden does not go away? There is only one way to have a free conscience.

"Having therefore, brethren, boldness to enter into the holiest by the blood of Jesus . . . let us draw near with a true heart in full assurance of faith, having our hearts sprinkled from an evil conscience, and our bodies washed with pure water" (Hebrews 10:19, 22).

GOD SPEAKING

DAILY BIBLE READING: EXODUS 33:8-11

"And the LORD spake unto Moses face to face, as a man speaketh unto his friend" (Exodus 33:11).

Passages like this make us feel a bit wistful. Imagine speaking face to face with God, actually hearing God's voice. For Moses, it happened again and again. On the day God instructed Moses to build the ark of the covenant, God promised, "There I will meet with thee, and commune with thee." Whenever Moses entered the tabernacle and stood before the ark, God would speak to him.

Throughout the Old Testament, God kept on speaking. He spoke to Noah; He spoke to Abraham; He spoke to the prophets. Weren't they privileged people?

But before we let our wistfulness run away with us, let's turn to the powerful words of Hebrews: "God, who at sundry times and in divers manners spake in time past unto the fathers by the prophets, hath in these last days spoken unto us by his Son" (1:1, 2). Jesus is the Word of God—the Word that was in the beginning, the Word that created the universe from nothing. God broke into history and spoke through His Son, who came to earth to redeem us.

God's speaking through His Son is more powerful, more wonderful, than any previous speaking had been. Why? The earlier speaking was only "in part." That's the meaning of the original Greek translated as "at sundry times"—God spoke only a portion at a time.

To each prophet He revealed some truth about Christ's coming. To Abraham He revealed the nation that would produce the Saviour. God revealed to David and to Isaiah from which family Jesus would be born. He told the Prophet Micah the town where Jesus would be born. He told Daniel the exact time of the Saviour's coming. Christ's death and resurrection also were revealed to the prophets.

Speaking, ever speaking down through the ages, God revealed His plan bit by bit. But what privileged people we are! By His Son, God has spoken the fulfillment of His plan!

"Of which salvation the prophets have inquired and searched diligently, who prophesied of the grace that should come unto you" (1 Peter 1:10).

HOW WILL WE FACE DEATH?

DAILY BIBLE READING: 1 SAMUEL 13:5-13

"Thou hast done foolishly: thou hast not kept the commandment of the LORD thy God" (1 Samuel 13:13).

Already this early in Saul's kingship, we can start detecting the sort of character he had. Samuel had instructed Saul not to start fighting the Philistines until he came to offer sacrifices to God. But after waiting seven days with no sign of the prophet, Saul felt he needed to act. So he took matters into his own hands and made an offering by himself. We can see that God's commandments were not very important to him. Saul was a man who lived for himself, not for God.

Other incidents in Saul's life show how selfish and arrogant he was. Just think how he treated David. Then in 1 Samuel 31, we read about Saul's death. Watching him take his own life, we are struck by this realization: Saul died the way he had lived, by taking matters into his own hands. He died serving himself, not God.

How will we face death? You might have many more years to live. But think of it. How we live our lives determines how we will face death.

On our dying day, we hope to trust only in the Lord, who saves us by His grace. We want to have peace with Him. When He says it is time for us to die, we want to meet Him with joy.

Will that be possible if we have been disobedient and headstrong in life? Will it be possible if we are used to depending on our own strength and taking matters into our own hands? Will it be possible to die peacefully if we have not lived in peace with God?

I am afraid not. At death's door, our response to God will be according to the way we have responded to Him all through life.

"Christ shall be magnified in my body, whether it be by life, or by death. For to me to live is Christ, and to die is gain" (Philippians 1:20, 21).

LEARNING CONTENTMENT

DAILY BIBLE READING: PHILIPPIANS 4:11-13

"For I have learned, in whatsoever state I am, therewith to be content" (Philippians 4:11).

There is no happier state on earth than to be content. Why, then, do we struggle so much with discontentment? I think our problem stems right back to Eden. Look at Eve. She lived in a large garden full of lovely things. She had all she could possibly need, and then some.

But Satan started questioning Eve. In effect he asked, "How can you be contented when you're not allowed to eat from that certain tree?" Eve made a terrible mistake. She stopped thinking about all God had given her, and instead started thinking about the one thing He had forbidden. She kept thinking about it until she felt sure she needed that one thing yet too.

I must admit this sounds all too familiar. How prone I am to forget my many blessings and focus instead on the one or two things I can't have!

But if we are in Christ, such a state of discontentment can change. In fact, it must change. Like Paul, we can learn to be content both when we have abundance and when we are in need. The two conditions can be equally challenging. If we are prosperous, we must learn not to be proud. But we can also learn to be serene and accepting during poverty and affliction.

From verse 12 we could get the impression that Paul learned these valuable lessons through his own strength. "I know how to be abased, and I know how to abound." But we must read on, and in verse 13 we see who enabled Paul to be so content: "I can do all things *through Christ.*" Paul also wrote in 2 Corinthians 3:5, "Not that we are sufficient of ourselves to think any thing as of ourselves; but our sufficiency is of God."

The secret is to live in the center of God's will. When our highest ideal is to fulfill God's will, we can live in utter contentment, secure in the faith that God will supply our need.

"But godliness with contentment is great gain. And having food and raiment let us be therewith content" (1 Timothy 6:6, 8).

FROM PRINCE TO SHEPHERD

DAILY BIBLE READING: EXODUS 2:15-21

"And Moses was content to dwell with the man" (Exodus 2:21).

The story of Moses gives us an example of the words of Paul we read yesterday: "I know both how to be abased, and I know how to abound." Can we grasp what a contrast Moses' new life in the desert was to his life as the son of an Egyptian princess? I imagine in the court of Pharaoh, Moses never had to do any work. Of food and raiment he probably always had far more than necessary. He would have been constantly surrounded with people who looked up to him and served his every whim.

Most poignant of all: in Egypt, Moses would have been taught to despise shepherds. We can gather that from Genesis 46:34: "For every shepherd is an abomination unto the Egyptians."

Then Moses fled to Midian and sat down by a well. Along came seven shepherdesses to draw water for their father's flock. Far from despising such lowly work, Moses got busy and helped those girls. Their father invited Moses into his home, and Moses was content to live there. The prince from Egypt's crowded courts became a shepherd who spent his days in solitude in the wilderness.

God had a purpose in bringing this enormous change to Moses' life. Moses was to be a great leader, but first he needed to learn humility. He needed to learn how to commune with God. In becoming a shepherd, he learned to identify with the Israelites, who were also shepherds. What's more, a shepherd's life inured Moses to wilderness existence.

During those long solitary years, did Moses realize what God was doing? Probably not. So also, we do not always understand why God allows drastic changes in our lives. But if we are content—trusting in God and seeking His will—He will work out His purposes. God has lessons He wants to teach us; let us learn them gladly.

"Better is little with the fear of the LORD than great treasure and trouble therewith" (Proverbs 15:16).

WATCH WITH ME

DAILY BIBLE READING: MATTHEW 26:36-39

"My soul is exceeding sorrowful, even unto death" (Matthew 26:38).

We can hardly imagine how difficult this night was for the Man Jesus. He was human, one of us, with feelings and fears like ours. How would you and I feel if we knew that in a few hours we would hang on a cross?

The Bible's language is very vivid in describing Christ's agony. "Sorrowful and very heavy . . . exceeding sorrowful, even unto death." Another version says, "My soul is overwhelmed with sorrow to the point of death" (NIV). Still another says, "He became anguished and distressed . . . My soul is crushed with grief" (NLT). Words are not adequate in the face of such intense emotions.

Was Jesus in His humanity rebelling against the Father's will when He asked that the cup might be taken away? No, He was not. If anything, He reaffirmed His desire to do God's will—at any cost.

"Watch with me." Christ's plea to the disciples comes down through the years and touches our hearts. How can we watch with Him? By doing as He did— surrendering our will to God in complete obedience.

"O Father, if this cup may not pass away from me, except I drink it, thy will be done" (Matthew 26:42).

IN SEARCH OF CONSISTENCY

DAILY BIBLE READING: PSALM 33:10-13

"The counsel of the LORD standeth for ever" (Psalm 33:11).

In the world there is so much inconsistency. New fads come along daily, and as people rush after them, things keep changing. The world's system seems as fickle and inconsistent as the shadows that shift their way across the face of the earth.

The trouble is, we also see a lot of inconsistency in ourselves. Our moods shift and change, and thus our actions vary from day to day. If you are a schoolteacher, you know how hard it can be to deal consistently with the children in your charge. One day you may feel quite loving toward them; another day they simply exasperate you.

Or perhaps you are a mother and need to discipline young children. How challenging it is to stay consistent in loving discipline, rather than merely scolding and nagging! It is just not in human nature to remain truly consistent.

Yet God calls us to consistency. How can we grow in that direction? There is only one way: we must look to the Lord, because He is consistent. He does not change. "They that trust in the LORD shall be as mount Zion, which cannot be removed" (Psalm 125:1). And as today's reading reminds us, "The counsel of the LORD standeth for ever"—as opposed to the fickle "devices of the people."

God is not like a wavering shadow. That's what James tells us in 1:17: "Every good gift and every perfect gift is from above, and cometh down from the Father of lights, with whom is no variableness, neither shadow of turning." Some manuscripts read, "who does not change like shifting shadows."

So if we want to learn consistency, we must disregard earth's shifting shadows and focus instead on the steady heavenly Light—the Father of lights Himself.

"They shall be changed: but thou art the same, and thy years shall have no end" (Psalm 102:26, 27).

TWO SPRINGS

DAILY BIBLE READING: JAMES 3:8-12

"Doth a fountain send forth at the same place sweet water and bitter?" (James 3:11).

The logical answer to James's question seems to be no. In nature, good water and bad do not flow from the same spring. By the same token, in nature a fig tree doesn't produce olives, nor will a vine produce figs. And yet—almost in bewilderment— James says that the same tongue will bless God and curse man. How can this be?

To try to understand, let's picture two springs. The one flows pure and refreshing. That symbolizes the new nature given us in Christ. Wise, loving words fall from the tongue of a regenerated man.

In our picture there is another spring close by. From it flows a foul and poisonous stream. It's a picture of the old, carnal nature. Bragging, complaining, exaggerating, flattering, putting others down, gossiping, lying—who among us has not allowed such things to cross our tongue?

James has a severe rebuke for this: "My brethren, these things ought not so to be."

Can the poisonous spring be cleansed? By the grace of God it can. Jesus promised, "He that believeth on me . . . out of his belly shall flow rivers of living water" (John 7:38). Isaiah tells how this transformation can come about, "Therefore with joy shall ye draw water out of the wells of salvation" (Isaiah 12:3). Drink from the fountain of life! Drink deeply and constantly, and thus the bitter water can be made sweet.

Also we must remember Marah. Thirsty Israel was so happy to find a spring, but they could not drink the water because it was bitter. What healed the bitterness? God showed Moses a tree; when it was cast into the waters, they became sweet. That tree symbolizes the cross of Christ. Let us submit to the cross so that it can do its cleansing, healing work upon our tongues.

"The water that I shall give him shall be in him a well of water springing up into everlasting life" (John 4:14).

TRUE FRIENDSHIP

DAILY BIBLE READING: DANIEL 3:13-18

"Be it known unto thee, O king, that we will not serve thy gods" (Daniel 3:18).

In Shadrach, Meshach, and Abednego, we have a clear picture of true friendship. What makes friends? Usually there are common bonds that draw them together: bonds of faith, family, or common interests.

What common bond drew these three men together? Along with Daniel and some other young Hebrews, they were captured and brought to the land of Babylon. In this strange land far from home, they became servants to the Chaldean king, who was determined to make good Chaldeans out of them.

But these four young men had convictions. They had faith. They wanted to stay true to their God. And I believe that was the deepest bond of their friendship.

The test came soon enough: "Bow down to this statue, or you will be thrown into the burning fiery furnace."

Shadrach, Meshach, and Abednego could have valued their lives and their friendship above their faith. They could have reasoned, "Maybe we should give in to the king's demand, so that we can keep our friendship."

But they realized that if they started worshipping idols, they would lose the bond that made them friends. God was more important to them than anything else. They believed God could deliver them; but deliverance or not, they kept on trusting Him.

We know the outcome. Not a hair on their bodies was singed by that intense fire.

The only basis for true friendship is faith in God. A friendship based on anything else is hardly worth preserving.

"Then Nebuchadnezzar spake, and said, Blessed be the God of Shadrach, Meshach, and Abednego, who . . . yielded their bodies, that they might not serve nor worship any god, except their own God" (Daniel 3:28).

YIELDED BODIES

DAILY BIBLE READING: ROMANS 12:1

"Present your bodies a living sacrifice" (Romans 12:1).

"Shadrach, Meshach, and Abednego . . . yielded their bodies, that they might not serve nor worship any god, except their own God" (Daniel 3:28). This verse reminds me of Romans 12:1: "I beseech you therefore, brethren, by the mercies of God, that ye present your bodies a living sacrifice."

When we think of sacrifices, we picture a priest offering slain animals on an altar. But those days are past. Jesus Christ, the Great Sacrifice, yielded His body to take away those dead sacrifices of yore. God wants living sacrifices, not dead ones.

How can we yield our bodies as living sacrifices? "Reckon ye also yourselves to be dead indeed unto sin but alive unto God through Jesus Christ our Lord" (Romans 6:11). There is, after all, some death involved: we must die to sin through faith in Christ. Then our yielded, living bodies are acceptable sacrifices to God.

From there we go to Romans 6:13: "Yield yourselves unto God, as those that are alive from the dead, and your members as instruments of righteousness unto God." The three Hebrews "yielded their bodies" through faith in God. Their whole lives were dedicated to the righteousness of faith.

From the thought of living sacrifices we go on to the thought of "living stones," found in 1 Peter 2:5: "Ye also, as lively stones, are built up a spiritual house, an holy priesthood, to offer up spiritual sacrifices, acceptable to God by Jesus Christ." There is the key to making the acceptable sacrifice: "by Jesus Christ."

In the previous verse, Jesus is called the "living stone." When we believe in Him, we become "lively stones"—part of the living Stone, part of the church, the family of God. Amazingly, we thus become priests, able to offer up spiritual sacrifices—the sacrifice of our whole lives surrendered to God.

It's mind-boggling. In Christ we are not only the priest (the one who offers the sacrifice), not only the altar (the lively stone), but also the living sacrifice.

"Who his own self bare our sins in his own body on the tree, that we, being dead to sins, should live unto righteousness" (1 Peter 2:24).

THE COURAGE OF FAITH

DAILY BIBLE READING: EXODUS 2:1-10

"She took for him an ark of bulrushes, and daubed it with slime and with pitch, and put the child therein" (Exodus 2:3).

What great courage Moses' parents had! It was a courage that resisted evil. For surely this plan of Pharaoh's, to exterminate all Hebrew boys, was exceedingly evil. They could have sighed and said, "Well, there's nothing we can do about this great evil. We'll just have to give up our son."

But Moses' parents didn't give up. I don't believe it was only because they didn't want to lose their baby. I believe they were inspired by God to do their small part in resisting evil.

Their courage came from their faith in God. We know that from Hebrews 11:23: "By faith Moses, when he was born, was hid three months of his parents, because they saw he was a proper child; and they were not afraid of the king's commandment." Who knows? Perhaps God had given these parents some revelation of Moses' future. And so they launched that little bulrush boat on the providence of God.

How greatly they were rewarded for their act of courage! Not only was their child restored to them to rear as they saw fit; but eventually Moses became the great leader who brought Israel out of bondage.

Today we don't have Pharaohs murdering babies, yet we do see much evil in the world around us. Shall we merely sigh and say we can't do anything about it? Or shall we be like Moses' parents who did what they could?

It is God who fights the battle against evil. In giving us the courage of faith, God may be working out purposes far greater than we can imagine. Our efforts against evil may appear insignificant and puny. But if the efforts are born of faith, God can use them in His all-wise plan.

"Wait on the LORD: be of good courage, and he shall strengthen thine heart: wait, I say, on the LORD" (Psalm 27:14).

HIS ARMS ARE UNDERNEATH

DAILY BIBLE READING: DEUTERONOMY 33:27-29

"The eternal God is thy refuge, and underneath are the everlasting arms"
(Deuteronomy 33:27).

What a sense of safety we can enjoy! In ourselves, we may feel as shaky and wobbly as a one-year-old learning to walk. Yet like a watchful mother, God is there, ready to catch us if we fall. "Underneath are the everlasting arms."

The trouble is, we too often don't trust those everlasting arms the way we should. We flail around and hang onto nearby props that seem to offer safety. What are the props that may distract a Christian from trusting the everlasting arms? We may be tempted to think we'd feel more secure if we had lots of money or a nice home or powerful friends.

But time teaches us that there is no lasting security in such things. All earthly props will eventually fail. What then? The everlasting arms are still there. We will find true security only in the solid rock of God's embrace.

The same verse that promises the safety of God's everlasting arms also promises that God will drive our enemies out. Originally, these words were spoken by Moses to Israel as they contemplated entering the promised land. As we enter the "promised land" of faith in Jesus Christ, we are like Israel. Many enemies threaten our souls. Those earthly props—they are enemies to our souls.

One by one, these cherished props are knocked out from under us. We may be tempted to fear and despair. But instead, let us do as God directed Israel—"Destroy them." Stop trusting in earthly things and trust only in the Lord. As long as our faith is in props and not in the everlasting arms, we will not know true safety.

"I will say of the LORD, He is my refuge and my fortress: my God: in him will I trust"
(Psalm 91:2).

THE ULTIMATE VICTORY

DAILY BIBLE READING: JOHN 16:29-33

"In me ye might have peace. In the world ye shall have tribulation" (John 16:33).

This last verse of John 16 has such a two-pronged message. Did you see the two prongs? One says, "In me [Christ] ye might have peace." The other says, "In the world ye shall have tribulation."

Jesus warned His disciples about tribulation. He told them they would soon be scattered, leaving Him alone. He knew their weakness and was not surprised by their failure.

The same is true for us. Jesus knows our weakness and our sin. And because sin is in the world, tribulation is inevitable. What Jesus predicted for the disciples is true for us too: "In the world ye shall have tribulation."

Yet regardless of any tribulation, we can possess peace in Jesus. How can this be so?

To help us understand, we must try to picture something of which we have very little experience—a battlefield. Perhaps we could picture an Old Testament battle between the Israelites and the Amalekites. Weary and discouraged, the soldiers are almost ready to give up the fight.

Then along comes their commander, riding a white horse. "Be of good cheer!" He calls. "The victory is already won! I have conquered the foe! Only keep on a little longer until you personally reach that point of victory. I have overcome the world."

What fresh courage that brings to battle-weary soldiers! Now they know it's worth it to keep on fighting. The victory is already won.

On the cross, Jesus won the ultimate victory. We need only keep on in faith. Because of His victory, we have peace in Him—no matter if earthly battles and tribulations still rage around us.

"For whatsoever is born of God overcometh the world: and this is the victory that overcometh the world, even our faith" (1 John 5:4).

SECOND MARRIAGE

DAILY BIBLE READING: ROMANS 7:1-6

"That ye should be married to another, even to him who is raised from the dead, that we should bring forth fruit unto God" (Romans 7:4).

Here in the first verses of Romans 7, Paul uses a second marriage to illustrate the Christian's change of allegiance from the law to the grace of Christ.

First Samuel 25 also tells about a second marriage. Abigail was a beautiful, sweet-tempered woman married to a foolish, evil man named Nabal. One day David, the refugee king, asked Nabal for food to feed his army. Nabal refused, and David flew into a rage.

Enter Abigail. With winsome apologies, she deflected David's anger. And when Nabal died, struck down by the Lord, David took Abigail for his wife. We don't read that Abigail had any regrets about losing her evil first husband.

Isn't that a picture of the second marriage we read about in Romans 7? Our "first marriage" was to the Law. Like Nabal, the law condemned us, provoked sin in us, and refused to offer any help or pardon.

But the condemnation of the Law can't extend beyond death. In our case, it's not the Law that dies—it's us. Because, you see, by faith we become united with Christ in His death on the cross.

By that death of our old nature, we are freed from the Law. Free to be married to the raised, exalted Christ! Free to live in newness of life—conformed to His resurrection. Free to bring forth fruits of holiness through the power of His life in us!

"But now being made free from sin, and become servants to God, ye have your fruit unto holiness, and the end everlasting life" (Romans 6:22).

THE BLOOD OF THE ETERNAL COVENANT

DAILY BIBLE READING: HEBREWS 9:11-14

"By his own blood he entered in once into the holy place, having obtained eternal redemption for us" (Hebrews 9:12).

Every year around the middle of May we celebrate Ascension Day. Here in Hebrews 9, we find the deepest, truest reason for celebrating this day. In Christ's ascension to Heaven, we see Him as our eternal High Priest, entering the holy place for us.

This great truth was foreshadowed in Old Testament times. The high priest would sacrifice an animal and enter the holy of holies to sprinkle the blood in God's presence, thus securing the remission of sins for the people. As it says in Hebrews 9:20, when Moses had sprinkled the people with blood, he said, "This is the blood of the testament which God hath enjoined unto you."

Those words remind us of Christ's words when He offered the wine to His disciples. "Drink ye all of it; for this is my blood of the new testament, which is shed for the remission of sins" (Matthew 26:27, 28). Jesus spoke of a "new" testament, or covenant, but it was new only to man. To God it was all a continuing part of the eternal covenant—a testament with no time. In Revelation 13:8 we read of "the Lamb slain from the foundation of the world." And Hebrews 13:20 tells us that God raised Jesus from the dead "through the blood of the everlasting covenant."

The timelessness of God's covenant fills us with awe. Throughout His Word we read again and again of the "everlasting covenant." To a casual observer it might appear that God made different covenants with different people: Noah, Abraham, David. Yet each "edition" of the covenant was only a glimpse of the great, preexisting "covenant of the blood": Jesus Christ in His crucified human nature entering the holy place of Heaven to secure eternal redemption through His blood. What tremendous importance is connected with Ascension Day!

"But this shall be the covenant that I will make...I will put my law in their inward parts, and write it in their hearts; and will be their God, and they shall be my people" (Jeremiah 31:33).

RECEIVING REPROOF

DAILY BIBLE READING: PSALM 141:5

"Let him reprove me; it shall be an excellent oil, which shall not break my head"
(Psalm 141:5).

Do you enjoy being reproved or criticized? Human nature doesn't take criticism very well. When someone points out our failings, we tend to get defensive or feel hurt.

But David had a good attitude toward criticism in this psalm. He seems to say, "It's a kindness if a righteous man smites me with his tongue." Can we learn from David to consider reproval as a kindness?

The words "which shall not break my head" are rather mysterious. What did David mean? We can't be sure, of course; but perhaps the scene in Mark 14:3 is a key to unlocking the meaning. Jesus was having supper in Bethany when a woman came with a flask of ointment. Mark says she broke the box in order to anoint Jesus. Apparently the only way to release the precious ointment was by shattering the flask.

So we could form this picture of criticism: it's as though a well-meaning friend takes a box of ointment and anoints you by smashing it against your skull. It hurts at first. But if we accept the criticism, it will be like an "excellent oil," a soothing medicine, to heal our sins and weaknesses.

For an example of a man who properly accepted criticism, look at Simon the sorcerer in Acts 8. Don't you think Peter's sharp criticism felt like a box being broken over Simon's head? "Thy heart is not right in the sight of God. I perceive that thou art in the gall of bitterness, and in the bond of iniquity" (Acts 8:21, 23).

How would you and I have reacted to such a pointed rebuke?

Simon's response is a lesson for us. He must have allowed the bitter medicine of criticism to become healing ointment, because this is how he responded: "Pray ye to the Lord for me." Let's remember when we receive painful reproof to accept it as a kindness and allow it to heal our mistakes.

"Give instruction to a wise man, and he will be yet wiser" (Proverbs 9:9).

LEARNING FROM REPROOF

DAILY BIBLE READING: PROVERBS 9:7-10

"Teach a just man, and he will increase in learning" (Proverbs 9:9).

Yesterday we looked at how we should receive reproof: even if it hurts, we should accept it meekly and not defensively. Today let's take the thought a bit further. We need to *learn* from reproof and criticism.

Proverbs 9 makes it plain that a scorner or wicked man doesn't learn from reproof. Rather, a scorner will hate the one who rebukes him. A scorner will respond with a quick retort, not allowing the criticism to reach his heart.

We dare not be like that! If we scorn reproof, we lose the opportunity to learn the highest wisdom, whereas if we learn from reproof, we are on the path of wisdom.

What is wisdom? The fear of the Lord is the first step. Wisdom means learning to know God. An alternate translation of the last part of verse 10 is, "The knowledge of the Holy One is understanding" (NIV).

That is why we should welcome reproof and be thankful for it. God is speaking to us through others, teaching us about Himself. We can never overestimate the rich treasures we receive from learning to know God better. Peter says that God gives us "all things that pertain unto life and godliness"—how? "Through the knowledge of him that hath called us" (2 Peter 1:3). It's in knowing God that we discover these treasures of life and godliness.

If we want to be wise, we must learn more about God. But that doesn't mean just knowing facts about Him. Our knowing must be in the form of a real, personal relationship with Him. Only through Jesus is that possible. If we grow in knowledge, we grow in grace. And if reproof and criticism can get our feet onto this path of knowing God—how gladly we should learn from it!

"Grow in grace, and in the knowledge of our Lord and Saviour Jesus Christ" (2 Peter 3:18).

BE FILLED

DAILY BIBLE READING: EPHESIANS 5:18-21

"Be filled with the Spirit" (Ephesians 5:18).

What does it mean to be filled with the Spirit?

Look at it this way. The question is not "How much of the Spirit do I have?" The question is "How much of me does the Holy Spirit have?" Your heart is a dwelling. Picture it with many rooms. How many of the rooms have you truly opened to the light of the Spirit?

There may still be rooms you have not allowed the Spirit to penetrate. Open wide every corner of every room! Allow Him to fill you more and more. Let Him draw aside all the dingy curtains that still obstruct His light.

It is not that the believer can gain more of the Spirit. He indwells us in His fullness. But we can continually allow Him to gain more of us to be in more complete control of our lives. And the more He fills us, the more we will sing and praise and give thanks and submit ourselves one to another.

"That ye might be filled with all the fulness of God" (Ephesians 3:19).

UPON TWO MOUNTAINS

DAILY BIBLE READING: DEUTERONOMY 27:4-13

"These shall stand upon mount Gerizim to bless . . . and these shall stand upon mount Ebal to curse" (Deuteronomy 27:12, 13).

Here is a picture so vivid that it becomes seared upon our souls. And that is exactly how God intended it. He gave these instructions to Moses as a means of deeply impressing His Law upon the people. Joshua 8 describes the people obeying what God commanded here in Deuteronomy 27. In my own words, this is what took place.

Beyond the Jordan in Canaan lay two mountains. Mount Ebal was a barren hill of white limestone, devoid of vegetation. Mount Gerizim was as fertile and green as Ebal was barren. Between the two lay a valley about three hundred yards wide. Here is where God staged this performance.

Half of the tribes—those descended from Leah and Rachel, the women of promise—stood before Mount Gerizim, the mount of blessing. The other half—the descendants of servant wives and of those who had lost their birthright—stood before Mount Ebal, the mount of cursing.

When all was silent, the priests in the valley beside the ark of the covenant were to read the Law. The reading was to be in the form of blessings and curses. "Cursed is he who . . ." All the wrongdoings were listed; after each, the tribes on Mount Ebal were to shout, "Amen!" So too with the blessings: "Blessed is he who . . ." For these, the tribes on Mount Gerizim were to shout, "Amen!"

Can you picture it? The great central truth was this: obey, and you are blessed. Disobey, and you are cursed. Don't you think it made a tremendous impression on the children watching? And ought it not make an impression on us today? God's message today is the same. Unless we obey His call to salvation, we cannot inherit eternal life.

Today, we have the true Mount Gerizim—the mount where Jesus told us, "Blessed are the . . ." And instead of Mount Ebal, we have the Lamb of God who gave His life to free us from the curse of the Law.

"Christ hath redeemed us from the curse of the law, being made a curse for us: for it is written, Cursed is everyone that hangeth on a tree" (Galatians 3:13).

SCOLDERS

"This man receiveth sinners, and eateth with them" (Luke 15:2).

Jesus got scolded rather often because of the people He associated with. Here we find the Pharisees aghast that He kept company with sinners. Why, He even sat down to eat with them!

On another occasion, Jesus' own disciples had a problem with His associates. They were miffed that their Master would take time for children. (See Mark 10:13-16.) Surely this was a waste of time!

Then there's the story of Zacchaeus in Luke 19. No Pharisee would ever associate with a hated tax collector! But Jesus had a friendly conversation with one and then invited Himself to a meal at the man's house. We read in verse 7, "They all murmured, saying, That he was gone to be a guest with a man that is a sinner."

What do these three accounts tell us about the people who did the murmuring and scolding? I'm afraid it shows that they were very status-conscious. They thought Jesus was too important to spend time with children, tax collectors, and sinners.

And what do we learn about Jesus? For one thing, He had no need to improve His position. He was God! For another thing, His only desire was to help those who needed Him most. His parables in Luke 15 show Him as Shepherd of lost sheep and Father of a lost son. To those who murmured at His association with Zacchaeus, He said, "The Son of man is come to seek and to save that which was lost."

What about us? Are we position-conscious? Or do we wish to help the most needy?

"They that are whole need not a physician: but they that are sick. I came not to call the righteous, but sinners to repentance" (Luke 5:31, 32).

ONLY THE SIMPLE

DAILY BIBLE READING: PROVERBS 9:1-6

"Whoso is simple, let him turn in hither" (Proverbs 9:4).

The Proverbs writer grows very poetic as he describes the beautiful mansion wisdom has built for her banquet-house and the sumptuous meal she has prepared. We can't help being reminded of the words in Revelation 21:2: "The holy city, new Jerusalem, coming down from God out of heaven, prepared as a bride adorned for her husband."

The church, the bride of Christ, offers a beautiful mansion and a delicious feast! Those seven pillars mean God's perfection. The wisdom of Christ lacks nothing; it is full and complete. The beasts that are killed and the wine that is mingled—are they not the body and blood of Christ, offered to save us from sin? "Come eat of my bread," calls the bride, offering the true pleasures found only in the knowledge and fear of God. Indeed, this banquet offers all the satisfaction a soul could desire: love, joy, peace, righteousness, grace, eternal life.

But think about who is invited to this great feast. Does wisdom call to those who are high and mighty in their own conceits? No. "Whoso is simple, let him turn in hither: as for him that wanteth understanding, she saith to him, Come" (verses 4, 5). If we want to partake of this feast, we must be poor and needy, hungry and thirsty. We must be aware that we lack understanding.

We should also notice that there is a condition. We must "forsake the foolish" if we want to live. We must repent of our sin and be washed in the blood. If we do not, we will be like the man in Christ's banquet parable of Matthew 22, who was turned away from the feast because he was not wearing a wedding garment.

"Come hither, I will shew thee the bride, the Lamb's wife" (Revelation 21:9).

THE OTHER "FEAST"

DAILY BIBLE READING: PROVERBS 9:13-18

"Her guests are in the depths of hell" (Proverbs 9:18).

Did you know that Proverbs 9 also tells us about another feast, another invitation prepared for humanity? What a contrast these two feasts are! As we saw yesterday, wisdom has a stately palace for her banquet place—the church—and offers the true feast of Heaven—the body and blood of Christ.

But here at the end of the chapter, we find that folly has set up a banquet-house next door. Her intention is to attract well-meaning young people on their way to wisdom's feast, "to call passengers who go right on their ways." Folly's invitation sounds much like wisdom's. Folly, too, invites the simple and those who lack understanding.

But oh, how deceitful is folly's feast! In reality she has only bread and water to offer, a contrast to the true heavenly nutrition offered by Wisdom.

Yet folly makes her feast sound inviting. Why? She is offering illicit pleasures. "Stolen waters are sweet, and bread eaten in secret is pleasant," she coaxes. How many people have fallen for the allure of enjoying forbidden things? How many have become entangled by dishonest gain?

At the very end of the chapter comes a realization that makes us shudder. Like a spider drawing a hapless creature into its net, folly has drawn a "simple" young person to her door. Peering inside, he makes a horrible discovery. The guests inside are the dead! Those who are "dead in trespasses and sins," as Paul writes to the Ephesians.

Will folly's victim turn away and escape before the tentacles of eternal death wrap themselves around him? Oh, let us listen to wisdom's invitation and spurn the allure of folly and sin!

"See then that ye walk circumspectly, not as fools, but as wise" (Ephesians 5:15).

Christian Light is a nonprofit, conservative Mennonite publishing company providing Christ-centered, Biblical literature including books, Gospel tracts, Sunday school materials, summer Bible school materials, and a full curriculum for Christian day schools and homeschools. Though produced primarily in English, some books, tracts, and school materials are also available in Spanish.

For more information about the ministry of Christian Light or its publications, or for spiritual help, please contact us at:

ADDRESS :: P. O. Box 1212
Harrisonburg, VA 22803
TELEPHONE :: 540-434-0768
FAX :: 540-433-8896
EMAIL :: info@christianlight.org
WEBSITE :: www.christianlight.org

CHRISTIAN LIGHT
PUBLICATIONS